An Introduction to Philosophy of Education

This introductory text, now in its fifth edition, is a classic in its field. It shows, first and foremost, the importance of philosophy in educational debate and as a background to any practical activity such as teaching. What is involved in the idea of educating a person or the idea of educational success? What are the criteria for establishing the optimum balance between formal and informal teaching techniques? How trustworthy is educational research? In addition to these questions, which strike to the heart of the rationale for the educative process as a whole, the authors explore such concepts as culture, creativity, autonomy, indoctrination, needs, interests, and learning by discovery. Updates to this edition include new chapters on religious education and moral education, as well as questions for reflection at the end of each chapter.

Robin Barrow was previously Reader in Philosophy of Education at the University of Leicester, UK, before moving to Simon Fraser University, Canada, as Professor of Philosophy of Education where for ten years he was also Dean of Education. He was elected a Fellow of the Royal Society of Canada in 1996. He became Emeritus Professor in 2019.

Ronald Woods was Senior Lecturer in Philosophy of Education at the University of Leicester until his retirement in 1980.

Other books by Robin Barrow available from Routledge

An Introduction to Moral Philosophy and Moral Education
Utilitarianism: A Contemporary Statement
Understanding Skills: Thinking, Feeling and Caring
Injustice, Inequality and Ethics
The Philosophy of Schooling
Happiness
Radical Education
Common Sense and the Curriculum
Plato and Education
Moral Philosophy for Education
Plato, Utilitarianism and Education

Also by Robin Barrow

Plato
Language, Intelligence and Thought
A Critical Dictionary of Educational Concepts (with Geoffrey Milburn)
Giving Teaching back to Teachers
Plato's *Apology*
Athenian Democracy
Greek and Roman Education

An Introduction to Philosophy of Education

Fifth edition

Robin Barrow and Ronald Woods

Fifth edition revised by Robin Barrow

Routledge
Taylor & Francis Group

NEW YORK AND LONDON

Fifth edition published 2022
by Routledge
52 Vanderbilt Avenue, New York, NY 10017

and by Routledge
2 Park Square, Milton Park, Abingdon, Oxon OX14 4RN

*Routledge is an imprint of the Taylor & Francis Group, an informa
business*

© 2022 Robin Barrow

First edition published by Methuen & Co. 1975
Fourth edition published by Routledge 2006

Library of Congress Cataloging-in-Publication Data
Names: Barrow, Robin, author. | Woods, R. G. (Ronald George), author.
Title: An introduction to philosophy of education / Robin Barrow and
Ronald Woods.
Description: Fifth edition / revised by Robin Barrow. | New York, NY :
Routledge, 2021. | Includes bibliographical references and index.
Identifiers: LCCN 2020057543 (print) | LCCN 2020057544 (ebook) | ISBN
9780367637385 (hardback) | ISBN 9780367637361 (paperback) | ISBN
9781003120476 (ebook)
Subjects: LCSH: Education–Philosophy.
Classification: LCC LB880 .B34 2021 (print) | LCC LB880 (ebook) | DDC
370.1–dc23
LC record available at https://lccn.loc.gov/2020057543
LC ebook record available at https://lccn.loc.gov/2020057544

ISBN: 978-0-367-63738-5 (hbk)
ISBN: 978-0-367-63736-1 (pbk)
ISBN: 978-1-003-12047-6 (ebk)

DOI: 10.4324/9781003120476

Typeset in Times New Roman
by Taylor & Francis Books

For Brigitte

Contents

Acknowledgments

I am most grateful to my friend and colleague Robert Manery for the help he has provided in preparing this edition.

Preface

A Brief Summary of Changes from the Fourth Edition

There are four chapters on new topics (Religion; Moral Education; Skills and Critical Thinking; Multiculturalism and Racism).

The previous 'Introduction' has been replaced by Chapter 1 'On Reading This Book'.

Chapter 10 ('Needs, Interests and Experience'), has been enlarged, split into two and placed earlier as Chapters 4 ('Do We Need Schools?') and 5 ('Needs and Interests') on the grounds that students in the past have found these topics more approachable than others.

'The Concept of Education' and 'Knowledge' (Chapters 6 and 7) have been rewritten, though the argument remains the same.

Chapter 14 ('Freedom and Autonomy') is a substantially revised version of the previous Chapter 8 ('Self-determination'), including a new section on academic freedom.

Chapters 8 ('Curriculum Theory'), 12 ('Rationality'), and 18 ('Culture') have been modified considerably.

Only Chapters 2 ('Thinking about the Educational System'), 3 ('What is it to be Human?'), 11 ('Indoctrination'), 15 ('Relativism', previously 'The Postmodern Challenge'), 16 ('Creativity'), 19 ('Research into Teaching'), and 20 ('Conclusion: Theory and Practice') remain relatively unchanged.

Prefaces to the previous editions are included as an appendix.

Besides the new topics mentioned above there is new material relating to a utilitarian approach to the question of what is worth studying in Chapter 7.

I have finally (and reluctantly) conceded that, although the generic use of 'he' (to mean 'he or she') is grammatically unassailable, the majority of readers will feel more comfortable without it. Therefore, in this edition the reader will be faced with various aesthetically unattractive and occasionally confusing alternatives. Sorry about that.

1   On Reading This Book

This book is intended as an introduction to philosophy of education for students in colleges and university departments of education who have had little or no previous instruction in philosophical methods and techniques. We shall therefore be at pains to explain any technical or semi-technical terms we introduce. There will not be many such terms, and readers need have no fear that we shall blind them with jargon. Anyone with a modicum of common sense who is prepared to exercise thought should find no great difficulty in understanding what we have to say, always provided that he or she comes to the book with an open mind. Terms that may be regarded as technical or semi-technical will be printed in *italics* when they are first introduced. (Italics are also used for *emphasis*, for the *titles* of books, and for the occasional foreign phrase such as *a priori*.)

Objectives

Our main objectives in writing this book are:

1. *To develop understanding of the nature of analytic philosophy*

There are various different uses of the word 'philosophy' and associated terms such as 'philosophical' and 'philosophically', as, for example, 'she took the news philosophically' meaning 'calmly', and 'his philosophy of life is to take what he can' meaning that that is his 'view of life'. There are also different schools of philosophy, such as Marxism and Existentialism, different emphases as between, say, Continental and Anglo-Saxon philosophy, and different branches of philosophy such as philosophy of religion and philosophy of science. None of that need concern us; the focus here is on analytic philosophy in the context of education.

2. *To enable readers to recognize and appreciate its practical value*

There is a common assumption that philosophy may be all very well in its way, but that it is an abstract, theoretical activity for dreamers, which has

DOI: 10.4324/9781003120476-1

little bearing on practical questions such as how to get children to behave. It is true that philosophy is an abstract and theoretical activity, but we hope to convince the reader that it is nonetheless of great practical value, indeed indispensable, if we are to base our actions on sound reasoning.

3. To provide an argument for a particular view of the educational enterprise overall

While a certain amount of philosophical work is critical in the sense that it exposes weaknesses and flaws in other people's arguments, it is ultimately as concerned as any other discipline to get at the truth and arrive at positive conclusions. Though we do not necessarily expect to convince all readers of our conclusions about education, and though we stress that our prime objective is to get readers to philosophize for themselves, we nonetheless argue for specific conclusions on the various educational questions we raise.

Concepts

We take philosophy to mean 'inquiry into the meaning of concepts and the logic and coherence of arguments'; philosophy of education thus becomes inquiry into the coherence of concepts and arguments in respect of education.

Some critics of philosophy argue that it is really just about words. This is mistaken. Words and concepts are not the same thing. One may be familiar with the word 'zygote', but, not being a biologist, have no idea what it means, which is to say one lacks any conception of a zygote. If we look up the word 'zygote' in the dictionary, we find this definition: 'the cell resulting from the union of an ovum and a spermatozoon.' Providing we have some grasp of the meaning of the words in this definition, we have a basic understanding of the concept. But to get a real grasp of the concept we will need to study biology. The *concept* of a zygote, in other words, is the fully articulated account of the idea to which the word refers. We sometimes refer to the meaning of words in this book, but our ultimate interest as philosophers is in concepts, not words. Furthermore, as philosophers, we are not in fact interested in a concept such as zygote, which, as indicated, is best understood by engaging in biological research. Philosophy is primarily interested in concepts of abstract ideas as opposed to concepts of physical objects, and in concepts that are not central to some other specialized discipline like biology.

In this book, when we refer to a word it is placed in single quotation marks (as in 'zygote' has six letters); when we are concerned with the concept no quotation marks are used. (We should add that we use "double" quotation marks when quoting another author or introducing an imaginary remark or statement.)

Educational discussion is full of concepts (including education itself) that are by no means clear or fully articulated. English language speakers know what the word 'gifted' means in some sense, but most of them would be unable to provide an account of the idea that makes it quite clear what we are saying when we refer to someone as gifted. They cannot provide the criteria that have *necessarily* to be met for a person to count as gifted, nor the set of criteria that are *sufficient* to establish that a person is gifted. Does a truly gifted person have to achieve something, for example? If so, does it matter what kind of achievement? The distinction between *necessary* and *sufficient* conditions, our first piece of semi-technical terminology, is basic to analysis, for ideally we seek to establish the set of conditions or criteria that are necessary to something being an instance of the concept in question and that taken together are sufficient to conclude that we have such an instance. Note that we say 'ideally'; the ideal is not always attainable.

Further Features of Philosophy

The focus on fully understanding concepts of important abstract ideas is one key feature of philosophy. Another is that it is not an *empirical* form of inquiry. Biology and the other branches of science invest heavily in testing or establishing conclusions by experiment and observation. And most other subjects, such as history, sociology, business studies and psychology, also involve a certain amount of empirical work. Philosophy does not. Philosophers of education may refer to empirical claims such as that children can only perform certain mental operations at certain stages of development, and make use of these claims in building an argument; but to carry out any type of empirical inquiry is not in itself to engage in philosophy.

Many people think of philosophy as being concerned with big questions such as 'What is the meaning of life?' and they are not entirely wrong. Philosophy is concerned to explore such questions. But you will be disappointed if you expect this or any other philosophy book to provide unequivocal answers to many such questions. What philosophy does, generally speaking, is clarify such questions and indicate what can be safely concluded in relation to them and what cannot. In the case of this example probably the first thing that a philosopher would do is point out that it is not clear what the question is actually asking for, and proceed to discriminate or distinguish between various different senses that the phrase 'the meaning of life' might have. But, generally speaking, the philosophical consensus would be that such dramatic and bold questions as 'What is the meaning of life?' 'Does God exist?' and 'What is the moral truth?' cannot be said to have received a clear and certain answer in the way that leading questions in various other disciplines have. However, far from this being a failing or shortcoming inherent in philosophy, this is one of its most important achievements. For what philosophy is telling us is that such questions cannot be answered definitively, and we need to recognize and face up to that fact. And, of course, to acknowledge that we cannot *prove* the existence of God, for example, is not to say that there are no particular philosophical claims and arguments concerning religion that can be satisfactorily resolved, as we shall see in Chapter 9. What philosophy can do is ensure that the discussion around religion is clear, coherent, and to the point.

So, there will be plenty of answers to educational questions in this book, and some of them will be indisputable; but it depends upon the question, since some questions, as philosophy will reveal, are by their nature unanswerable, some will yield answers that are the most reasonable we can come up with rather than demonstrably true, and some will yield the conclusion that there is no truth to be found on the matter, only opinion, as for example on the question of whether something is amusing. One thing philosophy teaches us is that we have to learn to live with a degree of uncertainty, because many things, including some things that we tend to be most passionate about, just are areas of uncertainty. For that reason alone, open-mindedness, tolerance and freedom are to be valued.

Philosophy in Action

The aim of this book is not to provide readers with information on a set of topics for regurgitation in an examination, but rather to attempt to show philosophy in action. Of course we believe in what we have to say positively; but the stress is on how to do philosophy. Hence we have not attempted to review the literature in the field, and the topics chosen for discussion are in a sense simply vehicles for the exercise of philosophizing. One of our main objects will have been achieved if we can help readers to become more skillful at philosophical debate, which is to say able to think about and discuss issues in a philosophic manner. Philosophy is not to be thought of as a fixed body of information waiting to be digested, but as an activity through the exercise of which men and women can think things through, in concert with others, for themselves.

Different Types of Meaning

The importance and centrality to philosophy of conceptual analysis is to be emphasized. It is not simply a recent fad or phenomenon in the subject. It has always been a part of philosophizing, at least as far as the Western world is concerned (and here it should be acknowledged that, though available to all, the kind of philosophy that we are engaged in is particularly associated with Western thought.) Thus, consider this passage from Plato's *Republic*:

> "What you say, Cephalus, is excellent," I said. "But as to this justice, can we quite without qualification define it as 'truthfulness and repayment of anything we have received'; or are these very actions sometimes just and sometimes unjust? For example, if we have been given weapons by a friend and he went mad and reclaimed them, it would surely be universally admitted that it would not be right to give them back. Anyone who did so, and was prepared to tell the whole

truth to a man in that state, would not be just." "You are right," he said. Then this – speaking the truth and restoring what we have received – is not the definition of justice.[1]

This passage makes it clear that one of the things Plato was up to in the *Republic* was to get at the meaning of justice, and this concern on his part links him directly with a great many contemporary philosophers, for as Gilbert Ryle observes, "the story of twentieth-century philosophy is very largely the story of this notion of sense or meaning".[2] There are three different kinds of meaning which it would be well to distinguish at the outset.

Consider the seemingly fact-stating statement "Education consists of molding individuals into obedient members of the state". Despite appearances, this might not be a statement of fact but an evaluation on the part of the person making it, meaning that "Education *ought* to consist of..." We need, then, to distinguish fact-stating language, which we shall refer to as the *descriptive* use of language, from the *evaluative* use of language.

Descriptive meaning is concerned with supplying information. For example, "The book is on the table" or "Snow is white". Note that the information concerned does not have to be true: "Santa Claus is coming tonight" is equally an example of descriptive use of language. We can get a little clearer about the nature of descriptive meaning by comparing it with *emotive* meaning. If a speaker says that a certain film lasts for an hour and a half, then this would be correctly classified as a descriptive remark, regardless of whether it is true or false. But if he says of the same film "it was sickening and disgusting", he is giving vent to his feelings; he was disgusted and sickened by it. Because he is expressing his emotional reaction rather than describing anything about the film, this utterance is classified as an instance of the emotive use of language. But now suppose that he says, "It was not a particularly good film." This is not an emotive use of language, for he says nothing about his emotional reaction to it; it is a judgment about the quality of the film, which we classify as an *evaluative* expression. Finally, we may note that the question "Why do you say that?" which is generally a perfectly reasonable and sensible question to raise in the context of an evaluative statement, is not appropriate in the case of a descriptive statement. For example, "Why do you say that?" in response to the descriptive statement that the book is on the table is puzzling. The book just is on the table, and that is obviously why it was said. The same is not true of "Why do you say that?" in respect of the evaluative statement that it was a good film. All that 'Why?' does here is ask for the reasons for rating the film as good, and that is not at all puzzling.

Many words can be used both descriptively and evaluatively (not to mention emotively), as for instance 'natural' can be. If I claim that aggression is 'natural' in humans, it is not clear whether I mean simply that it is part of our nature, whether I mean to imply that it is morally acceptable, or both (see Chapter 4). But certain words logically or necessarily imply evaluation, whether positive or negative. Thus, 'beautiful' and 'ugly', 'good' and 'bad', and 'right' and 'wrong' all obviously and inescapably involve evaluation. We may disagree as to what is beautiful, but we cannot get round the fact that in calling something beautiful we are commending it or giving a positive evaluation. Such terms as necessarily imply evaluation are frequently referred to as *normative* (because they imply standards or norms).

The distinction between descriptive, evaluative, and emotive meaning, and the ability to recognize normative terms, is important in philosophy generally, and particularly so in the philosophy of education. This is because education is shot through with questions of value. As Max Black puts it, "All serious discussion of educational problems, no matter how specific, soon leads to a consideration of educational aims, and becomes a conversation about the good life, the nature of man, the varieties of experience."[3] We need to be on our watch to detect occasions on which statements that appear to be merely descriptive are in fact also evaluative, on which statements are little more than emotive outpourings, and on which the words we are using necessarily imply evaluation.

Further Features of This Book

Finally, a few brief points about the various conventions we adopt in this book. This is not a history of philosophy of education, nor is it a review of educational theories or policies and practices. It is idealistic in the sense that it is concerned with what ideally we should be trying to achieve in the name of education, and it is focused more on aims than on means. Our references to other philosophers, whether alive or dead, are generally few and sparing. They are cited for the most part only when they are particularly associated with the issue being discussed, and they are cited not as authorities to be uncritically accepted but as opinions to be considered (whether we are personally in agreement or disagreement).

However, some readers may be surprised to find that the references that we do make are very often not particularly contemporary. In this chapter alone, we have referred to Plato, who lived some 2,500 years ago, and neither of the other people quoted is alive today. This might be of some concern if we were dealing with a subject that overall clearly accumulates knowledge and steadily progresses as does our knowledge of physics or medicine. But this is not the case with philosophy where questions such as what is the nature of the good life or what counts as being well educated are forever being debated, and various views and arguments come and go as individual philosophers seek to modify and defend them, or alternatively kill them off again. On some topics contemporary philosophers might agree Plato was plainly off his head; but on others he might still be judged as being correct or at least more plausible than anybody since. So, there is no particular reason to assume that contemporary work on a topic is the best.

Examples that are introduced may sometimes seem far-fetched or unreal to readers who are new to philosophy. That is because, for the most part, examples are introduced to make a general point and not for their own sake. When we introduced the example of a person making various statements about a film, for instance, we were not remotely interested in anything to do with films as such. We wanted to focus your attention on the difference between descriptive, evaluative, and emotive language; to that end we deliberately did not even name a particular film, for fear that the reader might be distracted by thoughts about the particular film referred to. The use of examples being frequent and commonplace in philosophy, we have tried to vary the phrasing from time to time. So, besides the phrase 'for example' itself, you will find 'e.g.,' and 'for instance'. For the sake of variety we also employ phrases such as 'surely it is the case that...', 'it seems to me that...', and 'we would not say that...'. These are all to be taken as appeals to readers to think for themselves whether they do or do not agree with the point being advanced. Thus, 'surely it is the case that...' should not be interpreted to mean 'it is a sure fact that...' but rather to mean 'we hope the reader will, after reflection, see the plausibility of this view.'

Note also that in the following chapters we have adopted the use of the first person singular ('I') rather than the first person plural ('we') that we have used in this introduction. This is partly for stylistic reasons, partly because, starting with the second edition, the book has been the responsibility of one author alone, and partly to distinguish clearly between authorial claims and opinions and the use of 'we' just referred to that signals a suggestion to the reader about the claims and opinions of people in general. For example, "I would argue that education necessarily involves knowledge" indicates where the author stands, while "we surely would not deny that education involves knowledge" means, surely you, the reader, agree with this. Note also that phrases such as 'I think' and 'it seems to me', which are generally used when we regard something as self-evident or clearly reasonable, are nonetheless not intended to settle the matter in question; they should be interpreted as invitations to the reader to reflect on the issue and decide for themselves whether or not they agree.

In summary, we have set out our three main objectives, explained our use of italics and quotation marks, and provided a working definition of philosophy of education. We have introduced and explained the difference between *necessary* and *sufficient* conditions, and between *descriptive, evaluative*, and *emotive* meaning. We have explained what is meant by a *normative* term. Most importantly we have distinguished words and concepts and stressed that analysis of concepts is central to philosophy.

We have pointed out that our goal is not to provide an overview of various theories of education, but to engage the reader in the activity of philosophy as we seek to come up with some clear and sane thinking about education, while acknowledging that it is a subject involving many value judgments and that some of our answers must be regarded as provisional. But even if provisional or uncertain, they can be more or less reasonable.

Notes

1   Plato, *The Republic* (Penguin, 1974) p. 65.
2   Gilbert Ryle, *The Revolution in Philosophy* (Macmillan, 1956) p. 8.
3   Max Black, 'A Note on Philosophy of Education' in C.J. Lucas (ed.), *What is Philosophy of Education?* (Macmillan, 1969) p. 11.

Further Reading

John Wilson, *What Philosophy Can Do* (Macmillan, 1986) provides a valuable contribution to the debate on the nature and purpose of philosophy. On meaning, Charles L. Stevenson, *Ethics and Language* (Yale University Press, 1960) has much to offer the advanced student.

On philosophical analysis, see Michael Beaney, *Analytic Philosophy: A Short Introduction* (Oxford University Press, 2017) and Robin Barrow, 'Philosophic Method and Educational Issues: The Legacy of Richard Peters', in *Journal of Philosophy of Education*, 54 (3), 717–730 (2020).

For comprehensive guides to the field of philosophy of education, see Richard Bailey, Robin Barrow, David Carr, & Christine McCarthy (eds.), *The Sage Handbook of Philosophy of Education* (Sage, 2010) and Harvey Siegel (ed.), *The Oxford Handbook of Philosophy of Education* (Oxford University Press, 2009).

Given the premise that we need to speak and think more clearly than we do, readers might enjoy Francis Wheen, *How Mumbo-Jumbo Conquered the World* (Fourth Estate, 2004).

Questions and Answers

It has been suggested that it might be helpful to student readers to add a section on how to write a philosophical essay. Unfortunately, we do not believe that this is the kind of thing that can effectively be taught by description and prescription. One develops one's ability to write a philosophical essay primarily by engaging with philosophical argument.

But what we can do is offer a little guidance in the form of a few tips and some questions framed in such a way as to invite an appropriately philosophical response.

First tip: almost any philosophical question will invite an answer that involves some kind of conceptual clarification. (E.g., Q: "Is democracy desirable?" A: "It depends partly on what counts as democracy...").

Secondly, as a general rule, if you are not discussing the work of a particular author keep direct quotation to a minimum. (E.g., If you are asked to summarize the argument of this chapter, do it as much as you can in your own words.) The fact that X said something does not make it true, however eminent X may be.

Thirdly, focus as much as possible on meaning (first tip) and coherence of argument. Remember that philosophy in itself is not concerned with making empirical points. (E.g., To say "A state system of schooling is desirable because it has been proved by X & Y that it makes people happy" is not to proceed philosophically. Philosophers would want rather to explore such things as what is involved in being happy, whether one can hope to measure it, and whether it should be a criterion of value in respect of schooling.)

Fourthly, wherever you think you see a flaw in an argument you are discussing, whether it is a matter of self-contradiction or other incoherence, of irrelevant points or points that could be made not being made, or lack of clarity of either particular concepts or reasoning, seize on it!

Finally, when answering questions in relation to a particular text (as in the case of this book), you are naturally expected to show first that you have understood the text. But there are no marks for the mere fact of agreeing or disagreeing with it. Your answer should make it plain whether you think the text faultless, partly convincing and partly inadequate, or plain wrong.

So, in response to this chapter, we might ask:

"What do you understand the authors take philosophy of education to involve?"

In answering this, one would expect you to make some reference to exploring meaning, noting both the difference between types of meaning and between words and concepts. What kind of concept particularly interests the philosopher? What does one ideally try to provide when analyzing a concept? And don't forget the concern with rational argument. All in your own words of course! And if you think that you can show by reasoning that this is somehow an inadequate conception of philosophy of education, make sure you spell that out too.

2   Thinking about the Educational System

All 12-year-olds at a comprehensive [school] were told that homework is being scrapped... [The Headmaster] who has already scrapped subject teaching... told them that, to make their schooling more 'relevant to life in the 21st century', they are to be given responsibility for 'managing their own learning'... [The School] is testing a futuristic project... which rejects the notion that a teacher's role is to transmit a body of knowledge to pupils. The project aims instead to encourage pupils to 'love learning for its own sake.'

(Daily Telegraph 2005)

For those new to philosophy, the subject is likely to seem somewhat abstract and removed from day-to-day concerns at first, and I therefore want to begin by drawing attention to the quotation above. Here is an example of an actual policy decision: Students will no longer do homework (and apparently are no longer taught 'subjects'). The decision is driven by a point of view or theory to the effect that schools should be relevant to contemporary life, that in order to achieve that students need to 'manage their own learning', and that the object of schooling is not to 'transmit a body of knowledge' but to encourage pupils to 'love learning for its own sake'. I hope that most people will agree that, in broad terms, this is an interesting contention – something manifestly worth arguing about, and, particularly if you happen to have children at school, something that you might feel pretty strongly about, one way or the other. The kind of argument this decision might give rise to is decidedly *not* 'airy-fairy', 'merely academic', 'purely theoretical', or 'irrelevant' to practical matters.

Ultimately, it is dealing with claims and counterclaims such as this with which philosophy of education is concerned. But it does not go straight to the question of whether it is correct or incorrect, for example, to claim that 'managing one's own learning' is necessary for a 'relevant education'. It starts a step earlier. It tries to make sense of this 'argument'. It asks, in particular, such questions as what is meant by 'an education that is relevant to life', by 'managing one's own learning' and by 'love of learning for its own sake'? It asks why there is a presumption that loving learning for its own sake is incompatible with learning subjects. It asks what is the argument for saying

DOI: 10.4324/9781003120476-2

that the teacher's job is not to transmit a body of knowledge. (It might also ask what scrapping homework is supposed to have to do with any of this.) Only by making sense of the argument, in particular understanding what some of the key words and phrases are supposed to mean, can we proceed to assess its merit or lack of it. And that is what philosophy is concerned with: making sense of arguments and ideas.

The Sphere of Education

The sphere of education today is extensive and education is generally highly valued. In most countries, in addition to a developed system of state schooling, there is a rapidly expanding system of higher education, including institutions focused on such diverse things as art, computing, gender studies, cooking, fashion design, and business, and a constant call for further qualification and accreditation in a variety of practices and pursuits, such as the hospitality industry, paralegal and paramedical services, mechanics, psychological services, accountancy, and horticulture. Alongside the state system a number of private education establishments at all levels, from kindergarten to teacher training, has arisen. Self-education manuals and books are one of the more lucrative sides of publishing, and educational programs of one kind or another abound on television and the net. Governments, by and large, maintain or increase their spending on education regularly, and proclaim it to be one of their first priorities. Similarly, world organizations and authorities ceaselessly emphasize education as crucial to poor or troubled areas throughout the world. A great deal of money, too, is pumped into educational research of one kind or another, in addition to the enormous basic investment in educational establishments of all kinds. Education, in short, is widely pervasive, takes a good slice of our resources, and is fairly indiscriminately valued. It is very big business, although we seldom think of it in that way.

But do we have a common understanding of what this thing called 'education' is? Is your assumption about what educating yourself involves the same as your neighbor's? Is studying the history of Greece part of 'education' in the same sense that learning how to cook is part of 'education'? If we have different understandings of what education involves, are these various views all equally clear, and, if they are, are they all equally important or valuable?

If we do not know what counts as being educated, how can we make judgments as to whether we are being more or less successful in our various attempts to educate people? If we are not clear what constitutes education, how can we assess whether a new course in health, a new program on road safety, or a new college for aspiring comedians should be regarded as educational? Debate about whether physical education deserves more curriculum time than mathematics or chemistry, or whether we can reasonably forego teaching grammar in English classes, cannot coherently take place in the absence of a clear idea of what is involved in a successful education. And how on earth can we design research into such things as the most effective methods of teaching or classroom organization, let alone evaluate the significance of our findings, except in the light of some notion of educational success?

Whether we ultimately agree on a definition of education is not the primary concern. We can get along, understanding one another and even making reasonable accommodation to one another, provided that each of us can make clear to others what we presume educating people involves. But we must at least clarify our own idea or conception of education if we are going to do any further thinking about it. It is the primary, the crucial, question in educational thought; and if practice is going to be based on sound reasoning, then it follows that it is the fundamental question for any educationalist, whether she sees herself rather as a practicing teacher or as a theorist. If you cannot give an account of what you mean by a 'well-educated person', then we can make no sense of any claim you go on to make about education, such as that it matters, that it is well-provided in this school, that another isn't really contributing to it at all, or that good teachers should proceed in this way rather than that.

I have deliberately used a variety of phrases as synonymous with 'knowing what education means': 'knowing what it is to be educated'; 'knowing what constitutes education'; 'what education is'; 'what we presume education involves'. For our purposes at the moment it is safe to regard these different phrases as interchangeable, along with some slightly more technical formulations such as: 'recognizing the defining criteria of education'; 'analyzing the concept of education'; 'establishing the necessary and sufficient conditions of being educated'. All of these different ways of speaking have this in common: they refer to the need to define education, not in the way that the dictionary does it (which usually simply refers to some examples of the word's use and provides a broadly equivalent synonym or synonymous phrase), but in the sense of establishing what is essential to its meaning. How do we distinguish education from other related but distinct concepts such as training, indoctrination, or socialization? To use my own preferred way of phrasing it: what precisely counts as being well educated?

The funny thing is that raising and answering this question is the least common, and the least well carried out, aspect of all our thinking about education. Everyday, one can encounter people who will readily tell you that studying poetry is a waste of time, that in today's schools we should focus on technical knowledge, that students should learn how to learn rather than learn particular subjects, that instruction doesn't work, that this school is better than that, that this teacher is useless, another brilliant, that homeschooling is the way forward, that university is too academic, and so on. Yet these same people, as likely as not, cannot begin to explain, let alone justify, the idea of educational success that they have in mind in making such judgments. They know, apparently, that this is more effective than that at achieving or contributing to a result, but they have no clear idea of what result they are talking about. Nor is this simply a problem for the proverbial man in the street: equally commonly, we find educational researchers claiming to have demonstrated or proved that a particular method of teaching is or isn't effective, without providing any explicit account of what we should be looking for in students who have been effectively taught in the sense that they have become better educated.

My first premise, then, is that the first and one of the most important tasks for those who wish to understand and contribute to sound educational policy and practice is to analyze the concept of education; to give an account of the idea; to determine what precisely counts as being well educated.

Schooling

I have used the word 'education' very broadly in the previous section, more or less as a synonym for 'the educational system'. We refer to the *'educational system'*, but that organization of schools, colleges, and universities in fact does a number of other things besides educate. Conversely, education doesn't only take place in some part of the system: people's education may be advanced in all sorts of ways, through their friends, by travel, on the web, by reading, by experience, by parents, or by self-reflection, to name but a few. So, before we attempt to analyze the concept formally (Chapter 6), it may be useful to distinguish between education and some related concepts, which, though distinct, may also be the concern of the educational system.

A typical dictionary definition of education might refer to it as 'upbringing' or 'acquiring knowledge'. In this sense practically anything one experiences, hears, or reads may be said to be part of one's education whether sensible or silly, coherent or incoherent, true or false, and regardless of how one came by the knowledge. It is in this sense that we refer to the education system, implying no distinctions between various things that might be learnt or how they might be taught. The most telling aspect of this broad concept of the educational system is that it is value-free. By contrast, the concept of education itself is *by definition* a good thing (it is a *normative* term). Why it is necessarily desirable and what makes it so will be considered when we analyze the concept fully, but for the moment we need only note the distinction between the value-free concept of the educational system or schooling and the normative concept of education itself.

Schools and other educational institutions have many purposes and do a number of things besides educate. Some of what they do may not be the result of anybody's deliberate or conscious aim so much as a by-product of having a system of education at all. For instance, schools do as a matter of fact serve as child-minding facilities, regardless of whether that was anybody's intention or wish. Similarly, at least in most systems, they play a part in categorizing and stereotyping individuals: schools just do tend to throw up the class clown, the computer geek, the sporting and the intellectual type, and they play a part in making individuals see themselves in particular lights, without anyone necessarily wanting to mold particular people into particular forms. And fairly obviously, the educational system may also make a significant contribution to the immediate and often the long-term happiness of people.

But there are also purposes that we consciously expect the school or similar institution to serve and deliberately try to enhance. Schools deliberately contribute to classifying people as relatively clever, hardworking, lazy, etc., for instance. But they also consciously aim to advance emotional development, socialization, training, and character development. Emotional development is concerned with achieving a satisfactory emotional equilibrium: it is a personal internal matter to do with reacting in an appropriate way and to an appropriate degree to varying situations and events. One is emotionally developed, for example, insofar as one recognizes cause for but can nonetheless handle upset; one is emotionally undeveloped if one is laid low by any disappointment or sent into a rage by the slightest obstruction. Character development refers to the cultivation of a wider range of habits and dispositions, such as being kind, truthful, or determined.

I am not at present trying to analyze these concepts or give a full account of what is involved in these notions. If I were, I could and should be criticized both for doing no more than giving examples, and for failing to address questions of value. You cannot define a term simply by giving an example of it: to say that ' being courageous' is 'to seek out and attack an intruder in one's house' is not to tell us anything about why this is courageous, which is what we need to know if we are to understand courage: what is it about 'seeking out and attacking an intruder' that is courageous, is the question. By the same token, any attempt to answer that question will have to tackle the implicit value question: courage is, by definition, a commendable quality, but is it actually commendable to seek out and attack an intruder in one's home? (It may well be. My point here is simply to illustrate that to define a term or analyze a concept, you need to do more than give examples, you need to explain why they are examples and, if values are involved, you need to support the implied value judgments with reasoning.) So, all I am doing at this juncture is drawing attention to some functions the school and similar institutions may perform, which can be distinguished from education and each other, without attempting to fully describe them.

Training and Socialization

Just as schools in most people's view should be partly concerned with character development even though that is not the same thing as education, so it would be hard to deny that they both do and should *train* and *socialize*. To train is to perfect by practice, the most straightforward example being physical training, whereby the body is kept fit and develops various basic skills through repeated exercise. Indeed, the change of name in educational discourse from 'physical training' (PT) to 'physical education' (PE) in the last fifty years illustrates an aspect of the point. 'Physical training' was and probably still is a more appropriate phrase for much of what is actually taught, but those with an interest in the subject were quick to see that if 'education' and 'training' were recognized as distinct, and the former being value loaded had more cachet, then what they did would have more prestige if known as 'physical education'; to bolster the claim to education, in many cases the teaching changed to include study of more theoretical matters such as physiology, fitness, or sport itself. Be that as it may, some of what goes on in schools, particularly at the more junior levels, should more properly be seen as physical training than physical education.

Schools train students in a variety of basic skills, particularly at the elementary level. In teaching the young to tie their shoelaces, do press-ups, form letters, recognize numbers, raise their hand to ask a question, and in other cases where we attempt to inculcate a discrete or self-contained skill without necessarily involving explanation or understanding, we may be said to be training them. Even as adults, a great deal of our behavior remains 'trained', as when we look both ways before crossing the road, clean our teeth for a minimum of two minutes, use a library reference system, keep our household accounts, sew on a button, greet people politely, or burn the garden rubbish. (On skills see Chapter 13.)

Training can be more or less complex and relate to more or less important skills, and the line between educating and training is not always straightforwardly clear in practice: the good historian, for example, is partly a product of skill training (how to locate references in the library, how to present references) and partly a product of education (coming to understand history), and sometimes it is hard to disentangle the two (e.g., should we talk of training a person to use historical sources, or is that a part of educating them?). There is an important general lesson here: we must not make the mistake of thinking that, because there are borderline cases when we don't know whether to describe someone as bald or not, it follows that there is no distinction between baldness and hairiness (sometimes referred to as the 'slippery slope' fallacy). In the same way, while it may be difficult to classify some human abilities as being clearly the product of either training or education, there is nonetheless a clear distinction to be made between perfecting particular self-contained practices by repeated exercise, and grasping or understanding patterns of reasoning. The former constitutes training, the latter provides us with an initial statement of what education involves.

Socialization might be said to be a species of training, but relating specifically to acceptable social behavior. What is meant by socialization is the development of certain attitudes, habits, and behaviors that are regarded as an integral part of the culture or society in question, primarily by a process of example and expectation, without any particular attempt to provide understanding of or any reasoning to support such behavior (other than along the lines of 'this is how we do things', or 'you wouldn't like people to do that to you'). No doubt a large part of who we are, judged in terms of how we behave, what we expect of ourselves and others, even what we think is right and wrong or true and false, is the product of socialization. Most people are socialized into the habit of being co-operative or polite long before they cultivate any views or arguments relating to the question of whether they should be. Once again, the basic distinction is between acquisition of attitudes and beliefs through the example and influence of the social environment, and the acquisition of some degree of understanding relating to our assumptions, which characterizes education.

I am not suggesting that because some functions of school, such as child-care, training, and socialization, are distinct from education that they are unimportant. The value of some of them, such as categorization or stereo-typing of individuals, might be debated, but training and socialization seem in themselves to be desirable, even necessary and unavoidable, aspects of upbringing. (Of course, one might take exception to features of a particular culture into which people are socialized. But to object to socializing people into the ways of the cultural revolution in Chairman Mao's China, for example, or to training people to torture, is to object to the cultural revolution and torture rather than to socialization and training.) There are other possible functions of the school, such as conditioning, indoctrinating, and closing the mind, which are inherently objectionable and antithetical to education, as we shall see (Chapter 11). But training and socialization are in themselves proper and desirable functions of schooling.

However, I want to suggest from the outset that the provision of education needs both to be distinguished from these other functions and to be recognized as a most important purpose of schooling. A system of public or state schooling is not in fact necessary to education, nor is it to training and socialization. All of these functions can be provided, and historically often have been, by the family, self-study, or some other informal means. But it is far easier for most parents to teach basic skills, to train their children, and to socialize them than it is for them to educate them, given that at minimum this means helping them to understand complex and abstract bodies of thought: I can take my child to the library and teach her how to look for and take out books (training) rather more easily than I can teach her the history, literature, and science contained in them. Similarly, she can teach herself science, literature, and history, by reading the books, but most people will not make much progress without the help of other trained and educated people. (Why do I say both 'trained' and 'educated'? Because I would argue that to become a good teacher one needs to be trained in some respects, for example, to write legibly on a board, to project one's voice, but overall one needs to be educated oneself, particularly in respect of the subjects one teaches. It is a surprising fact that in many places people are able, sometimes required, to teach subjects that they have never themselves fully or adequately studied. A small part of the implicit argument of this book is that that makes no sense at all and borders on the scandalous.) So at rock bottom I am claiming that the justification for a free state system of schooling is the practical one that this is the most likely way to ensure that all children, of whatever background, have an equal opportunity to enter an educational environment, and that emphasis should be placed on the educative function of schooling. In other times and places it has been clearly demonstrated that socializing and training the young to follow in the father's trade can be effectively done through the family. However, there is little reason to suppose that most people (especially the poor and relatively disadvantaged) will have a realistic chance of becoming well educated without a public system of schooling.

The Rational Tradition

Any school system, and any theory or argument about schooling and education, takes place within a particular social and historical context. This has a bearing on what is said and done. The educational practice of medieval religious communities owed something to the fact that that is what they were, just as the very different educational practice and thought of the Enlightenment owed something to the changed nature of society and general beliefs in the eighteenth century. Schools in the Soviet Union during the twentieth century provided a quite different kind of upbringing from that provided in Europe at the time (so different that one might question whether they provided a true education at all, although they undoubtedly trained and socialized citizens effectively). That difference arose out of the extreme differences in culture or the nature of and beliefs about society and people. Within Europe there were of course also differences between individual countries or, sometimes, between different religious, non-religious, or other distinguishable communities, and these too led to differences in schooling. And today the differences between schooling in, say, China and Canada are clearly partly the consequence of different overall cultures. There was a period (during the 1960s) when it was fashionable to focus on the importance of cultural difference and to argue that everything – all opinions, judgments, knowledge, and hence all consequent practical decisions – were purely and simply a product of their time and place, and, in a different form, this rejection of a standard notion of truth or knowledge is still with us. This extreme position, which will be considered in more detail below (Chapter 15), is quite untenable, indeed is rather childish in its willfulness and overstatement.[1] But it is important to acknowledge that to some extent we are all products of our place in history and have to make an effort to see beyond it. It is also necessary to recognize from the outset that we in the West are heirs to a particular tradition of thought, centuries old, that emphasizes and values rationality and believes that through detached and abstract reasoning we can hope to distinguish between sense and nonsense, between the plausible and plainly false, between the reasonable and unreasonable, and between what there is good reason to presume is true and what there is not.

   For these two reasons – the fact that we are part of a particular historical tradition that needs to be acknowledged, and the fact that that happens to be a tradition that values rationality – I want to conclude this chapter with a brief account of the rational tradition. For, notwithstanding globalization, the revolution in communications, the multicultural nature of our world, and the distinctive cultures within many countries, the system of schooling and the view of intellectual activity in most English-speaking parts of the world belong to and have been predominantly shaped by what is generally referred to as the Western tradition. It was not always and everywhere this way and it does not have to be this way. There have been, and are, societies that do not practice rational argument or scientific inquiry, relying instead on magic, religious inspiration, ideology, the commands of others, or historic tradition. Where does our commitment to rationality come from?

The Western tradition effectively begins in Athens in the fifth century BC. What may reasonably be said to be the beginning of civilization, implying living in a settled and ordered community as distinct from, say, a nomadic existence, is usually identified with the appearance of the cities of Uruk and Ur in Mesopotamia (a Greek word meaning between rivers, namely the Euphrates and Tigris), which is modern Iraq, in about 3500 BC. From here come the earliest examples of writing, consisting essentially of symbolic pictorial representation of commodities, and not of use for much more than inventories or lists. Between about 2500 and 2000 BC the Egyptian pyramids were built. While all of this attests to thought and design, it was not until somewhere between 1800 and 1600 BC that we find our first evidence of some kind of science, in Babylon where systematic planetary observations are made. In Greece, at about this time, the Minoan culture, associated with the famous palace at Knossos on Crete, is superseded by the Mycenaean Age, centered on the city of Mycenae, where King Agamemnon, according to tradition, was king. It was Agamemnon who led the Greeks to Troy to recover his brother Menelaus' wife Helen, and it is of this period that the Homeric poems, the *Iliad* and the *Odyssey*, tell, although they were probably composed and certainly written down later.

For comparative purposes, we may note that in China this was the period of the Shang Dynasty, during which there is evidence of extensive cities and the development of bronze work and writing, but the latter is still limited to strictly practical uses as, for example, on oracle bones and inscriptions. There is no evidence anywhere of the use of writing to tell stories, let alone to engage in discursive reflection. It is some time between 1500 and 1400 BC that an alphabetic script first emerged in the Middle East, and this, having reached Greece, is used in writing down the Homeric poems at Athens in the seventh century BC.

This brings us to the truly remarkable story of Athens in the fifth century BC. Greece was not then a unified country as it is today. It consisted of a number of quite independent and small city-states, with different histories and sometimes different racial backgrounds, and often at war with one another. The city-state of Athens covered an area of about 1000 square miles, and had somewhere in the region of 50,000 adult males (outnumbered by 100,000 slaves and 20,000 resident foreigners, not to mention the women). Yet within a period of little more than one hundred years this tiny state gave to the world democracy, trial by jury, tragedy, comedy, history, theology, art as an aesthetic category in the form of architecture, pottery and pottery painting, and sculpture, grammatical study, rhetoric, medicine, and natural science. This last was really the culmination of inquiry that had its roots in Babylon and Egypt, and which then developed among the Greek-speaking thinkers of Ionia (modern Turkey) at the end of the sixth and beginning of the fifth centuries. The major concern of these first scientists was not however what we associate with science today, although they were immersed in mathematics and, for example, predicted an eclipse in 585 BC; they did not do much in the way of empirical investigation, and focused rather on the speculative questions of how the world originally arose, and how change could come about, culminating in the first version of an atomic theory put forward by Leucippus and Democritus.

Here then is the beginning of systematic rational inquiry into questions to do with the nature of the world, though it should be noted that many did not write anything down, many of those who did still used poetry rather than prose, and all of them, however 'scientific' or 'modern' we may judge them to be, still reasoned in ways that made a lot of reference to gods, goddesses, chance, and necessity.

Then came Socrates, Plato, and Aristotle, who are the true known founders of the Western tradition. Socrates wrote nothing down himself, but is credited with being the first to emphasize the importance of moral and humanistic questions rather than scientific or natural ones. Plato, a disciple or pupil of his, did write, however, using a dialogue form that involved the character of Socrates, and it has been said and often repeated that there is a sense in which all of philosophy is a series of footnotes to Plato.[2] At any rate, Socrates, Plato, and Aristotle (who was not a native Athenian, but studied with Plato before founding his own school there) between them gave birth to what we know as philosophy.

Plato's theory of Ideas or Forms insists (as did many of his scientific predecessors) that the world of the senses is not to be trusted: a stick looks different from different angles, or if placed half in water, or as time passes, so we can never apprehend the true stick – the stick as it really is – with our senses. In fact, the senses often deceive, as when a person with an amputated limb nonetheless feels the presence of the limb. Looking for certainty and truth, Plato put forward the view that while no particular stick could be said to be perfect, there is an Idea or Form of a stick (or of stickness) to which all everyday sticks conform to an imperfect extent; similarly while no human action is entirely, uncontentiously, unequivocally courageous, courageous acts are courageous in so far as they partake in the Form or Idea of courage. The Ideas are real, unchanging, permanent, and as such must be the proper objects of knowledge, while about the shifting, deceiving, sensible world we can only have a belief or opinion: these opinions may sometimes be correct, but correct opinion is not the same thing as knowledge.

The theory of Ideas is not without its critics (and never has been; Aristotle was among the first to criticize parts of it), but it may be said that one's view of its plausibility depends mainly on how one interprets it. What is indisputably the case is that embedded in this theory is the claim that thought on any subject can only advance with absolutely clear conceptions: you cannot talk about, observe, or otherwise investigate anything from education to elephants without being clear about what counts as education or an elephant. And at one straightforward level it is correct to say that the idea of elephant is more 'real' (it is certainly more precise and timeless) than any actual elephant, though perhaps it would be better to say that it is more 'perfect' than more 'real', since for some the latter necessarily implies corporeal form (which Plato did not attribute to his Ideas).

There are those, even within the Western tradition, who deny even the basic assumption that one can meaningfully or usefully recognize or describe the characteristics of a concept, such that one can give an account of what an elephant or an education ideally is. And there are certainly other traditions of thought that do not place the same or perhaps any value on the giving of reasons. But, essentially, the Western tradition has been forever and consistently shaped by the two most important assumptions of the Greeks: that there are rational aspects of the Universe, which we should seek to understand, and that a necessary and vital part of understanding anything is to have clear concepts.

Notes

1 On this important topic, see Simon Blackburn, *Truth: A Guide* (Oxford University Press, 2005).
2 The remark was originally made by Alfred North Whitehead. For a study of Plato's educational philosophy, see Robin Barrow, *Plato* (Continuum, 2006).

Further Reading

There are many books that consider the scope of education in a broad social and political context. Harold Entwistle's *Education, Work and Leisure* (Routledge, 1970) is still worth reading. See also, Harry Brighouse, *On Education* (Routledge, 2006), J.P. White, *What are Schools for and Why* (Philosophy of Education Society of Great Britain, 2006), Roger Marples, *The Aims of Education* (Routledge, 2012), and Richard Pring, 'Liberal Education and its Aims' in J. Suissa, C. Winstanley, & R. Marples (eds.), *Education, Philosophy and Well-being: New Perspectives on the Work of John White*, pp. 1–13 (Routledge, 2015).

Other volumes of interest include Ruth Jonathan's *Illusory Freedoms* (Blackwell, 1997), James Tooley's iconoclastic *Reclaiming Education* (Cassell, 2000), David Carr's *Making Sense of Education* (Routledge, 2003), and Christopher Winch & John Gingell's *Philosophy and Educational Policy* (RoutledgeFalmer, 2004). See also James Marshall, *What is Education?* (Danmore Press, 1981).

Tara Westover, *Educated* (HarperCollins, 2018) is the compelling story of an indigenous Canadian who, having had no formal schooling, finally graduated with a doctorate from Cambridge University.

Questions

What does this chapter suggest the main aims of schooling should be?

What do you think the main aims of schooling should be and why?

Should any of these aims be prioritized? If so, on what grounds?

3   What is it to be Human?

Humans form a unique species. We are not just animals, although we are a species of animal, and we are not super-complex machines, or, more specifically, computers, although some analogies may be drawn between our brains and computers. Though some other animals have brains and genetic codes that are very similar to ours, none has exactly the same brain or code. More to the point, notwithstanding many fascinating discoveries in the field of animal research, it remains clear that there are things that humans can and other animals cannot do. Only a human has the ability to use a language that allows us to do such things as hypothesize, imagine, predict, and lie. Washoe the chimpanzee, for example, has been 'taught' to 'recognize' ('react to'?) certain signs, and other animals could similarly be said to have acquired a language in the minimal sense of allowing some form of communication or at least response or reaction between them and us; as every dog owner knows, the sound 'walk' can produce a reaction. But there is absolutely no evidence to support the notion, and absolutely no reason to suppose, that any non-human animal can formulate thoughts of the type 'you promised to take me for a walk, and now you have broken your promise'. An animal can certainly experience pain, but it cannot say to itself 'if you would just stop hitting me' or 'if you would return my sister to me, I would feel fine'. Similarly, while computers can calculate to a degree and at a speed that is amazing, no computer can 'say' to itself 'oh, I'm so tired of this calculation; I'm going to take a break; see how you people feel about that'.[1]

This is not because we haven't yet designed computers that can formulate such thoughts or because non-human animals have not yet mastered a complex enough language. It is because, so far as we know, no other animal has the capacity to use our kind of language, and because computers are, however sophisticated, programmed calculating machines that do not use our kind of language (although we tend to confuse the issue when we use human terms in talking about them). To say this is not to challenge or disparage the work that has been done in recent years on the brain, artificial intelligence, computers, and animals. It is simply to say that what this research shows, time after time, is that human beings are unique. Whatever the similarities that truly exist or the analogies that less securely may be

DOI: 10.4324/9781003120476-3

drawn between non-human and human brains, artificial and human intelligence, computers and people, and other animals and ourselves, there remains this ineluctable difference: the capacity to use a unique kind of language. From an educational perspective, we can add that if this is ever shown to be incorrect, if, for example, another species of animal is found that does have this capacity, or another familiar species develops it, or somehow a computer acquires it, what follows is that the animal or computer in question has become in this respect 'human' and therefore needs to go to school, because the distinctive linguistic ability of humans is at the core of the possibility of their being educated. You can design or program a machine and train a monkey, but, strictly speaking, you can educate only a human, or, to be precise, a being with a capacity for a hypothesizing language.

We are animals, then, and as such we have physical bodies that can be scientifically studied and explained. We have brains, which are also physical and can likewise be studied and explained in terms of cause and effect. Our brains in fact differ only slightly from those of certain other animals, so it is probably fair to say that it is not in our brains that our uniqueness really lies. It should also be acknowledged that we can identify certain parts of the brain with certain types of activity. But here we draw on the important distinction between *necessary* and *sufficient* conditions. Science has established that a particular part of the brain is associated with creative activity, for example. What this means is that without this part of the brain functioning properly one cannot display creativity; it is therefore a necessary condition of being creative. What it does not mean, what is not in fact the case, is that to have this part of the brain in good working order is sufficient to give rise to creative activity. Being creative means more than having a certain part of the brain functioning. A complete description of the brain can never capture the whole of the idea of creativity (see Chapter 16).

Nature or Nurture?

We are also genetically endowed individuals. Current evidence suggests that the particular people we are, our individuality, owes something to this personal genetic endowment. But we are not simply the product of that endowment, and we should not think in terms of being determined by it. Our individual genetic endowment is refined and modified by experience. The answer to the old question (very old; it was considered extensively by the Greeks) of whether nature or nurture makes us who we are, our innate self or the environment, is both; it is a matter of our given nature being developed in a specific way by its distinctive nurture. We are not determined by our genes; they are rather potentialities or tendencies that place limits on who we can become, but do not dictate specifics. To take a straightforward and simple example: I may have been genetically disposed towards some kind of cerebral way of life. To that extent I am partly where I am today because of my genes. But it does not follow that I could not have done other than pursue a cerebral career. I might not have had the opportunity to develop in such a way as to follow my genetic bent.

The Linguistic Capacity of Humans

But now we come back to the crucial point: the most important thing that humans and humans alone are genetically endowed with is this capacity for a distinctive kind of language. It is this ability to formulate propositions that may be true, false, or imaginary, and by extension, to promise, imagine, and hypothesize, and the consequent ability to explain our world and to some extent predict and control it, that makes us who we are. This unique feature is the most striking aspect of humans, and it is difficult to think of any more powerful and important feature.

The nature of our language, as contrasted with the communication systems of other animals, has enabled us to build up an understanding and explanation of our world. But the formidable web of understanding and insight that we have built up over the centuries includes truths that once articulated come to have control and direction over us. We have come to see, for example, that prime numbers have certain properties: having seen that, there is nothing we can do about it; we can't change anything; they have the properties they have. We have grasped that any argument of the form 'All men are mortal; Socrates is a man, therefore Socrates is mortal' (i.e. any syllogism of the form All As are B; C is an A, therefore C is a B) must be valid, just as any argument of the form 'All cows are four-legged; this is four-legged, therefore it is a cow' (All As are B; this is a B, therefore it is an A) is invalid. We, you might say, 'discovered' this or even 'invented' it, but that does not alter the fact that now we recognize that it must be so, and therefore here we are subject to the constraints and demands of that knowledge.

Humans, then, uniquely employ and can respond to reason. Being animals we also behave sometimes in terms of simple stimulus–response; but our distinctive characteristic is the use of reason. That is our essence: our mind, as distinct from brain. (Usage of the words 'mind' and 'brain' unfortunately doesn't follow any consistent pattern, particularly where different disciplines such as psychology and philosophy are concerned. The distinction that matters, however, is between the physiological organ that is necessary to but is not to be identified with the various aspects of reasoning, which I refer to as the 'brain', and the 'mind', which I reserve for the non-corporeal notion of our actual reasoning capacity in its widest sense. Fairly obviously, if you don't have a brain you can't have a mind; but having a brain does not guarantee having much of a mind.)

It is in virtue of the fact that we have minds that we may be said to have 'autonomy' which, though often thought of as 'freedom' actually means 'self-governance' or 'self-direction', as opposed to being directed, governed, or driven by external factors, whether inanimate or other people. Other animals have a limited number of responses to various stimuli; they are therefore in a literal sense governed by circumstances. So, no doubt, are we very often, but we are also able to act in response to our own reasoning, and in so doing we control rather than respond to circumstance; in so doing we are free in the specific sense of 'not a victim of circumstance'. (We are not here talking of free will and determinism as traditionally conceived. That is historically and primarily a problem for certain religious views. If God is all knowing, he knows what is going to happen; if he knows what is going to happen, in what sense can I be said to choose? Interesting as such a conundrum may be, it need not detain us here.) The argument here is simply that, notwithstanding the fact that we are partly shaped by our genetic inheritance and social pressures, insofar as we follow the dictates of our minds we are autonomous in the sense of self-directed rather than other-directed.

The Inclusive Classroom

The purpose of this brief consideration of what makes us human has been to focus attention on the distinctive linguistic capacity that (with a few very rare exceptions) is common to us all and central to our educational development, as we shall see in more detail in remaining chapters. But we are also unique individuals. Given the extent to which we are genetically endowed and given the close similarity between our individual genetic codes, some might be inclined to conclude that we must all be in reality very similar and that there is little room for individuality. Nothing could be further from the truth. Despite the fact that it has been calculated that the difference between individual DNAs is on average 0.1 percent, the evidence suggests that the consequence of the interplay between each DNA and its unique environment ensures a real and ineradicable difference between each one of us: our individuality is both explained and seemingly guaranteed by our understanding of genetics.

This raises the question of whether it is appropriate for everybody to receive the same schooling and/or education. Should there be a common system of schooling for all? Should all students follow the same curriculum? How inclusive should the classroom be?

Since we live in societies in which people come from various social, religious, cultural, ethnic and linguistic backgrounds, these differences need to be understood and respected (Chapter 17), but since we nonetheless presumably want to nurture a coming-together and some sense of common identity, we surely want a system of schooling that brings us all together, rather than separate schools for people from different social, ethnic, intellectual, or economic backgrounds. I believe that reasonable grounds can sometimes be provided for sending particular children to certain selective schools, for example the musical prodigy to a school for musicians, a child from a dysfunctional family to a boarding school, or an 'at-risk' child to a single-sex school (possibly even a child from a religious family to a school of a particular denomination, but see Chapter 11). In general, however, I would argue that children of all types from all kinds of background should merge together in school in a way that mirrors society at large, on the assumption that in the long run familiarity will breed togetherness rather than contempt. A common language in particular is crucial (or two if, as in the case of Canada, one is trying to pull off the difficult trick of two or more official languages). It is no service to either individuals or society to have citizens who cannot communicate freely with one and all. Cultural diversity, if it is to be successful, requires a degree of understanding, which is best provided by shared experience. Socialization, if it is to be true and effective, must apply to all.

However, examples of differential schooling are not uncommon. Consider, for instance, the tripartite system put into place in England and Wales by the 1944 Education Act. That system divided children at the age of eleven into those with a bent towards abstract academic and intellectual pursuits, who would attend *grammar* schools, those with a scientific and mechanical bent, who would attend secondary *technical* schools, and those less suited to either of those options for whom the emphasis would be on developing more practical skills for the workplace, who would attend secondary *modern* schools.

There were in practice grave defects in the implementation of this scheme: selection at the age of eleven was perhaps rather arbitrary, the mode of selection by a series of IQ-type tests was highly questionable, the intention that individuals should be able to move between types of school as they developed never effectively materialized, many jurisdictions failed to fully provide secondary technical schools, and, while each type of school was supposed to be held in equal esteem, from the beginning the secondary modern acquired the reputation of being second best. So it was not particularly surprising that in 1976 the government formally abolished the system.

Admittedly, some of these defects could in principle be put right. Nonetheless, I would not advocate a return to the tripartite system as such, since it is inevitably divisive in that it typecasts individuals in different categories (and tends to do so along socio-economic lines). But, accepting that a common school (i.e., one that embraces all manner of student, reflecting the nature of society) is desirable, that still leaves the question of whether a heavy emphasis on inclusion, such that virtually all children of a given age, regardless of their talents, mental, social or physical problems, special needs, inclinations, different stages of development, etc., are educated together in the same classroom, makes much sense. Even if there are good reasons for having a common school, might there not be a case for considerably more use of differential setting?

I would distinguish 'setting' from 'streaming', the latter involving labeling and grouping individuals as A, B, C, students overall. By 'setting' I mean allocating children to particular groups for particular subjects based upon aptitude (meaning a combination of specific ability and inclination), so that a child might be in one set with other highly able students at math, but in a set of different students less able in respect of history. In such a system the social mix in individual classes would very likely remain much the same as in the school at large. However, it must be acknowledged that children with extreme learning difficulties or with marked special needs, whether the result of social, mental or physical problems, would tend to be grouped together in many classes. This, I would argue, would be educationally beneficial, while the social advantage of all kinds of children intermingling on a daily basis would be maintained in the common school context.

Placing all children of a given age in one setting for all subjects as seems to be the norm in most jurisdictions places an enormous burden on both teacher and student. It is impossible to find a manner of teaching that suits all students of widely differing ability and interest equally well, and very difficult to adopt one's style and methods of teaching in relation to different individual students in the same class. Equally, individual students are going to be dissatisfied with having to work either at or around the pace of others. The truth is that social concerns (very proper in themselves) often outweigh educational concerns. But it is arguable that schools should not be set up and organized with a view to directly correcting social problems and that in any case they cannot effectively do so. A system in which all children are taught together in the same classroom in the same way regardless of aptitude will not produce school leavers of equal attainment; still less will it lead to a society without people of differing ability or without privileged and advantaged groups. Besides, as was suggested in the previous chapter, while schools do rightly serve other functions, including socializing the young, their distinctive feature is that they provide education, and one might reasonably argue that therefore the primary concern should be to give every individual the best education possible.

Finally on this particular issue, I am not assuming either that all students should be taught in the same way or that they will necessarily get the same out of their education. Nor do I wish to imply that such things as vocational study, technical and practical skills (which, as we shall see, are distinct from education) are relatively unimportant. On the contrary, they are extremely important both to society as a whole and in respect of individual satisfaction. Indeed, I regret the widespread tendency to group together all sorts of different institutions of higher education (e.g., polytechnics, colleges of further education, teacher training colleges, schools of art) as 'universities', since this suggests that every individual and every form of study should be immersed in theory and that there is something inferior about, say, a training school. I should be disappointed if any reader concluded that I disparage practical know-how. However, this book is focused on education as distinct from training and socialization, and it is my belief that (with the obvious and sad exception of a few extreme cases) all students are capable of getting something worthwhile out of a truly educational curriculum.

Thus, in the remaining chapters I shall be arguing for a particular curriculum that should be common to (almost) all, but taught in different ways to students according to their different aptitudes in the context of a common school.

Note

1 For more on Washoe and research into apes generally, see Paola Cavalieri & Peter Singer (eds.), *The Great Ape Project: Equality beyond Humanity* (Fourth Estate, 1993). On computers and minds, see John Searle, *Minds, Brains and Science* (Harvard University Press, 1984).

Further Reading

Matt Ridley, *Nature via Nurture* (HarperCollins, 2003) is a good basic text on genetic research. See also Rainer Born (ed.), *Artificial Intelligence: The Case Against* (CroomHelm, 1987), J.Z. Young, *Philosophy and the Brain* (Oxford University Press, 1987), and John Searle, *Mind* (Oxford University Press, 2004).

Taking a very different view to that presented in this book is John Gray, *Straw Dogs* (Granta, 2002). To different degrees, also wedded to a material view of mind, are Rodney Cotterill, *No Ghost in the Machine* (Heinemann, 1989), Steven Pinker, *The Blank Slate* (Viking, 2002), and Antonio Damasio, *Looking for Spinoza* (Harcourt, 2003).

Particularly interesting in respect of animal intelligence is Peter Godfrey-Smith, *Other Minds: The Octopus, the Sea and the Deep Origins of Consciousness* (Farrar Strauss and Geroux, 2016).

Questions

Do you accept that their particular linguistic capacity distinguishes humans from other animals? Are there other capacities that might be considered more important in relation to education?

What grounds might there be for what kind(s) of selective school? Can there be good grounds for treating different children differently? How inclusive should the classroom be?

Should educational considerations come before social considerations when it comes to schooling?

4   Do We Need Schools?

Nature

Do we actually need schools? Surprising as it may seem, some educators argue that we don't. In 1762, for example, Jean-Jacques Rousseau published an educational treatise entitled *Emile*. In it he argued that the boy Emile should have what he called a 'natural' education or an education in accordance with nature, as distinct from a formal education in a traditional classroom setting. Emile would live on his own, free of any specific program of study, and free of any book-learning until about the age of fifteen. His tutor is an ever-present example and influence, but he would not instruct or directly impose his views on the child. Emile would be free, for example, to break the windows of his bedroom if so inclined, but he would learn how foolish he had been when the winds blew or snow fell and his bedroom became freezing cold.

This summary does not do justice to either the complexity or interest of Rousseau's thesis, but it does convey its radical nature. And it does legitimately suggest that there are serious problems in the thesis, not least of which are the questions of how we are to determine what is natural and whether what is natural is necessarily good.

Nature has rightly been described as one of the most elusive concepts there is. One problem, as noted in Chapter 1, is that there is a purely descriptive use of the word, as in 'acorns grow naturally on oak trees', and an evaluative use as in the claim by some that 'homosexuality is unnatural'. Another is that in many cases, including on occasion a claim such as that homosexuality is unnatural, it is not clear whether the term is being used descriptively or evaluatively (or both). Yet a third problem is that it is not always clear what is or is not natural in the descriptive sense. Is envy, for instance, a natural human emotion or a product of social conditions? Given such obscurity, it is far from clear what demanding that we educate our children naturally amounts to in practice.

Nonetheless, in broad terms a viewpoint such as Rousseau's persists to this day. In 1969 John Holt in *How Children Fail* wrote as follows:

Behind much of what we do in schools lie some ideas that could be expressed as follows i) Of the vast body of human knowledge, there are

DOI: 10.4324/9781003120476-4

certain bits and pieces that can be called essential, that everyone should know; ii) the extent to which a person can be considered educated and be a useful member of society, depends on the amount of this essential knowledge that he carries about with him; iii) it is the duty of schools therefore, to get as much of this essential knowledge as possible into the minds of children. Thus we find ourselves trying to poke certain facts, recipes and ideas down the gullets of every child in school, whether the morsel interests him or not, even if it frightens him or sickens him, and even if there are other things that he is much more interested in learning. These ideas are absurd and harmful nonsense. We will not begin to have true education or real learning in our schools until we sweep this nonsense out of the way. Schools should be a place where children learn what they most want to know, instead of what we think they ought to know.[1]

Holt was not alone in believing that our guiding principle should be what children want to learn. At that date there was a prominent movement advocating what was called 'child-centered' education (nowadays generally referred to as 'student-centered'), which called for recognition of the child as a distinct kind of person rather than simply a miniature adult, and furthermore a person in his or her own right who needed to be understood on their own terms. On this view, emphasis should be on allowing innate individual potential to develop and flourish as opposed to what was seen as the traditional attempt to train and mold the young so as to make them serve a useful purpose in society as adults. Central tenets of this approach were that the curriculum should be 'relevant', and that learning should be through discovery and experience rather than through instruction.

Then, in 1973, Ivan Illich published *Deschooling Society* in which, as the title indicates, he returned to something like Rousseau's radical rejection of school altogether. It is important to note that Illich is not opposed to education. His thesis, and that of others loosely grouped together as 'deschoolers', is that the *institution* of schooling is incompatible with the provision of a true education.

Illich was a Roman Catholic priest, who, like Martin Luther and John Calvin before him, felt that the institution of the Catholic Church, far from advancing the faith, actually hindered and corrupted it. He felt, likewise, that an institution such as the army indoctrinated recruits and destroyed their independence of mind. So, in turning his attention to schooling, he was contributing to a wider thesis to the effect that institutional settings destroyed free and independent thought. The idea that he and other like-minded educationalists promulgated was that the formal school setting and traditional mode of transmitting knowledge through accredited professional teachers should be replaced by a host of informal means of transmission, drawing on a wider field of resources, including many unaccredited private individuals as teachers. Technology, then about to expand its capacity rapidly and monumentally, was one obvious and vital resource to be utilized. But so too were local individuals who were willing to share their enthusiasms and skills with others, while libraries and informal discussion groups could also be drawn upon. Overall, in place of compulsory schooling, the young will voluntarily educate themselves by means of such resources.

Deschooling

There are four main contentions in the argument of those who believe that the system of schooling should be abolished and replaced with a variety of informal routes to learning.

1 First, it is maintained that there is a *hidden curriculum*. On the face of it the school curriculum consists of subjects such as science and history, but it also teaches a number of other things, such as belief in expertise being vested in professional groups, deference to authority and various other values, which it does not explicitly advertise. (Hence the label 'hidden'.)
2 Secondly, partly arising out of the former point, it is asserted that institutionalization is effectively a means of *social control*.
3 Thirdly, knowledge is *artificially fragmented* and rendered unrealistic by breaking it down into separate subjects, by classes always being of a regulation length, and by frequent testing.
4 Finally, the culminating and central charge is that schools teach *conformity* and stifle independent thought.

As to the first point, it must be conceded that there is a hidden curriculum, inasmuch as schools deliberately and consciously set out to teach many things that are not explicitly referred to in timetables or curriculum plans.

But we do not have to accept the implication that this part of the curriculum is hidden for some devious reason. And surely the question of whether we should be concerned about things that are being taught without being explicitly advertised depends upon what those things are. If children are learning such things as the value of punctuality, the wrongness of cheating, respect for expertise in a field, and the importance of politeness, why should we be concerned? In other words, there is nothing wrong with a so-called hidden curriculum in itself; much of it may be positively desirable, and if there are some values being conveyed to which we take exception, that is what we should worry about, not the fact that there is inevitably a hidden curriculum. There is admittedly also the possibility that there is a part of the hidden curriculum of which the school and teachers are themselves unaware. Perhaps, for example, the system is conveying the idea that manual skills are inferior to intellectual skills, which was not anybody's deliberate intention. But again, this is an argument for considering whether we are teaching things that we do not wish to teach without realizing it, and taking appropriate action if we are. It is not an argument against having a standard curriculum, which will inevitably include some unadvertised elements.

Equally, there is no question that schools try and to a large extent succeed in exercising a degree of social control. As we have seen (Chapter 2), as well as aiming to educate, the school system aims to train and develop various behaviors and habits. It avowedly aims to help individuals develop into good citizens, which necessarily involves a degree of conformity. There is nothing wrong with this, unless one wishes to argue that society does not require or benefit from any degree of cohesion or conformity.

The point about the artificiality that the timetable involves is, I think, true as far as it goes, but it does not seem to me a particularly worrying point, and it is not clear why replacing the school with disparate individual learning opportunities would solve that problem. It may be true, as some educationalists maintain, that all knowledge is an 'integrated whole', but the fact is that we have to approach it in a piecemeal fashion. (And I have to add that, nice-sounding as it may be, it is far from clear what the claim that knowledge is an 'integrated whole' actually means.)

Everything therefore hinges on the final claim. Does schooling necessarily inhibit independent thought? If it does, for most of us that would be damning, because independent thought, as is reiterated in different ways throughout this book, is of supreme importance to us.

But this is where the thesis that it is institutionalization itself that necessarily leads to conformity breaks down. It is true of the army, because that is an institution that is avowedly committed to instilling obedience and deference to authority. It may have some truth in the case of religion, because every faith demands allegiance to its view of life. But the whole point about a school is that, while it may certainly encourage commitment to specific things such as honesty, loyalty, respect, and good citizenship, it also explicitly aims to encourage and enable people to think for themselves. In other words, if there are schools that indoctrinate (see Chapter 11) and crush independent thought, as there may be, that is a *contingent* matter and requires us to do something about those particular schools. But it is not a *necessary* feature of schooling, as Illich's thesis maintains. (A 'contingent' matter or factor is one that happens to be the case but does not have to be; it is a contingent fact that most elementary school teachers are female. A 'necessary' matter is one that could not have been otherwise, often a matter of definition; it is a necessary truth that the angles of a triangle add up to 180 degrees.)

Furthermore, it is far from clear that the alternatives proposed by those who would deschool society would be any more free from possible failure. Deschoolers of the 1970s deserve credit for having foreseen the potential power of the Internet; technology certainly brings a massive amount of information about the world to our fingertips and it can also provide exciting and innovative ways to learn. It is true too that many people who are not accredited teachers might nonetheless make a great contribution to the education of the young. So the notion of the community as educator is not absurd. But one of the main functions of a schooling system is to organize and evaluate the vast body of information available so that it is manageable and meaningful. Good teachers help students to make sense of information and to develop their own powers of inquiry; in one of today's clichés, they 'enable' their students. Experience in recent years has surely taught us that using the computer as a primary resource is hazardous in the extreme, since the Internet is as full of nonsense as sense, and the experience of virtual education sadly brought about by the Covid-19 crisis has not proved very successful.

One particular fear that one might have of a deschooled society would be that it would be detrimental to any goal of equality of opportunity. If learning were to be a matter of the individual pursuing knowledge for him or herself, it is a fair bet that those from privileged backgrounds, with more access to technology, more access to individual expertise, better educated parents, more opportunity to travel widely, more able to buy books and other educational material, and so forth, would be better able to educate themselves than those from poorer backgrounds, whether economic or cultural. One of the arguments for a state system of schooling has always been that it is instrumental in providing equality of opportunity. Again, we must not confuse legitimate complaints that for various reasons it does not always ensure total success with the suggestion that it is not overall beneficial.

I would conclude that there is no case for deschooling. However, the suggestion that we should deschool society does serve to remind us of some of the dangers that we want to avoid. In particular, while certainly wanting a degree of homogeneity in society and general acceptance of certain values and ways of behaving, we want to avoid bringing up a generation of conditioned individuals who do not think for themselves, but slavishly follow established convention and question nothing; and we want to minimize the sense of alienation from school that some individuals undoubtedly feel. But if deschooling is not the answer, perhaps we should return to the view associated with student-centered approaches that it is not schooling as such that is the problem so much as the nature of the curriculum and the traditional style of teaching. Student-centered theorists argue that curriculum content should not be decided and implemented by adults, and teachers should not adopt a didactic or instructive approach. Instead they advocate an approach that is based on responding to initiatives and features of students themselves such as their needs and interests (see next chapter). But let us first consider the claims that the curriculum needs to be 'relevant', that children need to be 'ready' for whatever it is we wish to teach, and that they will learn best through experience and by discovery.

On the face of it, such pronouncements seem eminently reasonable. Who would argue that the curriculum should be irrelevant or that children don't need to be ready to engage in an educational exercise? And surely there is something to be said for discovering things for oneself rather than simply being told them, while it is indisputable that we can learn very well from experience. All true enough. But on closer examination it can be seen that these claims, while being true, are of little or no practical value in helping us to form educational policy.

Relevance

The call for a relevant education or curriculum is often made as if it answered the question of what and how we should be teaching children in our schools ("What kind of curriculum do we want? Why, a relevant one"). But it doesn't answer the question at all; it merely reintroduces it in different words. For what constitutes a relevant curriculum is as open a question as what constitutes a good curriculum.

There is a tendency for people to talk as if relevance were a quality that is inherent in something, as color or shape are inherent in a particular object. But nothing is relevant or irrelevant in itself. It has to be relevant (or irrelevant) for some purpose. So if the call is for a relevant curriculum we need to ask relevant for what purpose? Since the main purpose of the school is to educate, it follows that the curriculum that is relevant is one that contributes to the successful education of the individual. And since the question of what kind of a curriculum will contribute to a successful education is not likely to be best answered by young children, we need to add that it should be relevant as a matter of fact and not simply felt to be relevant by students. For what students feel or call relevant is very often just what they enjoy, the more so the younger they are. And while we no doubt wish to make learning as enjoyable as possible, it is not a criterion of the value of a curriculum. What is actually a relevant curriculum depends not on student attitude to the material but on whether it serves our educational aims.

Readiness

Certain concepts often associated with student-centered and deschooling viewpoints, such as readiness, experience, and discovery, are in principle more concerned with teaching methods than with curriculum content. I say that 'in principle' these concepts provide prescriptions for method, but if one is not careful one can imperceptibly drift into the habit of using them as criteria for content. From the view that learning by discovery methods may be a valuable way of learning, some child-centered enthusiasts seem to come to the conclusion that whatever is learnt by discovery is worth learning, and that whatever is not learnt by discovery is not worth learning. Obviously the conclusion does not follow, and it is well to be on one's guard against this confusion at the outset.

The claim that teaching should proceed according to children's readiness seems at first glance unimpeachable. We surely have to agree that it makes little sense to get students to study Shakespeare when they are not ready to do so. But although we may all agree with this formal statement that does not mean that we are all going to agree as to when various children are ready to study Shakespeare (or pop music, social studies, or anything else). What does it mean to say that somebody is ready for something or ready to do something? What does the concept of readiness involve?

To say that somebody is ready to do something is to say, if nothing else, that that person is able to do something or capable of doing something, and of doing it with some degree of success. It is not necessarily to say that she will do it extremely well, but it is to say that she will succeed in doing it. If a person is ready for responsibility, she must be capable of exercising responsibility according to the criteria of success in exercising responsibility. A child who is ready to study Shakespeare must be able to study Shakespeare in such a way as to get something of whatever constitutes successful study of Shakespeare.

Findings of child psychology make it clear that children pass through various stages of mental development such that there will be certain ways of looking at things that they cannot achieve at particular stages, and hence certain types of things that they cannot do. For example, it is suggested that generally young children are not capable of understanding even simple parables as parables until about the age of eleven. Therefore, if our object in introducing parables to six year olds is to impart the point of the parables, we are wasting our time. The children cannot assimilate the point of the parables *qua* parables. They are not ready for them. In addition, one can think of many thousands of things that children are not ready to do for many reasons besides psychological limitations, such as lack of knowledge and lack of physical strength.

Now it is plainly absurd to insist that children should do what they cannot do. But an emphasis on children's readiness in this sense is not going to be a great deal of practical help. First, besides the knowledge of child psychology, we should need to have a clear idea of what the study of Shakespeare involves before we could begin to assess whether particular individuals were capable of doing it. Secondly, because claims about age-readiness are generalizations, one cannot conclude that because a particular child is only six years old it is impossible that she should be ready to understand parables as parables. Thirdly, and most importantly, the criterion of readiness cannot help us to decide between the various things that they might do at any particular age. Let us assume, as experience would seem to indicate, that at the age of fourteen many children are capable of playing various card games, carrying out some kind of survey into the political allegiances of members of the local community, studying Shakespeare, studying pop music, studying math, and so on. The notion of readiness is not going to help us decide which of these activities to encourage children to pursue.

Going beyond these considerations that limit the value of readiness as a significant criterion for making educational decisions lies an even more serious problem. How do we tell when a particular child is ready to do something? Rousseau wrote blandly of Emile not being allowed to read books until he was about fifteen and 'ready' to tackle literature; similarly, he was supposed to be 'ready' to undergo some elementary scientific training at the age of twelve. On what grounds does Rousseau claim, by implication, that children cannot be ready to read literature until the age of fifteen? We know that children can read – and understand – literature before that age. John Stuart Mill could read Greek by the age of four. What does it mean say that he was not ready to?

It is clear that what Rousseau is doing is extending the meaning of 'readiness'. He is providing what is sometimes referred to as a *persuasive definition* in that he is taking advantage of the evaluative overtones of 'readiness' and providing his own preferred definition. For him an individual is only ready to do something when he has reached that stage which, in Rousseau's view, is the ideal point to undertake the task in question. On this view, to say that children are ready to read at the age of fifteen is a covert way of saying that in the speaker's opinion it is best that children should not learn to read until that age. There may be arguments to support this opinion, but if there are they need to be given and we have clearly passed a long way beyond the normal meaning of 'readiness'.[2]

When, therefore, we hear some specific claim such as that children should not start to learn to read until they are ready to, we need first of all to know precisely what is meant by 'ready to' in this context. Are we being advised to wait until children are capable of learning to read, in which case, presumably, we should agree and the phrase may have a certain value in reminding us that inasmuch as children differ there is no fixed age by which all children must be reading. Or are we being advised to wait until children show an interest in learning to read? If this is the case then surely, although we may agree that it is a factor to be taken into consideration (since if the interest is there the task will very likely be more pleasant and easier for the child, and hence the whole operation more successful), it is not the only consideration. There comes a point (assuming that one believes in the value of learning to read) at which if the child does not express a readiness the very least we should want to do is attempt to provoke his interest, and if that attempt gains no response we may even want to teach him to read despite his lack of interest. At what age such steps should be taken can only be decided by reference to the ability of the child and the degree of importance one attaches to reading both for its own sake and as a necessary means to further activities of educational value. What seems quite unacceptable is the view that nothing should be done in schools except what children express a readiness to do. (On interests, see Chapter 5.)

Discovery

The view that education should proceed by means of discovery methods seems altogether more comprehensible. Here nothing is necessarily being said about what content of education is valuable. Rather the argument is that whether we are dealing with mathematics, Latin, or video games, it is preferable that children should find things out for themselves rather than be told everything. For example, rather than telling children a particular rule of mathematics and expecting them to learn it by rote ("The square on the hypotenuse equals the sum of the squares on the other two sides"), the teacher gives them certain data (in this simple case, perhaps a triangle drawn to scale) and leaves them to discover the rule for themselves.

The claims for discovery methods involve the assertions that children learn better this way, are more interested, understand what they learn better, and in the process learn to think for themselves. These of course are empirical claims and can only be tested by experiment and observation. But despite one's intuitive feeling that the child who discovers the rule about the square on the hypotenuse for himself may have more understanding of that rule than the child who is simply told it, and hence in some sense may be said to have learnt it better, it is worth raising a few skeptical questions.

1   In what sense can the many thousands of people who learnt this and other mathematical rules by rote be said to have not learnt it very well? They acquired the rule, they used it, they understood it, and they know it still. Surely at the most the claim must be not that discovery methods are the most effective methods of learning, but that they are more effective for some children.

2   The general claim that an education based on discovery methods teaches people to think for themselves is rather obscure. In one sense of course it does so by definition. The child who works out the mathematical rule is thinking for herself. What is not clear is whether practice and skill at discovery or problem-solving in one area leads to proficiency at problem-solving in another area or whether such an education necessarily promotes good thinking or rationality. It must be remembered that the child does not just discover a mathematical rule out of thin air; she is helped towards its discovery by the guidance of the teacher who selects and provides relevant data. What she is really gaining practice in is the art of drawing conclusions from selected data in a given field. This *may* promote a general skill at drawing conclusions, but clearly this skill can only be of use in situations where the individual has access to the relevant data. And even allowing for this it is difficult to see why the individual who is skilled at drawing conclusions in one area, such as mathematics, should necessarily be so in another area, such as politics, where the manner in which conclusions have to be assessed is entirely different. (This important point is taken up in different ways in Chapters 7 and 13.)

3   Are there not various considerations that may count against an emphasis on discovery methods? For instance, do not considerations of time and the ability of children lead one to the conclusion that some things are better not left to discovery? Are there not some areas in which it is more important that children should have knowledge than it is to worry about how they acquire it, and are there not some areas of study that are less appropriate to discovery techniques than others?

These questions and observations do not amount to an attempt to discredit discovery methods in education. As already said, the value of such methods is in any case largely an empirical matter. The real point that is brought out by the questions raised is that there is a distinction between advocating discovery methods as the best way to gain certain objectives in particular areas of the curriculum and advocating discovery as an end in itself. The mere fact that a child discovers something for himself is not necessarily valuable.

Experience

Much the same may be said of the notion of educating through experience if what is meant by this phrase is that experience can constitute a valuable way whereby children may learn. That is to say, one can see *prima facie* value in attempting to relate one's teaching to the child's actual experience, in attempting to give her experience of what she is learning, and in attempting to let some learning arise directly out of her experience. Understood in this way the demand that education should be through experience would amount to the general injunction that what goes on in schools should be made to seem important to the child, and the injunction could be defended on the grounds that the child will gain more and learn more effectively if she feels that what she is doing is of some value to her.

But once again there is a great difference between arguing that as a matter of fact a great deal of what goes on in schools is ineffective, in terms of its own objectives, because it does not relate to the experience of children or because they do not see any connection with their present or future experience, and arguing that the child's experiences can serve as the criterion whereby to assess what ought to be taught in schools. Imagine that a class of fifteen-year-old boys from homes in which books are scarcely read are due to read a book during the course of the term. If the teacher has any choice in the matter one can at once see a case for selecting a book in the *Game of Thrones* series rather than Jane Austen's *Pride and Prejudice*. The former is likely to have a much more immediate impact on them, since it relates much more to their experience, and to be as useful in terms of the desired objectives as *Pride and Prejudice*. But it would be a different matter entirely to argue that, since these particular boys come from homes where reading is confined to a cursory glance at the sports pages of the newspapers, reading books does not relate to their experience and they should therefore not be encouraged to read books at all.

John Dewey

One is therefore a little chary of phrases such as 'education through experience' or 'education is growth' since they are so ambiguous. The last phrase is Dewey's and he characterizes education in terms of experience. But it is symptomatic of the danger inherent in using such slogans that Dewey seems to have been misunderstood by many who regard themselves as his followers.

For many take him to have advocated the view that education is taking place provided that the child is provided with an environment in which he is free to grow or in which a sequence of experiences can arise out of the child's original experience, without any imposition or control on the part of the teacher. In other words the view seems to be attributed to Dewey that the mere fact of growing or developing, in the sense of changing from a child to an adult, could somehow constitute becoming educated.

In fact Dewey offered a rather more plausible view than this. In the first place he took for granted certain objectives, which were broadly speaking based on the ideal of a democratic state. These objectives were that children should become tolerant and rational adults, able to cope with a relatively high degree of social freedom without abusing that freedom to interfere with the freedom or well-being of others. Given these objectives, Dewey argued, education must avoid stultifying the individual's capacity to think for herself and promoting in her the idea that for every question there was only one right answer, namely the answer handed out by those in authority. Therefore, education should not proceed by a series of dogmatic answers, rules, and fiats from the teacher. The school should order the child's development through experiences in a small-scale social setting that mirrored the democratic world. But the experiences in the school situation were not to be selected solely with reference to the children's actual present experience. They were to be selected by the teacher and the teacher was to select with reference to two criteria: first any experience which the children were to have must have an immediate appeal to them (in Dewey's terminology, 'interaction'), but secondly it must also have a propensity for leading on to further experiences that would also provide further interaction. And no experience that involved anti-social tendencies would at any stage be selected.[3]

It is at once apparent that, for Dewey at least, behind the casual and careless slogans about growth and experience lie strong qualifications. To say that the school should provide opportunities for children to experience situations or activities that are not anti-social, that are appealing to the child, and that will lead on to further experiences, is very different from saying that experience should be the sole criterion of education. One might still object to Dewey's view on the grounds that teachers should not only start from experiences that already appeal to the child but that they should also create or promote interest in experiences that do not have an immediate appeal to the child. Furthermore, even accepting Dewey's position, there is room for a great deal of argument as to which experiences measure up to his conditions. But our concern here is to question the view that experience alone can provide a sufficient criterion for deciding what ought to go on in schools. I suggest that it cannot. For the claim that the teacher is doing all that she needs to do and all that she ought to do, if she helps the child to explore his present experiences, involves the claim that there is no distinction between worthwhile and non-worthwhile experiences and that it is in some way improper for the teacher to enlarge the horizons of the child and to initiate him into experiences that he would never have come across if education were confined to an exploration of his experience.

When it comes to discovery and experience there is the ever-present danger of confusing an effective technique with an end in itself, and so far as the question of technique goes it is perhaps a more open – empirical – question than some would admit as to how far and in what circumstances and for what purposes they are effective. It may be suggested that a great deal more empirical research is needed into the efficacy of various styles of education than is in fact yet available. But this research cannot begin until it is clear precisely what claims we are supposed to be researching into.[4] When a teacher says that discovery methods are best, what is she claiming that they are best for? If she gives a specific reply, such as that discovery methods in mathematics produce adults who are better mathematicians, and remember more of what they learnt in school or find it easier to apply their mathematical skill to new problems as they confront them, does she actually have any evidence to support this claim? In relation to this point it may also be suggested that there is a certain lack of clarity in a great deal of educational theory as to whether various arguments are supposed to be empirical or evaluative. Whether we are talking about deschoolers, child-centered theorists, or traditionalists it is often unclear whether they are claiming that their approach and their methods will achieve better results in terms of certain broadly agreed objectives, or whether they are arguing for an entirely new set of objectives. In most cases, no doubt, a little bit of both is going on, but it is vital to keep the two types of argument distinct since they have to be assessed in entirely different ways: the former type of claim can ultimately only be tested by empirical means, the latter by philosophical.

Notes

1 John Holt, *How Children Fail* (Penguin, 1969) p. 171.
2 For a detailed study of Rousseau's educational views, see Robin Barrow, *Radical Education* (Martin Robertson, 1978) Chapters 2 and 3.
3 See R.S. Peters (ed.), *John Dewey Reconsidered* (Routledge & Kegan Paul, 1977).
4 Sadly, the warning implicit in this sentence has not been heeded. See Chapter 19. See also Robin Barrow, *Giving Teaching Back to Teachers* (Wheatsheaf, 1984).

Further Reading

The canonical text on deschooling is Ivan Illich, *Deschooling Society* (Penguin, 1973). Ian Lister (ed.), *Deschooling* (Cambridge University Press, 1975) provides a useful overview.

M. Sukarich & S. Tannock, in 'Deschooling from Above', *Race & Class*, 61 (4), 68–86 (2020), maintain that the concept of deschooling is making a comeback. Eric J. Weiner, *Deschooling the Imagination: Critical Thought as Social Practice* (Routledge, 2014) certainly advocates it.

See also Harold Entwistle, *Child-Centered Education* (Methuen, 1970), Richard Pring, *John Dewey* (Continuum, 2007), Roland Meighan, *John Holt* (Continuum, 2007), and Jurgen Oelkers, *Jean-Jacques Rousseau* (Continuum, 2008).

Questions

What arguments can you provide for and against a free public system of schooling?

Since most of us agree that children should be ready to study and that their study should not be irrelevant, why does the text argue that these terms are not useful as guides to curriculum content?

In what way(s) is experience important in education?

5   Needs and Interests

Another popular line is to argue for a curriculum based on children's needs. Once again, *prima facie,* the suggestion seems unexceptionable. It would surely be very odd to say that education should *not* take account of children's needs. But what are children's needs?

Needs

It is easy to talk as if there can really be no doubt as to what children's needs are, and as if, in order to identify them, we only have to conduct some empirical survey. But needs, whether children's or anybody else's, are by no means always obvious and indisputable. There are some things we need, such as food and drink, which we are liable to forget we need since we have them. One might think one needs something and be mistaken, as, for example, one might think one needs plastic surgery, only to discover that one has made a bad mistake. I might need something and have absolutely no view on the matter as to whether I need it or not: for example, if I am unconscious, I may nonetheless need medical attention. Do I need to have a sense of humor in this day and age? Do I need a car? How much money do I need? Do I need to have access to libraries? And what about the question of the connection between wants and needs? Some seem to treat the two concepts as synonymous, which they are certainly not – I want an expensive iPhone, but it is by no means clear that I need it. I might need something and not want it, for instance a penicillin injection.

These uses of 'need' make it clear that, although needs may be important, it is by no means clear what people's needs are, how one sets about assessing them, and therefore what education according to children's needs would actually consist of. They also make it clear that one point about the logic of the concept of need is that an objective is presupposed. One needs something *for* something, or one needs something given some prior assumption. One does not have needs in a vacuum. Even such needs as the need for food and water can only be regarded as needs on the prior assumption that one wishes to survive. One does not need food if one intends to starve oneself to death. Similarly, in so far as we take it for granted that we want everybody to survive

DOI: 10.4324/9781003120476-5

without acute discomfort, then, in our society, we all need money since money is the means of obtaining various necessities for comfortable survival. But how much money we need is a difficult question to answer, since it depends on such factors as who we are, what we regard as comfortable survival, and various other objectives that we might have.

Wants and needs are to be distinguished essentially in that one may talk of wants without specifying any particular objective (although it may be true that in general we happen to want things for particular purposes), whereas to talk of needs necessarily implies some specific objective. I need a paintbrush rather than paper-hanging equipment, if my intention is to paint my room rather than paper it. If this specific objective is changed then I cease to need the paintbrush. In many cases the selection of an objective itself will be a matter of wants rather than needs. In general people do not need to paint their rooms rather than paper them, that is to say they do not have some further objective that necessitates paint rather than paper; they simply want one rather than the other. Our wants, then, become needs in the light of specific further objectives. I want a car: it would give me pleasure to have one. But we do not start talking of my need for a car unless specific objectives are brought into the matter, for instance that I have to make a long and complicated journey to work by public transport.

The fact that a need logically implies some objective has two important consequences: first, it is not necessarily desirable to fulfill needs. Whether we think that a particular person's particular need at any given time ought to be satisfied will depend on our evaluation of the objective at which this need is directed. A man who wants to commit murder needs the opportunity and the means to do so, but we should presumably not feel inclined to satisfy that need. A drug addict needs his drugs, but we might reasonably argue as to whether this is a need that should be satisfied. To put the same point another way, we may disagree as to whether a particular person does need something because we have different values. One important point that emerges from this is that assessing needs is not simply a matter of empirical research. Estimating children's needs requires consideration of evaluative assumptions as well as psychological and sociological data.

The second consequence of the fact that needs presuppose objectives is that, in order to assess needs, one also has to have knowledge about what is in fact required for a certain end. Before I can know that I need penicillin, I do not only have to assume the value of being healthy, I also have to know that penicillin will in fact restore my health. Furthermore, I have to recognize that I am sick. I have to have knowledge about myself as well as knowledge about means to ends. Just as I could not know whether my next-door neighbor needs financial assistance without knowing what his financial resources are, so I cannot know whether I need to take a job as a teacher without knowing myself pretty well. I may want to be a teacher, I may feel that I need to be a teacher rather than an insurance clerk but, on the assumption that this need is related to the general objective of feeling self-fulfilled, I can only be right in claiming that I need to be a teacher if I am reading my own personality accurately. It may transpire that teaching makes me anxious and depressed, and that a job as a teacher was not what I needed for my fulfillment as an individual.

It follows that one may not be the best judge of one's own needs. Perhaps in general people are – that would be an empirical question – but it is not necessarily true that they will be: they may lack self-knowledge and consequently assess their own personality inaccurately, they may be mistaken about means to ends, or they may assume that certain ends are desirable which turn out not to be. There is then the further question of whether the ends that people set up for themselves, and therefore the needs that they have in relation to those ends, are morally desirable or more generally worthwhile.

It is at once clear that, whatever the case with adults, young children at any rate are very unlikely to be the best judge of their own needs. In so far as they are not very self-aware, do not have a great deal of knowledge or experience about means to ends, do not tend to look into the future, and do not have the ability or experience to make an informed choice between ends, they are not likely to be very good judges of what they need, particularly if we assume that we are thinking of what they need from a long-term point of view. In many cases at least, what children think that they need will be indistinguishable from what they want. But, as we have seen, what people want or think they need is not necessarily what they do need. A child, for example, may feel that she does not need to learn to read. She is not necessarily wrong. We could only say that she was wrong if we could confidently predict that she will need it for some objective that at some stage she will embrace. But as a matter of fact, and despite the arguments of some deschoolers such as Goodman, it is highly likely that she is wrong.[1] In many ways life will be more difficult for her if she cannot read, and on the assumption, surely a reasonable one, that she will not want a difficult life then one thing that she does need to do is to learn to read – and that is all there is to it. (Goodman's argument is based upon the point that information can be gained through television and other aural and visual media. Allowing that this is so, and allowing that all education could be carried on through audio-visual aids, it should nonetheless be noted that to argue that children do not need to learn to read is to deny the objective of giving individuals the opportunity to pursue arguments and interests that go beyond and that may challenge the point of view of those who are responsible for programming information.)[2]

What then does the demand that education should be according to children's needs amount to? Very little. In the first place it is purely formal: it does not tell us what children's needs are. We might all agree with the demand in principle but disagree violently as to what children do need, for one's view of what children need is one and the same thing as one's view of child psychology, one's sociological knowledge, one's knowledge of means to ends, and one's view of what are desirable objectives all rolled into one. For example, if one held the view that traditional teaching techniques of drill and instruction were efficient and not harmful to the child's psychological make-up, if one believed in the value of reading Cicero in Latin (either for its own sake or for some further objective), if one believed that it was good to be cultured and that cultured people should have read Virgil, and if one believed in the value of going to a particular university that required a knowledge of Latin as an entrance requirement, then a most old-fashioned Latin course could be said to be part of an education according to children's needs. To convince a particular teacher that such a course did not meet children's needs one would have to convince her that what she valued was not valuable.

Secondly, as is clear from the previous paragraph, it is not going to be very easy to arrive at agreement on what children's needs are. There may well be agreement on certain basic needs simply because there is a degree of agreement on certain broad objectives and the means that are necessary to meet these objectives. For instance, we all agree that one objective is to provide children with the means and ability to survive. Children, like other people, therefore need food and shelter and certain basic skills. But even over the question of what basic skills they need there may be disagreement, as we have seen in the case of reading. Once we go beyond such an uncontentious objective, we lose any kind of consensus as to what children's needs are. Even if we agreed that children should be enabled to flourish or thrive, rather than merely survive, in a complex industrial society, we should immediately open the door to rival views as to what 'flourishing' or 'thriving' actually involved, and hence as to what we needed to meet this objective. But to ask the sorts of question that one would need to ask to construct a curriculum according to children's needs – Do children need to study English literature? Do they need to do math? Do they need to do what they feel like doing? – would simply be to open up the question of what should be done in the name of education.

Thirdly, talk of education according to children's needs is likely to obscure what might be an important distinction between what children need now for certain immediate objectives, and what they need for certain long-term objectives. Fourthly, there is considerable lack of clarity about alternative phraseology such as 'based on', 'according to', and 'taking account of'. It is one thing to take note of children's needs and another to subordinate everything to them. Finally, although the phrase 'children's needs' may have the merit of reminding us that it is children we are concerned with and what *they* need rather than what we need for them, there is also the danger that we shall ignore the question of whether there are not other needs besides those of the child to be taken into account. In other words, is 'education according to children's needs' to be understood as meaning education with reference to the needs of children only, or does it also allow consideration of the needs of, say, parents or society as a whole?

Needs Assessment

A word should be added about needs assessment. A number of programs of, and strategies for, assessing the needs of various groups or individuals in various contexts have been developed and put into practice over the years. Because some means of assessing needs employ techniques that are familiar to social science research (such as the use of questionnaires and various types of observation), there is a tendency to think of assessing needs as a reasonably sophisticated technical business, such that experts in the field can furnish information that is fairly accurate and objective. In response it might be questioned whether the procedures in question really are reliable as means of getting at the truth. The most important thing to appreciate is that such techniques of needs assessment, despite the words used, are not in fact even attempting to assess people's needs but rather people's *opinions* on people's needs (whether their own or others').

If, for example, we hear that a certain district in Northern Ontario wants to set up a new curriculum, suited to the particular needs of people in the area, we might welcome the additional news that what those needs are is going to be established by some rigorous and organized manner of assessing those needs. But, in fact, in nine cases out of ten, whether the researchers in question favor informal means of gathering information or formal means, the information will relate to what various people *think* are the needs that children in the locality have. Whether the children truly have the needs suggested is an entirely different kind of question. And, as we have already seen, to answer it requires sorting out and justifying various aims and values, as well as empirically establishing what the nature of life in the area may be, what people do lack and what are efficacious means to the chosen ends.

None of this is to say that education should not take account of children's needs. It is simply to say that such talk does not really get us anywhere since virtually any school from the most traditional to the most progressive could make out a reasonable case for saying that it was based on consideration of children's needs.

Interests

Unfortunately, the idea of education according to children's interests is not much more helpful. Just as there is a distinction to be drawn between needs in the sense of felt needs and needs in the sense of objectively assessed needs (by which I do not mean the findings of needs assessment schedules), so there is an ambiguity between two possible senses of 'interest'. If I claim that my life is organized according to my interests, I might mean that it is organized in accordance with what interests me. That is to say I am interested in opera, Victorian literature, insurance, and swimming, perhaps, and my life is so organized as to give me scope to indulge these interests. Interests, in this sense, are those things with which I have a particular degree of interaction or engagement; things that provide satisfaction and pleasure for me. To claim an interest in something in this sense implies a degree of commitment to the activity in question.

But I might also mean, by the claim that my life is organized according to my interests, that it is organized in accordance with what is good or profitable for me. In this sense, a life organized according to my interests or in my interests, might mean such things as that I, rather than my wife, have the use of the car, that my next-door neighbor rather than me is responsible for the upkeep of the partition fence between our gardens, and that in general my advantage is secured. Obviously, what is in my interests and what interests me may happen to coincide: it is in my interests to write this book and it also interests me. But equally obviously the two may not coincide: it is in my interests to exercise daily but it does not interest me at all. Conversely, it interests me to study real-life crime, but it is difficult to see in what way it is in my interests to do so.

The question therefore is whether education according to children's interests is supposed to mean education in accordance with what as a matter of fact interests them or in accordance with what is in their interests. If we take the latter interpretation, a situation arises similar to that which arose over the idea of education according to needs. Few would dispute that education should be in children's interests. But agreeing that education should take account of children's interests in this sense would get us nowhere, for we should have the problem of deciding what *is* in children's interests still before us, and it is this problem on which there is so little agreement. Even those who propose what may seem *prima facie* to be the most bizarre or objectionable types of education seldom argue that they are unconcerned about what is in children's interests; they simply have their own view as to what it is that is in their interests. And, as with needs, to come to some conclusion as to what really is in children's interests would involve working through all the findings of educational psychology and sociology and working out one's overall philosophy of education. In other words, the slogan 'education according to interest', if it means according to what is in the interests of children, would not constitute a helpful dictum for ending the debate about what form education should take and what content it should have. It would merely be another way of starting the debate. Instead of asking what is it desirable that children should gain through education we are asking 'What is in the educational interests of children?' The words are different, but the question is the same.

But suppose we interpret talk of interests in education to mean that education should be according to what does as a matter of fact interest children. Here the situation is very different, for although we cannot simply write down a list of what does interest children, since different children have different interests, there is not a great deal of room for meaningful disagreement as to what does interest particular children. Two teachers might debate for a very long time about what is in the interests of a particular child, even though they both know the child well, for they may disagree about the value of various objectives. But they would have little excuse for arguing deep into the night about what interests that same child. All they have to do to find out what interests him is to ask him.

(Conceivably a person might make a mistake even as to what does interest him. He might claim to be interested in fishing on the strength of a one-day fishing excursion, which perhaps he enjoyed, without realizing it, for reasons that had little to do with fishing. A second outing might then cause him to realize that he was not interested in fishing. Allowing for this kind of mistake we should perhaps modify what was said above and say that the two teachers only have to give the child the opportunity to do various things and then ask him which interest him or alternatively observe which things he continues to do. For one indication that one is interested in doing something is that one freely chooses to do it when the opportunity arises.) The problem then with this view of education is not that it is unhelpful in practice, but that considerable disagreement will arise as to whether it is indeed desirable that education should be in accordance with what interests children.

An important point that would need clarification before many people would be prepared to commit themselves one way or the other, as was the case with needs, would be what precisely is meant by 'according to' or 'in accordance with', and whether the interests of children are supposed to be the only determining factor in what goes on in schools or merely one of many factors. If the claim is simply that education should among other things take account of what interests children, perhaps more than it has sometimes done in the past, then many people with very different overall educational view-points might happily agree. For the claim would be so vague as to allow the support of all except a few extremists – if they exist – who held to the peculiar view that schools should positively avoid taking any notice of what interests children. One might for instance consider that children ought to learn mathematics, on grounds that have more to do with what is *in* children's interests than what actually interests them, but then, having decided that, go on to attempt to teach it in such a way as to interest them, specifically by starting from some point that does already interest them. The desirability of some such general concern for what does interest children already and for making what they are doing as interesting as possible seems hardly worth debating. That people should derive some enjoyment from their education is not a particularly contentious ideal, and people's interest is one of the most obvious and helpful forms of motivation. But of course, the suggestion that we should show some concern for interesting children is only uncontroversial because it avoids all the crucial questions, such as when should we ignore the fact that something does not interest the child very much? In what areas should we actually start from what already interests the child rather than simply attempt to interest him in what we insist that he does for other rea-sons? What are the other considerations that may conflict with and override the question of the child's interest?

But what finally of the view that education should be according to chil-dren's interests in the sense that the *only* determining factor in planning an education should be what as a matter of fact interests the child? The view, in other words, that stands in opposition to any attempt to reply to the question 'What should be the content of the education that we provide for our children?' that is couched in terms of what we think they need, or what we think is in their interests or what we think it is good from society's point of view that children should do. Now this view of education *seems* to be a necessary condition of what some people mean by child-centered education. P.S. Wilson writes: "The point of calling education 'child-centered' lies in emphasising that even when a person who is being educated is a child, and even, therefore, when his interests often seem 'childish' or silly or undesirable from the point of view of his adult teachers, nevertheless his education can only proceed through the pursuit of his interests, since it is these and only these which for him are of intrinsic value".[3]

Wilson's position is both complex and, in my view, confused. But it deserves a brief mention since it is the only serious philosophical attempt to make sense of an extreme child-centered view. The reader is, however, referred to Wilson's book *Interest and Discipline in Education*, since the confusion may be mine rather than his. It should be stressed that Wilson does not commit himself to the view that the teacher should just stand back and *allow* children to pursue whatever interests come into their heads. In the first place the teacher has the positive task to perform of helping the child to see whatever may be of value in what interests him, and to develop in the child the inclination and the ability to pursue what is valued. All that Wilson is committed to is the view that the content of education has to be decided by reference solely to what individual children do as a matter of fact value. This, for Wilson, effectively means that what interests the child has to form the content since, as the quotation above indicates, the child can regard only what interests him as having intrinsic value.

Wilson might appear to gain some plausibility for his argument from such statements as 'There is always value, therefore, "in" my interest,'[4] for if one agreed that an individual's interests always had some value, one might at least begin to regard the notion of education according to children's interests, in this sense, as worthwhile. But the conclusion that there is always value in my interests, whatever they are, seems either badly phrased or simply mistaken. Wilson arrives at his conclusion by arguing that, since being interested in doing something can stand as a sufficient explanation of why one is doing it, a child's (or anyone else's) interest 'will always constitute a good reason for engaging in the activities which he sees as relevant'[5] to that interest. But this is either not true or else highly ambiguous. It is not true if by a 'good reason' we mean a reason that other people might regard as a sufficient *justification*, which is what we usually do mean. The fact that I am interested in torturing people does not constitute a good reason for doing so, in this sense of 'good reason'. What Wilson obviously means here by 'good reason' is simply an *explanation* or a motivation. It is true that my interest in torturing people will explain why I am doing so and serve as a motivation for my doing so. But then the fact that my interest will always constitute a good reason, in the particular sense of 'an explanation', does not lead to the conclusion that there is any value in my interest. At the very most one might say that people tend to see value in what interests them. But then why should we agree that education ought to consist simply of what children do as a matter of fact want to do, which is what all this talk of interest and value seems to amount to?

At this point we must note a second and most peculiar – in the circumstances – proviso laid down by Wilson. Not only should the teacher help the child to get something out of his interests, rather than simply allow him to indulge them, but he should also prevent the child indulging certain interests that are trivial or harmful. This seems at first sight a flat contradiction of the statement that education must proceed only through the child's interests. It turns out that it is not, because Wilson quite simply *defines* education with reference to interests. Anything else, such as imparting adult values, is to be called 'schooling'. But he agrees that we ought to do some 'schooling' as well as some 'educating'. In other words, for practical purposes the whole argument seems to pivot on an arbitrary definition of 'education' and to give us virtually no indication of how we are to decide when to educate and when to school.

The thesis is therefore considerably less dramatic and considerably less revolutionary than Wilson seems willing to admit. He is arguing that, although there may be some adult values that we ought to bring children to hold, although there may be some children's interests that we ought not to encourage because they are trivial or harmful, nonetheless we ought to take good note of children's interests.

However, regardless of the logic of Wilson's argument, there is not much doubt that what he and some others in practice are advocating is that the school curriculum should be based on what does interest children and what they do value and want to do, rather than on what we regard as valuable. What are we to say about this view of a curriculum based on children's present interests?

If children's interests were to be the sole criterion of what went on in schools, then unless we believed that all children necessarily must have worthwhile interests if left to themselves, we commit ourselves to the view that there is no such thing as a distinction between more and less worthwhile activities. We commit ourselves to the view that it does not matter what activities children engage in, provided that they are interested in whatever it is that they do. There can be no two ways about this: that is the necessary corollary of making children's interests the sole criterion of the content for education. (And at this point let us make a distinction between admitting, as many would, that establishing what activities are worthwhile may be very difficult and may invite considerable disagreement, and claiming that there is no such thing as a relatively worthwhile activity.)

Do we accept that if a child is interested in blowing up frogs with bicycle pumps or bullying smaller children the interest makes it an acceptable activity? These are examples in which the question of cruelty, or more generally moral considerations, might, for some of us, be thought to outweigh consideration of interests. Blowing up frogs might also be thought to be rather pointless. Do we accept that other examples of *prima facie* pointless activity, such as making paper darts, throwing stones in ponds and making mud pies, are worth pursuing in schools, just because they interest children? Do we accept the possible consequence that, at least in many cases, concentration on what does interest children now will deny them the opportunity of being introduced to activities which would interest them once they had been initiated into them? Jersild's empirical survey led him to the conclusion that 'the range of children's out-of-school interests' (i.e., of interests that arise without any deliberate attempt to create them) 'is quite restricted compared with children's potentialities'.[6] Do we accept that there is no point or good reason to develop, even create, potential interests? Is it a bad thing that I have an interest in the Classical world, since I would never have developed this interest at a school that concentrated exclusively on the interests that I had acquired simply through my peer and social group? Why, in any case, are interests that arise out of my interaction with my peers – which is presumably how some children's interests arise – more hallowed than interests that arise out of my interaction with my teachers? Do we accept that they are? Even if we accept that the fact that the child values something or is interested in it makes it valuable, do we accept the possibility that some children's education will consist of exploring interests that they themselves will later lose interest in and regard as less than valuable? Do we, in other words, accept that there is not even to be a distinction between the present interests of children that are temporary and the present interests of children that will continue to interest them and seem valuable to them?

Readers must decide for themselves. The point that is being made here is that if one or more of these conclusions seem unacceptable then children's interests cannot be the sole criterion for deciding the content of the curriculum. But if it is only one factor to be taken into account in constructing a curriculum, then talk of education according to children's interests has virtually no value until we have some more or less precise idea of what considerations are to override interests to what degree. Once we start to specify the considerations that might outweigh children's immediate interests – moral considerations, other value considerations, the adult's more experienced view of what will be of lasting interest and value (whether with Wilson we refer to these as schooling considerations or as educational considerations) – the stress on children's interests becomes meaningless, except as a general reminder to the effect that, as things are, a lot of what goes on in schools does not interest children, and that to gain their interest is to gain a most effective source of motivation. Only either by maintaining the thesis that the only criterion of value is what the individual of whatever age, experience or intelligence values, or by claiming it to be an empirical truth that children, given the freedom, select worthwhile interests, could the notion of education according to children's interests become more than a vague slogan that is useful only as a counterweight to the extreme view that whether children are interested or not in what goes on at school is unimportant.

Notes

1 Paul Goodman, *Compulsory Miseducation* (Penguin, 1971).
2 It is also to ignore the important question of the relationships between thought and language, and language and reading/writing. See Robin Barrow, *Language, Intelligence and Thought* (Edward Elgar, 1993).
3 P.S. Wilson, *Interest and Discipline in Education* (Routledge & Kegan Paul, 1971) p. 66.
4 Ibid.
5 Ibid., p. 63.
6 Arthur T. Jersild & Ruth J. Tasch, *Childrens' Interests* (Teachers' College Publications, 1949).

Further Reading

R.F. Dearden, *The Philosophy of Primary Education* (Routledge & Kegan Paul, 1968) includes a chapter on needs and interests. See also his article '"Needs" in Education' in R.F. Dearden, P.H. Hirst, & R.S. Peters (eds.), *Education and the Development of Reason* (Routledge & Kegan Paul, 1972).

Despite the concerns and problems alluded to in this chapter, emphasis on needs and interests is still popular, particularly in conjunction with the view that caring and promoting happiness are central to education. E.g., Nel Noddings, *Happiness and Education* (Cambridge University Press, 2003) and J.F. Goodman, 'Responding to Children's Needs: Amplifying the Caring Ethic', *Journal of Philosophy of Education*, 42 (2), 233–248 (2008).

See also Christine Doddington & Mary Hilton, *Child-Centered Education: Reviving the Creative Tradition* (Sage, 2007).

For a trenchant critique, see Kieran Egan, *Getting it Wrong from the Beginning: Our Progressive Inheritance from Herbert Spencer, John Dewey and Jean Piaget* (Yale University Press, 2002).

Questions

What does one need to know in order to work out what children's educational needs are?

Using those criteria, what are their educational needs?

What difficulties are there in the formula that education should be determined by children's interests?

6 The Concept of Education

There used to be considerable controversy as to whether the word 'education' was derived from the Latin word 'educere' or the word 'educare'. 'Educere' means 'to lead out', and those who favored some kind of student-centered approach saw this as the origin of our word 'education'. They appealed to this derivation as evidence that teachers, if they were truly educating, should seek to bring or lead out what was in some sense innate in the child, rather than to impose various preselected attitudes, characteristics, and values on him. The teacher was to regard herself as a gardener tending a plant, rather than as a craftsman making a product. She should encourage the natural flowering or development of the individual, rather than attempt to mold him.

This particular argument, conducted with reference to the supposed derivation of the word 'education', was more than usually silly, and provides us with an object lesson in one way *not* to analyze a concept. In the first place, the fact, if it were established as a fact, that the word 'education' is derived from a particular Latin word is not particularly compelling evidence to persuade one to teach in one way rather than another. Words change their meaning over time, sometimes dramatically, as for example in the case of 'gay' or 'stasis' (which is a Greek word that used to mean 'discord' among other things, but is now taken to mean 'stagnation'), and in any case the etymology of a word has got nothing to do with contemporary conceptions. In the second place, the Romans themselves used both 'educere' and 'educare' with reference to educating children, and it is therefore difficult to see how one can successfully establish one rather than the other as the source of our 'education'. In the third place, 'educere', besides meaning 'to lead out', was also used to mean 'train', and 'educare', besides meaning 'to train', was used to mean 'nourish' with reference to plants. In other words, either term could in fact be said to involve either of the contrasting views of education. One is glad therefore that this particular etymological game seems to be out of favor at the moment.[1]

Education

But we do need to get to the heart of the matter and to consider what exactly constitutes education. A quotation from Richard Peters will serve

DOI: 10.4324/9781003120476-6

as a starting point. But it should be stressed that Peters was concerned with the notion of education for many years, during which time he modified his views to some extent. I shall concentrate on an early statement of his position, since his ideas are cited only as a way into the discussion of education. It is not my purpose to review his work and no attempt will be made to chart his subsequent changes of view or emphasis.

In *Ethics and Education*, Peter asserts that the word 'education' has "the criterion built into [it] that something worthwhile should be achieved". He continues:

> It implies that something worthwhile is being or has been intentionally transmitted in a morally acceptable manner. It would be a logical contradiction to say that a man had been educated but that he had in no way changed for the better, or that in educating his son a man was attempting nothing that was worthwhile. This is a purely conceptual point. Such a connection between 'education' and what is valuable does not imply any particular commitment to content. It is a further question what the particular standards are in virtue of which activities are thought to be of value and what grounds there might be for claiming that these are correct ones. All that is implied is a commitment to what is thought valuable.[2]

Peters is here making the point that education and associated terms (or *cognates*) such as 'educate' and 'educated' are *normative* terms; that is to say they are by definition value loaded. To call someone educated is to compliment them, to call them uneducated is to put them down. It is true that one sometimes hears remarks such as "you get a rotten education at that school" or "thank goodness I didn't have your education", which on the face of it seem to be self-contradictory, for, if education is necessarily good, how can it be rotten and how could anyone not prize it? But such expressions are really disguised ways of saying, respectively, that what is taught at that school is not truly educational and that I don't regard what you have studied as worthy of the label education.

Peters goes on to argue that the word 'education' is *polymorphous* (from the Greek, meaning 'takes many forms') in the same way that, say, the word 'gardening' is. Whether I am pruning, digging, weeding, or cutting the grass, in each case what I am doing is legitimately described as 'gardening'. It doesn't make sense to say "She was pruning the rosebush, not gardening". It is thus a mistake to think of 'educating' as the name of one, and only one, particular activity.[3] One may be educating when one gets children to find out things for themselves, when one drills them (recitation of times-tables for example), when one instructs them (chalk and talk, showing them how to do things), when one gets them to make things, and so on. Each of these activities can be distinguished from one another but they may still be instances of the educative process. It is not, then, logically legitimate to ask a teacher "Were you educating those children or merely instructing them?" (note the emotive overtones of 'merely'), for this carries with it the implication that educating is one particular kind of activity and instructing a different particular kind of activity. There is, however, a qualification to be added here: while a number of different methods of or approaches to teaching may count as equally educational, some practices cannot count as educational, and that is because of the normative nature of the term. Certain approaches such as indoctrination (see Chapter 11) are incompatible with education because they are morally unacceptable, whereas education, being something we value, must proceed in morally acceptable ways.

'Education' and its cognate terms are also *degree* words: nobody is completely or perfectly educated, and few adults if any are totally uneducated. When we refer to someone as educated without qualification we mean relatively well or highly educated, and to call someone uneducated is to suggest that their education was minimal rather than that it was literally non-existent.

The Educated Person

The obvious questions that now arise are "What are the worthwhile things that are to be transmitted in education?" and "How do we tell whether a manner of transmission is morally acceptable or not?" An attempt at a full answer to these questions is going to take most of the remainder of this book, but let us begin by turning our attention away from the concept of education and concentrate instead on the concept of the educated person.

If we can establish what an educated person *is* or what constitutes being educated, we should get some idea of what the worthwhile things that education should provide are.

Peters' answer in broad terms is that an educated person is one with a *developed mind*, and what is meant by a developed mind is essentially *developed understanding*. He makes it clear that the understanding in question is not confined to what he terms 'how to' knowledge but must also involve knowing 'the reason why of things'. In other words, my skills as a mechanic or accountant, though admirable and vital in their way, do not in themselves establish that I am well educated; to be considered as educated I should also have some understanding of the science behind my mechanical skills or the math and economic theory behind my accountancy skills.

It is important to recognize, first, that Peters is not scorning practical 'how to' knowledge, but saying that in itself it is not enough to mark out an educated person. Secondly, it is clearly implied that there are a number of other ends that while they may be valuable in themselves do not count as criteria of being educated, such as physical fitness, sporting achievement, artistic talent, and possibly even moral probity (see Chapter 10). Many people who value such things naturally find it hard to accept this conclusion. But surely on reflection it makes sense: of course we want children to be physically fit, to develop any artistic talent they may have, and to behave morally, and these may indeed be legitimate goals of *schooling* as a whole, but it does not follow that we have to judge how well *educated* a person is by these criteria. And surely there is something very odd about suggesting that, say, the obese or the otherwise unfit cannot count as educated whatever their knowledge or abilities. Likewise it would seem very far-fetched to suggest that all artists are educated simply because they are artists.[4]

Peters then introduces four formal criteria designed to mark out the nature of the knowledge that characterizes the educated person.[5]

1   The first is the *breadth criterion*. The knowledge or understanding of the educated person has to be broad. There are people who are undoubtedly very clever in respect of some narrow specialism, but if that is all that they are we would not regard them as well educated. Educated people are by definition people with a breadth of understanding. (This view, incidentally, is familiar from Aristotle: "We ascribe education to one who is able to judge nearly all branches of knowledge and not one who has a like ability merely in some special subject." *Parts of Animals* 639a.)

2   The second is the *transformation criterion*. Peters writes that the broad knowledge in question must "characterise [a person's] way of looking at things rather than be hived off. It is possible for a man to know a lot of history in the sense that he can give correct answers to questions in class-rooms and examinations; yet this might never affect the way in which he looks at buildings and institutions around him. We might describe such a man as 'knowledgeable' but we would not describe him as 'educated'; for 'education' implies that a man's outlook is transformed by what he knows." Though naturally referred to as the *transformation criterion*, since 'transformed' is the word Peters uses, I would suggest that the notion of 'transformation', implying a major shift in one's character, is a little strong. What is important is that one's learning should not simply rest 'inert', to use another of Peters' words, but that it should have some effect on one's outlook on life, should make one in however slight a degree a different person.

3   Thirdly, the *caring criterion*. The educated person must *care* about the standards immanent in subjects or fields of interest. "A man cannot really understand what it is to think scientifically unless he not only knows that evidence must be found for assumptions, but also knows what counts as evidence and cares that it should be found. In forms of thought where proof is possible cogency, simplicity and elegance must be felt to matter. And what would historical or philosophical thought amount to if there was no concern about relevance, consistency or coherence? All forms of thought and awareness have their own internal standards of appraisal. To be on the inside of them is both to understand and care." The *caring criterion* is sometimes also referred to as the *commitment criterion*, since it is commitment to the standards and procedures appropriate to the various kinds of subject matter that the educated person cares about.

4   Finally, the educated person must have *'cognitive perspective'*. So, "a man might be a very highly trained scientist [satisfying the previous three criteria]; yet we might refuse to call him an educated man... [if he were] to work away at science without seeing its connection with much else, its place in a coherent pattern of life. For him it is an activity which is cognitively adrift". This criterion effectively extends the breadth criterion by saying that not only does an educated person have a broad understanding, but the component parts of that understanding should be integrated, so that, for example, the scientist brings his moral understanding to bear even as he engages in scientific research.

What can be said about the plausibility of these criteria? The insistence that an educated person must have some breadth of knowledge seems in accord with our sense that being a brilliant race-car driver, a brilliant chess player, or a brilliant mathematical scholar does not in itself show that one is well educated, if that is all that one knows. The common assumption that Albert Einstein was a well-educated person is based not on the fact that he was a brilliant scientist, but on the fact that he was also deeply musical, historically aware, had a deep sense of morality, and so forth. Conversely, Mozart, though a musical genius, was not obviously very well educated. Surely it is counter-intuitive to see the technical wizard, the brilliant sculptor or the aeronautical engineer as being well educated simply in virtue of their specialist expertise. One might add that if we do not accept this criterion, if we allow that any expertise is sufficient to indicate that a person is well educated, then the concept becomes so general as to be useless. Almost every individual has some developed knowledge of some kind, be it of opera, country music, reality TV, politics, gardening, or whatever; consequently, almost everybody would count as well educated. But "when everyone is somebody, then no one's anybody".[6] If everybody is well educated, what is so special about education?

A person with a broad range of factual knowledge or information, but who had no concern for or commitment to the norms and standards implicit in the disciplines of science, math, history, and so on that produced and backed up such knowledge, might be admired as a champion of pub quizzes or a successful contestant on a television game show might be. But it would be odd to regard any such fount of information as necessarily well educated.

After all, if they lack any commitment to and understanding of the nature of such things as historical or scientific inquiry (or in other words any appreciation of how their information was come by), they have no way of distinguishing true information from false. Likewise, a person lacking in cognitive perspective whose knowledge is compartmentalized so that her moral understanding never obtrudes on her scientific thinking, her historical knowledge is never brought to bear on her political thinking, and her familiarity with literature has no effect on her day-to-day thinking and conduct, besides being rather odd, would hardly be classified as someone with worthwhile knowledge, for there is not much value in information that is never brought to bear on life.

The contrast between being knowledgeable and being educated, which is emphasized by the transformation criterion, is a most important one. Some people criticize much traditional schooling on the grounds that the aim seems to be no more than to impart relatively recherché information for memorizing and subsequent regurgitation in written examinations. Education, it is rightly suggested, should have relevance to and should impact upon the lives that people lead. But, as Peters points out, in being transformed by the knowledge acquired the educated person is indeed being prepared for life.

> Those who make it [i.e., the contrast between education and life] usually have in mind a contrast between the activities that go on in classrooms and studies and those that go on in industry, politics, agriculture, and rearing a family. The curriculum of schools and universities is then criticised because, as the knowledge passed on is not instrumental in any obvious sense to 'living', it is assumed that it is 'academic' or relevant only to the classroom, cloister, study and library. What is forgotten is that activities like history, literary appreciation, and philosophy, unlike Bingo and billiards, involve forms of thought and awareness that can and should spill over into things that go on outside and transform them. For they are concerned with explanation, evaluation and imaginative exploration of forms of life. As a result of them what is called 'life' develops different dimensions. In schools and universities there is concentration on the development of this determinant of our form of life. The problem of the educator is to pass on this knowledge and understanding in such a way that they develop a life of their own in the minds of others and transform how they see the world, and hence how they feel about it.[7]

In sum, Peters suggests that an educated person is one who has understanding of a broad range of worthwhile subject matter, who cares about the standards implicit in the various subjects, whose knowledge is integrated rather than compartmentalized, and who is transformed (affected or changed) by this understanding.

These criteria, even if accepted, obviously give rise to further questions; questions, furthermore, that need to be answered if we are to arrive at any practical conclusions as to what we should study and how we should proceed in the name of education. Questions such as "How broad is the breadth of knowledge required of the educated person?" and, especially, if education involves the imparting of worthwhile knowledge, "What knowledge is most worthwhile?" I shall take up that question in the next chapter, but there is a prior question that needs to be addressed.

Is Peters' Case Proven?

Peters has put forward the view that education implies morally acceptable ways of imparting worthwhile knowledge of the reason why of things, and that the knowledge in question should involve breadth, transformation or change, care or commitment, and cognitive perspective. But has he put forward a convincing argument for this case or simply asserted it? Is he in fact simply drawing on his own educational background and values, and subtly (or some might say not so subtly) imposing them on his readers?

One particular criticism has focused on Peters' repeated use of phrases such as "we would not say...", "we would not call a man educated who has simply mastered a skill", and "yet we might refuse to call him educated".

To whom does the 'we' refer in such instances? It may be pointed out that, if it is meant to be an empirical claim to the effect that in general people don't say such things, then it is by no means proven to be true and, even if it were, one cannot draw conclusions about what we ought to do simply by following what people appear from their speech to think we ought to do.

I think this particular criticism of Peters ill-founded. It is certainly not an empirical claim, since Peters was well aware both that most people probably don't say the sort of things about education that he is suggesting are implicit in the concept, and that they think many things, such as that having a certain accent or nice manners is a mark of education, with which he would emphatically not agree. Nor is it an attempt to sneakily bypass argument by writing as if the point has been formally established. On the contrary, this is a form of argument or reasoning in itself. My presumption is that in using phrases such as "we would not say...", he is indirectly appealing to his readers, so that the phrasing is equivalent in meaning to "surely, reader, you agree with me that it would not make sense to say...". Thus, he is straightforwardly setting a thesis before his readers and asking them whether on reflection they find it convincing.

Still, the question looms: is Peters seeking to impose his values? The first point to make in response is that 'impose' is a somewhat loaded word in this context. 'Education' is a normative term. Therefore, anybody who engages in discussion of what it involves is necessarily going to introduce their values. So of course we must conclude that Peters values a broad understanding and so forth. But that is not the same thing as imposing his values or even his views on his readers. Nobody is being taken advantage of or obliged or forced to accept anything, which are the usual implications of imposing on people. He is putting forward a view of what it is to be educated in sufficient detail and based upon sufficient thought for it to be worth our consideration.

There now comes a most important moment in this introduction to philosophy. For at this point many readers are going to ask, "Has he *proven* the value of education in this sense? Is his account the *correct* account of what it is to be educated?"

These are the wrong questions to ask. They are the wrong questions because conceptual analysis does not lend itself to demonstrable truth in the manner of the sciences. What we have to ask is rather whether Peters' account is reasonable and convincing when carefully considered; and the criteria for determining whether it is or not are the *four Cs*: whether it is Clear, Complete, Coherent, and Compatible with our other beliefs.

The first thing that any reasonable analysis or account of a concept must obviously be is clear. It must avoid obscure jargon and language that is in any way opaque, but it must also avoid the kind of vagueness, unintelligibility, and ambiguity that can be present even when the words used are in themselves familiar. The suggestion that 'education is a kind of begetting', for example, does not strike me as clear, nor does the popular claim that it is 'of the whole person'. Even the philosopher and educationalist Alfred N. Whitehead's remark that "education is the acquisition of the art of the utilization of knowledge", though vaguely comprehensible as far as it goes, is not exactly crystal clear.[8]

By completeness I refer to the need to make sure that when a concept is analyzed any further terms introduced are themselves clearly explained. If, for example, education is to be defined partly in terms of the development of emotional maturity, we need to know what is meant by or what constitutes 'emotional maturity'. In the case of Peters' account of education, the analysis is not in fact yet complete, since, as I have said, to fully understand the conception of the educated person being presented we need to get a fuller understanding of the nature of the knowledge possessed by the educated person.

Coherence refers to the requirement that a satisfactory analysis is internally coherent and does not involve such things as self-contradiction.

Compatibility refers to the need to ensure that when one has arrived at a clear, complete, and coherent account of the concept in question it does not jar with one's other beliefs and values. For example, one could not consistently provide an account of education that claimed that it was a matter of developing innate potential, if one believed that the individual's self is entirely formed by the environment in which they grow up.

The general point being made is this: when it comes to the concepts that philosophers are interested in, namely concepts of non-specialist, abstract ideas such as love, happiness, and education, we are not in a position to establish any one analysis as the incontrovertible truth. We have to think long and hard about the matter, contemplating various different ideas and suggestions, and come to a conclusion as to which analysis is the most convincing. This is not because the question of what love is is very difficult to answer and we haven't yet found the answer. It is because there is no right or correct answer. There are only better or worse attempts to describe an aspect of human experience. And the better attempts are those that are couched in clear and complete terms and that are coherent and compatible with our other beliefs about the world.

In my view, Peters' analysis of the concept of education is presented in perfectly clear terms, is entirely coherent in itself, and does not appear to be incompatible with any other beliefs that are generally held. It does not, for example, lead to the conclusion that certain groups or classes of people cannot or do not deserve to be educated, which we would presumably not be willing to accept. However, the criterion of completeness has not yet been met, since, as noted above, we need a fuller understanding of the nature of the knowledge that the educated person is supposed to have. It is to that question that I shall turn in the next chapter.

Notes

1 Note however a variant of this game in Neil Postman & Charles Weingartner, *Teaching as a Subversive Activity* (Penguin, 1971). The authors claim (p. 67) that "the word 'educate' is closely related to the word 'educe'", evidently with the object of adducing this point as evidence in favor of their particular view of education. The idea of education as a process of 'leading out' what is already innate in the child can be traced back at least as far as Plato, who illustrates the contention vividly in his dialogue *Meno*. But Plato believed in reincarnation, which gives a specific meaning to the thesis.
2 R.S. Peters, *Ethics and Education* (Allen & Unwin, 1966) p. 25.
3 See R.S. Peters, op. cit., pp. 24–5.
4 I have no doubt in my mind that, e.g., physical fitness and artistic ability, though desirable in themselves, should not be regarded as criteria of being educated. However, in recent years, while still committed to the view of education posited here, I have become increasingly uneasy at the emphasis placed on 'knowing the reason why of things' *at the expense* of practical know-how. For an interesting attempt to argue against stress on a liberal education for all, see David Conduct, *Essays on a Liberal Education* (PublishNation, 2016).
5 R.S. Peters, op. cit., p. 30. To avoid endless notes I observe here that the quotations which occur in the next few paragraphs come from *Ethics and Education*, pp. 30, 31.
6 W.S. Gilbert and Arthur Sullivan, *The Gondoliers*.
7 R.S. Peters, 'What is an Educational Process?' in R.S. Peters (ed.), *The Concept of Education* (Routledge & Kegan Paul, 1967) pp. 7, 8.
8 These definitions are taken more or less at random from Rudolf Flesch (ed.), *The Book of Unusual Quotations* (Cassell, 1959).

Further Reading

R.S. Peters' work on this topic is pivotal. See in particular Chapters 1 and 2 of *Ethics and Education* (op. cit.), Chapter 1 of *The Concept of Education* (op. cit.), and the first paper in R.F. Dearden, P.H. Hirst, & R.S. Peters (eds.), *Education and the Development of Reason* (op. cit.). W.K. Frankena's paper on 'The Concept of Education Today' in J.F. Doyle (ed.), *Educational Judgments* (Routledge & Kegan Paul, 1973) is measured and balanced. For hard-hitting objections to Peters' thesis see J. Woods' and W.H. Dray's contributions to R.S. Peters (ed.), *The Philosophy of Education* (Oxford University Press, 1973).

For an excellent critical study of Peters, see Stefaan Cuypers & Christopher Martin, *Richard Peters* (Continuum, 2013). See also M. Katz, 'R.S. Peters' Normative Conception of Education and Educational Aims', *Journal of Philosophy of Education*, 43 (1), 97–108 (2010), R. Curren, 'Peters Redux: The Motivational Power of Inherently Valuable Learning', *Journal of Philosophy of Education*, 54 (3),

731–743 (2020), and J.R. Martin, 'The Path Not Taken', *Journal of Philosophy of Education*, 54 (3), 744–756 (2020).

Questions

What is wrong with using etymology to analyze a concept?

How would you judge the plausibility of a concept?

In your own words critically summarize Peters' view of education.

7 Knowledge: What is Worth Studying

Following Peters, I have argued that education involves the transmission of a broad range of worthwhile understanding in morally acceptable ways, while developing commitment to the standards and procedures inherent in different types of inquiry. Educated people will also have cognitive perspective and be transformed or changed to some degree by their understanding.

The next question is what constitutes this broad body of worthwhile understanding. What subject matter is most worth studying? And how broad is broad? The latter question cannot be answered in the abstract. The educated person is not to be defined simply in terms of a given amount of knowledge so as to enable us to say "you are less educated than her, since you are familiar with one less subject". But if we can find a way to determine what subject matter is most worth studying, and if we are lucky enough to find that this body of knowledge is not too broad to be studied in its entirety, then the question of how broad the breadth should be disappears; the body of worthwhile knowledge represents the breadth we are seeking.

So, what are the worthwhile subjects that education should be concerned with? Hundreds of subjects and pursuits can reasonably be said to be worthwhile, from sailing to Shakespeare, from chess to chemistry, from pop music to stamp collecting, and from mathematics to mechanics. How do we set about determining which of the many worthwhile pursuits open to us we should prioritize in the name of education?

Herbert Spencer

One way is to adopt a utilitarian approach, which is to say assess the worth of a subject by reference to its *utility* or usefulness, arguing for example that engineering is more useful than poetry and should therefore be judged more worthy of study.

An interesting example of this approach is provided by Herbert Spencer, who, in his short book *Education*, originally published in 1861, argued that schooling should enable individuals to look after themselves physically (self-preservation), to secure the necessities of life (including employment), to rear and discipline their young (parenting, as we would

DOI: 10.4324/9781003120476-7

say today), to maintain social and political relations (to be good citizens, which is taken to include playing an active role in political activity, such as voting), and to make good use of leisure time.[1]

In the interests of self-preservation, or ensuring that everybody could maintain their health and safety, he proposed that everybody should study physiology, so that they had understanding of the workings, needs, and nature of the body. With regard to securing the necessities of life, he argued that the prime necessity, particularly for securing employment, was to have an understanding of math, chemistry, geology, and biology. In this he was no doubt partly influenced by the industrial revolution taking place in his time, which led to a vast increase in work that was based largely on science and applied science. But it turns out that his proposed curriculum is more or less entirely a scientific one, because he regards both sociology and psychology as being genuine sciences, and surprisingly proposes science as the subject most appropriate to preparation for leisure time.

The last proposal is based largely on the fact that he seems to regard accuracy with respect to real life as the main criterion of art. The famous Greek statue of a discus thrower (the *Discobolos* of Myron, known through Roman copies), for instance, is criticized on the grounds that the athlete would actually fall over if he stood as depicted. Had the artist had a better understanding of the laws of physics he would not have made such an error. Similarly, the then emerging popular taste for delicate Chinese figure painting is dismissed as being unrealistic and grotesque.[2]

I shall have more to say on the subject of whether the 'social sciences' can be truly scientific later in this chapter. For the moment it is enough to note that Spencer believed that human conduct, including our relationships, our emotions, and our moral behavior, is subject to laws in the same way that the physical world is subject to laws. Hence his apparent belief that good parenting is a matter of learning various psychological truths about children and related facts about things such as the effects of various different forms of discipline and punishment. But such a view flies in the face of the overwhelming evidence that there is no *science* of parenting. There may perhaps be one or two undeniable truths about good parenting, but, if there are, they are likely to be either relatively obvious, or relatively trivial, or else *analytic truths* (which is to say true by definition) rather than empirically established. An example of a fairly obvious truth might be that children do not respond well to being lied to, while the observation that young children tend to like sweet tastes is rather trivial. In neither case does one feel that a parent needs to have studied psychology or sociology to be aware of these facts (and in fact of course neither are laws, but rather generalizations). More serious is the point that seemingly more important observations such as that children need to feel secure are not truly empirically based findings. It is a necessary truth, or true by definition, that good parents try to make their children feel secure, because we define parents who have no interest in making their offspring feel secure as bad parents.

Furthermore, what matters is not so much awareness that children need to feel secure as knowing how to make them so. But what develops a feeling of security may vary considerably from individual to individual, depending on their individual natures, those of their parents, and the overall particular circumstances of a given family. I am not aware of any finding about how a parent should proceed in order to foster a feeling of security in the child that is, at one and the same time, unexpected (i.e., not obvious), important (i.e., not trivial), empirically proven (i.e., not an analytic truth), and classifiable as a law that covers all parents in all situations. Nor should we ignore the extremely important point that there is room for argument on what the end or ends of parenting should be – in other words, what is to count as good parenting?

There is, in fact, no evidence to support the claim that those who study sociology and psychology necessarily learn what they need in order to conduct themselves as good parents, citizens, or friends, or that those who lack such learning cannot be good parents, citizens, and friends. (In philosophical terms that is to say that having sociological or psychological knowledge is neither *necessary* nor *sufficient* for good citizenship.)

Utility

I have mentioned Spencer's view, despite finding it unconvincing, because it serves to illustrate some general problems in taking a utilitarian stance on education.

In claiming that education is a normative term, one is claiming that it is good in itself or has *intrinsic* value, and, as such, does not need to be defended in terms of consequences or *extrinsic* values. It would seem self-evidently better to be educated than uneducated, just as it is better to be happy than unhappy. But one may nonetheless be concerned about the terms on which someone finds happiness (perhaps your happiness comes at the expense of everybody else's), and one may still see certain consequences of being happy as valuable (perhaps it improves your physical health, enables you to work more productively, or contributes to your ability to bring cheer to others). In the same way, acknowledging the intrinsic value of education is no reason for ignoring the question of whether it has extrinsic value. The problem with a utilitarian defense of education lies in deciding what it is supposed to be useful for. To what end or ends do we want education to be useful?

Spencer's view that it must be useful in that it contributes to survival, finding employment and good citizenship is very similar to what is today referred to as 'economic utilitarianism'; this is the view that the value of an education system should be judged by the extent to which it contributes to the economy, particularly in terms of producing individuals with the skills and knowledge required in the workplace. But this is a very limited conception of usefulness. What about ends such as enabling people to flourish or find happiness in life, or developing creative talent and aesthetic appreciation, or striving to achieve success in diverse areas, or cultivating moral probity, or developing autonomy or a critical spirit? Economic utilitarianism involves a very narrow and impoverished view of worthwhile human ends or aspirations, and for that reason alone is surely to be rejected as the sole determinant of what is worth studying.

When attempting to defend education in terms of utility, we also need to note that there are some areas of knowledge that are useful or necessary for the betterment of society as a whole, but which it is not necessary or useful for every individual to have. Knowledge pertaining to engineering and medicine, for example, is clearly most important to us all, but it doesn't follow that we all individually need to study these subjects. Spencer's reasonable concern for individual health does not necessarily lead to the conclusion that every individual should study health sciences. Then there is the danger that attempts to defend education on the grounds of utility will confine themselves to *short-term benefits*. In the short term, for example, given the current (as I write) coronavirus pandemic and consequent financial crisis, it might seem very useful to teach everybody economics or medicine; but even if that were so at a given point in time, it doesn't follow that it will be in the future. History is littered with examples of people who were trained or educated for roles and positions which no longer exist when their education is complete. Indeed, history itself is sometimes dismissed as a subject with little practical value. Taking the short-term view, that position might be arguable. But in *the long run* we all gain in terms of sensible social and political policy from a populace that has a broad understanding of history rather than one that in ignorance derides "every century but this and every country but its own"?[3]

Of equal concern is the tendency to focus on *direct utility* and to ignore *indirect utility*. Learning to tie my shoelaces has direct and immediate utility, but it may be less important than the value of studying poetry, if, for example, the latter were to lead to a more sensitive and sympathetic outlook.

In short, if we are to assess what is worth knowing on grounds of utility, let us at least remember (i) that some things may be worth knowing for their own sake, (ii) that there are other ends to be considered besides economic ones, (iii) that some things that do not have immediate utility may have long-term usefulness, and (iv) that some things that lack direct utility may have indirect utility. In fact, a proper assessment of what is useful should involve consideration of the nature of a good or worthwhile life, since ultimately it is what is of use to enabling us to live well that matters. The fundamental objection to the view that students should merely study whatever is deemed good for their survival in a flourishing economy is that there is more to life than economic survival. I may perhaps justify the study of a particular subject on the grounds that it will enable me to make a living, but then what am I living for? Perhaps, as US President John Adams said, we need two educations: one should teach us how to make a living, and the other how to live. Let us acknowledge that *schooling* overall should, among other things, be concerned to equip the individual to contribute to the economic well-being of society, but let us not define *education* in those terms. The question of how well educated a person is, is not to be answered by assessing how well off they are financially or what they contribute to the economy. Plenty of relatively uneducated people fare well in life economically, and, equally, many well-educated people can be counted among the poorer members of society.

What we are looking for, rather than a general admonition that education should be useful, is a way of discerning what subject matter is most useful in respect of the ends that we consider most important. The beginning of an answer to that question, I suggest, is to look for subject matter which not only provides knowledge of itself (as the study of chemistry provides knowledge of chemistry, the study of the hospitality industry knowledge of the hospitality industry, and so on), but which also has both the propensity to generate further knowledge and greater understanding in the future and wider significance for understanding and control of our world. Studying popular culture for example obviously leads to knowledge of its subject matter, but it does not have any significance beyond itself as, say, physics does, and it does not represent a kind of inquiry that can generate further knowledge as physics does.

Paul Hirst

Probably the foremost proponent of a position along these lines was Paul Hirst, and no inquiry of the kind that we are now engaged in would be complete without a critical appraisal of his central contentions.[4]

Hirst's basic contention is that there are some subjects or types of inquiry that between them have the potential to yield answers to questions about all aspects of our world, and are in that sense fundamental. Furthermore, fortunately for practical purposes, they are few in number, so that in principle an individual can be initiated into all of them (and thus possess the breadth of knowledge appropriate to an educated person). To take perhaps the clearest example, mathematical questions can and may need to be asked in many contexts from building to gardening, whereas one cannot ask gardening questions about mathematics. To study gardening might prove very enjoyable, and might ultimately contribute to satisfaction in life for individuals. But ignorance of the knowledge and skills of the gardener will in itself only deprive us of the pleasures of gardening, whereas knowledge of mathematics is essential to our understanding of most things and to our ability to engage successfully in most pursuits (including at times gardening).

Following this line of reasoning, Hirst suggested at one point that there are eight such fundamental subjects: math, physical sciences, human or social sciences, literature and the fine arts, philosophy, history, moral understanding, and religion.

Before proceeding to assess this thesis, a few points need to be clarified. First, as time passed and in response to various suggestions and criticisms from others, Hirst modified his position in various ways, including making some changes to his list of subjects. For instance, at one point 'interpersonal understanding' ("i.e., explanations of human behavior in terms of wills, hopes, beliefs, etc,") was on the list, while history was not. I shall ignore those changes since my main concern is with the nature of his reasoning.

Secondly, for the most part he does not use the word 'subjects' but refers instead to 'forms of knowledge'. This is important because his argument requires that he gives these subjects a label that indicates their unique status. Each of his forms of knowledge is a subject, but other subjects such as geography, women's studies, and book-keeping are not forms of knowledge in his sense. 'Subject' is in any case not a very useful term in this context since it is so broad as to cover any kind of study related to a particular subject matter. More or less anything can be called a subject. ('Discipline', which is sometimes used in this kind of debate, seems appropriate for some subjects, such as math, but less so for a subject such as literature.)

However, one modification that I propose to Hirst's thesis is to refer to 'forms of understanding' or 'forms of inquiry' rather than 'forms of knowledge'. These formulations do not change the nature of Hirst's thesis, and seem to me preferable because 'knowledge' has connotations of secure truth claims, which, as we shall see, it is not clear that a sphere such as religion can provide in the way that science can. Referring to a form of understanding makes equally good sense in either science or religion, since even if knowledge in the sense of proven truth is not possible in the latter case, one can still have a better or worse understanding of it. Perhaps the phrase 'forms of inquiry' is even more appropriate, because it puts the emphasis on the distinctive ways of proceeding when trying to understand certain particular kinds of subject matter, and that is essential to Hirst's argument.

Forms of Knowledge (Understanding or Inquiry)

Knowledge or understanding, according to Hirst, is separable into a number of distinct forms. These forms of inquiry are not mere collections of information (subject matter) but rather "complex ways of understanding experience which man has achieved" (p. 122). A form is distinguishable by four criteria, all of which need to be met.

1   First, it must have certain concepts that are peculiar in character to the form (as notions of integrity and wrongness are distinctively moral concepts, while gravity and hydrogen are distinctive of the physical sciences) (pp. 128–129).

2   Secondly, the form must have a "distinct logical structure". This comes about partly as a result of the central concepts that are peculiar to the form. Because of the nature of gravity there is only a limited number of things you can meaningfully say employing this and other

scientific concepts; you cannot for example start talking about gravity's color or questioning its integrity (p. 129).

3   Thirdly, a form, by virtue of its particular concepts and logic, gives rise to claims or statements that in some way or other are "testable against experience" (p. 129).

4   Finally, a form develops particular techniques for exploring experience and testing its distinctive expressions (p. 129).

The phrase 'testable against experience' has proved troublesome to many, since some take it to imply that the truth of a claim such as that God exists or that Beethoven is a greater musician than Mozart can be proved (or falsified) by some empirical means, which is certainly not what Hirst intended.

I suggest that we may avoid any such implication by running the third and fourth criteria together and phrasing it thus: the claims or conclusions that are put forward in relation to a specific form have to be approached in a distinctive way when we seek to establish whether they are true or false. One does not seek to establish whether it is true that the angles of a triangle add up to 180 degrees in the same way that one tests whether cigarettes cause cancer.

How plausible, then, is this thesis?

Math, Science, and Philosophy

It is surely indisputable that the physical sciences and math have their own distinctive concepts and adopt quite different procedures for establishing truth and falsity. Philosophy, in its turn, would seem to be equally *sui generis* or unique. A scientific claim such as that 'metal expands when heated' is tested by empirical means; we experiment and observe. At a higher and more complex level this remains true. In physics, for instance, concepts (mass, acceleration, density, force, etc.) are used to make statements comprising theories and these theories possess a logical structure in the sense that the statements which go to make up a particular theory can be so arranged that certain statements follow from others. It is also true that, relatively speaking, well-developed physical sciences have at their disposal refined experimental techniques so that predictions made on the basis of working hypotheses can be checked with the object of falsifying the hypotheses – this constituting Hirst's notion of testability against experience. And similar sorts of observation would be true of mathematics – namely a pronounced degree of logical structure exemplified in some such structure as "If a is greater than b, and if b is greater than c, *then* a is greater than c". But the radical difference between mathematics and the developed physical sciences lies in the fact that the statements of pure mathematics are not verified or falsified by reference to the external world. At no stage in pure mathematics reasoning does the mathematician break off to conduct experiments. Mathematics is essentially deductive. The pure mathematician is concerned with abstract symbolic systems, and explores the connections between axioms and postulates and conclusions by a process of deductive reasoning (exemplified in the "if a is greater than *b*" example used above). Mathematical propositions such as that 'the opposite angles of a parallelogram are equal', in other words, are confirmed by understanding the axioms and concepts of math rather than by empirical measurement, experiment or observation. And, as I hope readers are beginning to understand, the credibility of the philosophical claim that "being educated is a matter of having worthwhile knowledge" is neither empirically testable nor to be established or rejected in the way that mathematical claims are; rather, we have to clarify concepts and look to rational argument on the matter.

These three subjects, then, do seem to be distinct forms of inquiry or understanding, as delineated by Hirst. Each one relates to a different kind of question that has to be approached in a unique way. As such, they are of fundamental importance, for most questions of significance that arise in life are either in themselves scientific, mathematical, or philosophical, or they partially involve one or more of them. As a society we simply could not make progress of any kind without such understanding, and as individuals our ability to comprehend and control our world depends upon a degree of such understanding. To understand something of the nature of the physical world, to have a basic mathematical understanding and to be able to distinguish and handle philosophical questions surely has intrinsic value. It is better in itself to have such understanding than to be unable either to distinguish or come to grips with questions as different as "Is this drug harmful?", "How do I work out the angles I need for this bookcase?", and "Are there distinguishable forms of knowledge?" But clearly some degree of mastery of these subjects also has considerable extrinsic value or utility both for the individual and wider society. Putting it crudely, we can get a lot more done efficiently and effectively with such understanding.

The Social Sciences

As noted above when discussing Herbert Spencer's views, the very idea of social or human *science* is problematic. Can the study of humans be truly scientific in the way that the study of the physical world can be? There are of course some things pertaining to humans, such as questions about physical health, that can be approached scientifically, and one can make empirical studies of behaviors and attitudes. But is human interaction and conduct ultimately governed by laws as the natural or physical world is? Are the ubiquitous self-help books telling us how to be successful, how to make friends, how to save our marriages, and how to be happy, based on science, which is to say on empirical proof? Presumably not, since they all say different things, and none have turned out to provide infallible advice. Besides, if the study of humans were altogether scientific, it would not be a distinct form of knowledge, but a species of scientific knowledge.

In saying this, I am not suggesting that psychological and sociological questions are unimportant. On the contrary, I think them very important.

My argument is that in many cases when a question such as "What makes humans happy?" is treated as a scientific question we misrepresent and distort reality. We do this by defining the concepts we are concerned with in purely observable terms (so that we can observe them!), whereas something such as happiness cannot adequately be defined in terms of observable signs such as smiling and laughing, which are neither necessary nor sufficient since one can be happy without smiling and one can smile without being happy. But when the questions are not regarded as scientific, it is by no means clear that professional psychologists and sociologists actually have any reliable and distinctive expertise. A good novelist or an experienced historian, for example, might be said to have a better, or at least an equally good, insight into the human condition.

Be that as it may, it is clear, I think, that the social sciences do not constitute a viable form of knowledge in Hirst's sense on his own terms. And I would suggest that what the educated person needs is not familiarity with the academic subjects of psychology and sociology so much as an awareness of psychological and sociological issues which might be better developed through philosophy, history, and literature.

History

History does not seem to be a *bona fide* form of knowledge either. Rather, it is an amalgam of science and philosophy. A question such as "What is the date of this settlement?" is an instance of an historical question, in this case an archaeological question, that is scientific in nature, and to answer it will require empirical investigation. "Was Napoleon a great general?" is an instance of an historical question, the answer to which will be partly dependent on analyzing the concept of good generalship. "What were the causes of the Second World War?" is more of a hybrid question, since attempting to answer it will necessitate quite a lot of empirical work trying to establish the facts, as well as some philosophical work on cause and effect.

But, while I would argue that Hirst was mistaken to see history as one of his forms of knowledge, I would argue that it is nonetheless an equally fundamental area of inquiry. The statement that those who do not study history are doomed to repeat it has become something of a cliché. (The origin of the remark seems to have been the Spanish philosopher George Santayana's observation that "those who cannot remember the past are condemned to repeat it".)[5] But regardless of the preferred wording, it is surely the case that in describing and interpreting the past, historians are drawing on and organizing a vast wealth of data pertaining to the human condition. It may be somewhat fanciful to imagine that history repeats itself in an unqualified way, but it is certainly true that we can learn a lot about possibilities and potential dangers facing humankind from studying other times and places. History cannot be said and must not be used to prove or justify any particular practice, for it is a basic philosophical tenet, inspired in particular by the work of the Scottish philosopher David Hume, that one cannot legitimately derive an evaluative conclusion from a descriptive premise, or, to put it in a familiar colloquialism: "no 'ought' from an 'is'".[6] The fact that something is the case does not in itself establish that it is right or desirable that it should be so, and consequently arguments of the form "this happens in nature so it must be good" are invalid. (This is sometimes referred to as the '*naturalistic fallacy*'.) Equally we cannot use historical precedent to justify policy or practices. However, history clearly does help to illuminate and may provoke us into more imaginative thinking about contemporary issues. Furthermore, historical understanding is a necessary part of a rich understanding of human beings.

Moral Understanding

As with history, moral understanding does not seem to me to involve a unique or *sui generis* way of dealing with a certain particular kind of question in the way that math, science, and philosophy do. It is true that the moral sphere is defined by a specific subject matter, but that is also true of myriad subjects from stamp collecting to video gaming. If Hirst were correct in claiming that moral understanding is a form of knowledge, he would need to have established that there is a distinct way of dealing with claims to moral truth. But he has not been able to do that. In fact, as in history, there are different kinds of question one can raise in relation to moral issues, some of which are empirical (e.g., "What percentage of the population values freedom more than equality?"), some of which are philosophical (e.g., "Is happiness the supreme moral good?"), and some of which are partly historical (e.g., "Was the ancient Greeks' attitude to women morally acceptable?").

However, although I suggest that moral understanding is not a form of knowledge by Hirst's own criteria, I would argue, as with history, that it is nonetheless a fundamentally important subject; after all, its subject matter is nothing less than the issue of how ideally we should live our lives. Given its importance, Chapter 10 will be devoted to the topic.

Religion

The suggestion that religion is a form of knowledge should cause some surprise, since it is hardly controversial to point out that many people (and not just philosophers) would argue that it does not deal in *knowledge* at all. It is a matter first and last of *faith*. Of course, it is nonetheless possible to gain an *understanding* of religion, both as a general concept and of particular religions. But the former would seem to be a philosophical task and the latter a largely historical and empirical task.

Now, some would claim that understanding religion is the task of the theologian rather than the philosopher and is therefore a distinct type of understanding. But this is to confuse particular specialized knowledge with respect to subject matter or information with a particular methodology appropriate to a unique kind of question. Theology is indeed different from philosophy since its subject matter is the interpretation of religion or religious dogma. But theology is not a unique type of inquiry; rather it involves familiarity with and understanding of particular sets of belief and ritual. The theologian *qua* theologian never takes the position of looking in from the outside in an attempt to assess the plausibility or otherwise of religion. On the contrary, rather like the sports commentator, his expertise consists in understanding and explaining the rules of the game (the nature of the religion) rather than in justifying or establishing its truth.

Nonetheless, like morality, the sphere of religion is obviously of enormous importance to millions of people, and historically religion has had and continues to have an immense effect on human lives. For that reason alone, the study of religion would seem to be of major importance; and yet today it is a subject that schools (other than faith schools) almost go out of their way to avoid. It will be discussed in more detail in Chapter 9.

Literature and the Fine Arts

Hirst's positing of 'literature and the fine arts' jointly as one form of knowledge has led to much bewilderment among philosophers, and his apparent view that a work of art, be it a painting, a statue, a dance, a symphony, or a book, is somehow in itself a statement, the truth or falsity of which has to be examined and assessed in a unique way, is both difficult to comprehend and highly contentious. In what way is Mozart's 23rd Symphony a statement, and how on earth would one set about establishing whether it is true or false?

It is undoubtedly the case that many people are hard to convince of the value of the arts, and, since I share with Hirst the view that they matter a great deal, it is tempting simply to repeat the cry that they represent a unique form of knowledge and should therefore be given equal prominence with subjects such as math and science. But since I cannot really comprehend what it means to call it a form of knowledge, I cannot do that. I can, however, argue slightly differently that the various arts represent peculiarly human activity and achievement. Other animals behave in ways that may appear to be artistic, as for example when a bird arranges a pattern of flowers and other scavenged bits and pieces in a way that may strike us as beautiful and may serve the purpose of attracting a mate. But as far as we know the bird is engaging in genetically endowed behavior, it proceeds instinctively, and there is no evidence that it consciously sets out to create a beautiful pattern for the purpose of impressing a possible partner. Works of art by definition involve conscious intention on the part of the creator to produce something aesthetically pleasing. The case for including some kind of introduction to the fine arts in the school curriculum must surely at rock bottom be this point that artistic endeavor and achievement are uniquely human; but we may add that to initiate children into the fine arts is to open up the possibility of developing aesthetic awareness and the pleasure or satisfaction that may bring.

Another problem in Hirst's approach in this case is his throwing together of literature and the other fine arts. Though literature may not in fact be more important or valuable than any of the other arts, it is rather easier to explain its value. Literature is, like history, a vast depository of data about the human condition. If, with Matthew Arnold, we define literature as "the best that has been thought or said",[7] distinguishing it from badly written, inauthentic or unrealistic work, then by definition we are referring to work, of whatever century and whatever country, whether poetry, fiction, or non-fiction, that increases our understanding of some one or more aspects of the world. It can be truly said that to move easily through the world of literature is to engage with more varied and interesting characters, more mind-stretching ideas and arguments, and more imaginative possibilities than one is likely to encounter in everyday life. Of course, there is room for extended discussion and argument about which authors are the 'best' and the logically prior question of how one determines the best. But though we are never going to settle to everybody's satisfaction specific questions such as whether John Grisham is a good writer, or whether Zadie Smith is superior to Hilary Mantel, it is unconvincing to suggest that we can make no reasonable judgments about the value of certain books. Only ignorance or the confusing of taste with reason could lead one to deny that in their distinct ways the works of such different authors as Plato, Cicero, Montaigne, Shakespeare, Tolstoy, Isabel Colegate, Ernest Hemingway, Graham Greene, Anita Brookner, Evelyn Waugh, Oscar Wilde, Virginia Woolf, Margaret Forster George Gissing, Anthony Trollope, Richard Russo, and Philip Roth have value. But the point here is not to argue the merits of particular authors, nor to establish a canon. It is to maintain that one of the most useful things we can do to develop the mind is enable individuals to feel at home with, and therefore read, books that in one way or another open up and broaden their understanding of the world. It need hardly be added that the very reason for including literature on the curriculum implies that teaching the subject should first and foremost be directed to enabling students to be at ease with reading.

Conclusion

Given that educated persons are essentially characterized by their knowledge, and given that we cannot know everything, we need to establish what knowledge is educationally most worthwhile. Since 'knowledge' has connotations of certain truth, which is not necessarily attainable in every sphere of inquiry, it is preferable to think in terms of 'understanding', for it is possible to understand something without it being true. The understanding of the educated person may be said to have intrinsic value, but it may also have utility. However, the latter observation is not very helpful until we can determine to what end or ends it should be useful.

The contemporary tendency to emphasize economic utility to the exclusion of other considerations is to be resisted, as are all approaches that involve concern only for short-term direct pay-off. Schooling may legitimately have some concern for economic benefit, but education should look beyond such a limited horizon. In particular, understanding which enables individuals to both generate further understanding and to exercise greater control over their circumstances and to enhance their appreciation of human achievement is to be valued.

Hirst suggested that eight subjects between them served as the basis for all kinds of inquiry. If that were so, it would be a very strong reason for concluding that they represented the educationally worthwhile understanding we are seeking. Unfortunately, it seems that only science, math, and philosophy can truly be distinguished as forms in the sense that they involve a set of distinctive specialist concepts, a particular logical pattern, and a unique way of attempting to assess the truth of claims. But, with the exception of the so-called social sciences, his other candidates as educationally worthwhile subjects, namely history, moral understanding, religion, literature and the fine arts (now treated separately), do seem to merit categorization as definable subjects of fundamental importance. History and literature are to be valued as the prime and best source of our understanding of humans as individuals and social animals. Moral understanding is by definition necessary if we are to have any hope of creating a moral world (though, alas, not sufficient). Religious understanding is vital in a world in which religion is such a powerful phenomenon, and ignorance and misrepresentation surrounding it such a danger. The fine arts are a peculiarly human achievement, and incidentally a potential source of great satisfaction, whether through creation or appreciation, and as such would seem to earn a place in the distinctively human activity of education.

Some readers may be inclined to suggest that these subjects represent more or less the traditional school curriculum and they may consequently be disappointed in the conclusion. But even if the conclusion of my argument had been that the curriculum we should have is precisely the one we do have, to dismiss the conclusion for that reason would be to miss the point of the exercise. The point of conducting an inquiry into what we should be teaching is neither necessarily to support nor change the *status quo*; it is simply to see what there is good reason to do. If it establishes that current practice is what we should be doing, well and good.

But as a matter of fact, though there are certainly similarities, this is not the traditional curriculum. Currently, and generalizing, schools, as noted above, avoid teaching religion altogether. Little goes on in the way of moral education, although the school as a whole may be said to engage in a degree of moral training. Philosophy is not formally taught at all, and indeed in many jurisdictions philosophy is one of the few university subjects that does not qualify one to teach in schools. And in practice the fine arts are almost always treated as the poor relation.

It should be noted in conclusion that to introduce these various subjects as distinct, whether regarded as forms in Hirst's sense or not, is not meant to imply that they should necessarily be taught separately. One might well argue for an integrated curriculum of some kind that involves pursuing topics that demand different kinds of reflection and inquiry such as historical, literary, and scientific. But the questions of how these subjects should be organized or programmed, how they should be taught, and what level they should be taught to, are not to be confused with the philosophical question (what is most worth teaching?) with which we have been dealing. The questions of what degree or level of math, what branches of science, what specific litera-ture, or what periods of history should be studied, and suchlike, though answering them properly will involve some philosophical thinking, are prob-ably best left to subject specialists. I will have a little more to say about cur-riculum design and research into teaching (largely critical, I have to say) in Chapters 8 and 19, but for the moment it only needs to be pointed out that the reasoning provided for teaching these subjects does imply one particular point about how to teach them. Since many of the subjects do not obviously give rise to many, if any, proven conclusions, but at best yield more and less comprehensible or more and less plausible conclusions, and since the idea in every case is to empower the individual, enabling her to increase her own informed decision-making, it surely follows that the subjects need to be taught in ways that encourage the critical and reflective response of students, and not in ways that merely require acquiescence on their part.

Notes

1 Herbert Spencer, *Education* (Watts & Co, 1929). Worth noting is that Spencer was an early advocate of what became known as 'social Darwinism', i.e., the view that human social norms and behaviors are the product of an evolutionary process. He was allegedly the originator of the phrase 'survival of the fittest'.
2 "What gives the grotesqueness to Chinese pictures, unless their utter disregard of the laws of appearances?" (Ibid., p. 38).
3 W.S. Gilbert and Arthur Sullivan, *The Mikado*.
4 Hirst has written at length on the nature of knowledge, at various times. Not surprisingly, his views have been modified with the passing of time and in response to critical appraisal. I am not, however, intent on following through in detail the progression of Hirst's thought, and I shall take as representative of his position his influential and often-quoted paper 'Liberal Education and the Nature of Knowledge', which is to be found in R.D. Archambault (ed.), *Philo-sophical Analysis and Education* (Routledge & Kegan Paul, 1965) pp. 113–38. I shall not refer in these notes to specific pages of Hirst's paper; I shall instead give the necessary page references in the body of the text.
5 George Santayana (1863–1952), *Life of Reason*, Vol 1, Ch 12.
6 David Hume (1711–76). See *A Treatise of Human Nature* (1739), Bk 3, Pt 1, Sec 1. See also Chapter 17 below.
7 Matthew Arnold (1822–88). Arnold used such phraseology on several occasions. See in particular *Culture and Anarchy* (1869) or 'The Function of Criticism at the Present Time' in *Essays in Criticism, First Series* (1865).

Further Reading

Besides works cited in the notes, I suggest that readers consult Paul Hirst's contributions to J.F. Kerr (ed.), *Changing the Curriculum* (University of London Press, 1968), and to Richard Hooper (ed.), *The Curriculum: Context, Design and Development* (Oliver & Boyd, 1971). His *Knowledge and the Curriculum* (Routledge & Kegan Paul, 1975) contains both the paper 'Liberal Education and the Nature of Knowledge' and a paper on 'Literature and the Fine Arts as a Distinct Form of Knowledge'.

See also Richard Smith 'Unsettling Knowledge: Irony and Education', *Journal of Philosophy of Education*, 54 (1), 757–771 (2020) and Christopher Martin, 'Educational Justice and the Value of Knowledge', *Journal of Philosophy of Education*, 54 (1), 164–182 (2020).

J. Derry, 'What is Educationally Worthwhile Knowledge?', in D. Guile, D. Lambert, & M.J. Reiss (eds.), *Curriculum Studies and Professional Knowledge*, pp. 84–96 (Routledge, 2018), tries to make sense of Michael Young's notion of 'powerful knowledge'.

Charles Bailey, *Beyond the Present and Particular* (Routledge & Kegan Paul, 1988) and M.A.B. Degenhardt, *Education and the Value of Knowledge* (Allen & Unwin, 1984) both pursue the question of a liberal education. J.P. White, *Towards a Compulsory Curriculum* (Routledge & Kegan Paul, 1973) is provocative and very interesting, while Robin Barrow's *Common Sense and the Curriculum* (Allen & Unwin, 1976) offers a sustained critique of White as well as positive curriculum proposals.

R.C. Whitfield (ed.), *Disciplines of the Curriculum* (McGraw-Hill, 1971) consists of a useful collection of papers concerned with different subject areas and arguments for including them in the curriculum.

Studies of specific subjects are legion, but worth particular mention are E.H. Carr, *What is History?* (Penguin, 1964), R.F. Atkinson, *Knowledge and Explanation in History: An Introduction to the Philosophy of History* (Cornell University Press, 1978), and M.I. Finley, *The Use and Abuse of History* (Hogarth Press, 1986). On literature, see James Gribble, *Literary Education: A Re-evaluation* (Cambridge University Press, 1983) and Richard Beach, Deborah Appleman, Rob Fecho, & Rob Simon, *Teaching Literature to Adolescents* (Routledge, 2016). On religious education, see John Sealey, *Religious Education: Philosophical Perspectives* (Allen & Unwin, 1985).

Questions

What is problematic about making educational decisions in terms of utility?

Critically examine Paul Hirst's Forms of Knowledge thesis.

What criteria would you use to determine curriculum content? Why?

8 Curriculum Theory

To most people the word 'curriculum' probably means the subject matter to be studied or the school syllabus. Thus, in the previous chapter I argued that the school curriculum should essentially comprise science, math, philosophy, history, and so forth. But, as we saw in Chapter 4, there is also a 'hidden curriculum', and some educationalists argue that we should extend the meaning of curriculum to include various other things (such as the hidden element) besides the stated outline of subject matter. Furthermore, in educational discourse the word is sometimes used as a short-hand way of referring to curriculum theory or the study of a wide variety of issues relating to that subject matter, such as how it should be organized, how it should be taught, and how it should be assessed. These questions are sometimes related to specific branches of curriculum theory with their own specific labels such as 'curriculum development', 'curriculum evaluation' and 'curriculum implementation'. And sometimes, just to add to the confusion, a phrase such as 'curriculum and instruction' or simply the word 'curriculum' itself is used to refer to the study of curriculum generally. In this chapter I shall argue that there is good reason to continue to define 'curriculum' simply in terms of the subject matter to be studied, that the notion that there are a number of distinct areas of expertise relating to such things as implementation and design of curricula is suspect, and that none of this concern for questions about the curriculum makes sense without prior clarity on the question of what subject matter the curriculum should contain.

Curriculum: The Word and the Concept

The first issue is to settle the meaning of 'curriculum' itself, for obviously what constitutes curriculum has some bearing on what constitutes curriculum theory. This question also conveniently allows us to draw attention to and stress the distinction between a verbal question and a conceptual question, for the issue here is not that we have some complex idea that needs careful examination, but that different people are using the word in straightforwardly different ways.

As already stated, commonly the word 'curriculum' refers to the subject matter to be studied. Some, as has also been stated, would extend the term

DOI: 10.4324/9781003120476-8

to include reference to the hidden curriculum. But there are those who would also include the *desired* outcomes of study in the definition. Then there are those who prefer to think in terms of *actual* outcomes. There are those who would define it in terms of the learning experiences of students. And the list of possible definitions is not exhausted by these examples. There may be many reasons why different people want to define the word in different ways, but one of them is that a person adopts a particular usage in order to make an evaluative point: in defining 'curriculum' in terms of, say, student learning outcomes, I am making the point that in my view learning outcomes are something that we ought to be concerned about. It is obviously useful to one's cause to define key words in an enterprise in ways that reflect or reinforce one's point of view – in short, to provide a persuasive definition.

Here we may note that concepts may be of different sorts, which is to say that we have concepts of different types of thing. Some concepts are conceptions of what is to a large extent given and unalterable in nature: mountains, for example, are what they are, and, if it is the concept of mountain that one is trying to understand, one is largely governed by physical reality. Some concepts are primarily governed by the laws of logic: whatever a circle is, it cannot be square. A third group of concepts are clearly devised by humankind: they are ideas conceived, developed, and defined by us, as the concept of chivalry has been. It is into this third category that curriculum surely falls.

It is not written in heaven how the word 'curriculum' should be used. Neither logic nor the laws of nature can decree that curriculum should be understood to mean one thing alone. It is therefore not my intention to try and tease out the meaning of 'curriculum'. But, while it would not be appropriate to pursue the question 'What is curriculum?' as if it had some fixed and determinate answer, one may nonetheless produce reasons that incline one to defining the term in one way rather than another. In this case, broadly speaking, I suggest that there are reasons for keeping our definition of curriculum simple and specific in scope.

A Definition of Curriculum

The main reason for resisting the temptation to define curriculum very broadly so as to cover, for instance, all the experiences that a child encounters at school is that it is useful in itself to have a number of relatively narrow or specific concepts to work with in an area that one is trying to understand. The more specific a concept is in relation to others in the same area, the more fully it characterizes or delineates something. For example, the general concept animal tells us far less about any particular animal than the more specific concepts of duck, snake, rabbit, and so forth. Knowing what an animal is tells us less about animals than knowing what a duck is tells us about ducks. Of course, we need general terms too, precisely in order to note and fix our attention on similarities. Without the concept of animal we might fail to note that by certain criteria ducks and rabbits are similar and comparable. But a proper understanding of any field is hampered by reliance solely on general concepts. It may, for example, be argued that it is difficult to have serious and illuminating discussions about popular music, precisely because the concept of popular music itself is so broad as to cover a variety of forms which do not really resemble each other in any way other than that they are popular. The explanatory power of a concept is seriously affected by its degree of generality. As historians used to be taught, anything that allegedly explains everything (such as God or market forces) in fact explains nothing.

The desire and tendency to widen the concept of curriculum arose at least partially from an honorable cause. Those who were interested in the curriculum in the old-fashioned and relatively simple sense of the syllabus or program of study saw, correctly enough, that what is on the syllabus is never totally identifiable with what is actually taught, still less with what is learned, and in some cases is barely comparable. The curriculum may, for example, include the study of the American war of independence; but what that actually comes to mean in classrooms and individuals' experiences throughout the world will vary enormously as a result of such diverse factors as who is doing the teaching, how they choose to do it, the material resources available, where it is being taught, who the students are, their backgrounds, their prior knowledge, and their frame of mind. There is a perfectly straightforward and reasonable sense in which using the term 'curriculum' to mean the program of study and to refer to such things as 'reading, writing, and arithmetic' in the elementary school, or 'quadratic equations and trigonometry' for a secondary math curriculum, is less in touch with reality, or what actually happens, than some definitions based on what particular students actually get out of the provision of various courses.

However, the great disadvantage is that in lumping everything together the term 'curriculum' becomes unmanageable and diverts attention away from what is after all the key question, namely what is the content that ideally we want to impart to students? Granted that it is also important to pursue such questions as whether particular styles of teaching or certain individual psychological states of mind may in various ways affect the outcome of our program, we have to start with some idea of a program. We want to consider what content or subject matter students ought ideally to study, not only because it is an important question in its own right, but also because our answer to this question is logically necessary to conducting inquiry and research into other related matters. Whether certain techniques of teaching are desirable, for example, may depend at least partly on what one is teaching and why – two questions that are at the heart of inquiry into content.

My view is that the key question in the domain of curriculum is 'What should the content be?' and that consequently the term should be used to refer to the content that we intend to put before students. The main argument for this, as I say, is that it forcefully reminds us that we have to focus on that question, and that ideally we should do so in isolation from all the other kinds of question that will undoubtedly subsequently arise. Let us examine what happens when we teach x in certain situations by all means, but let us do it when we are certain that we *want* to teach x and clear about what we mean by teaching it.

Curriculum Expertise

We must note three quite distinct uses of 'curriculum'. It can be used to refer to the school curriculum; it can be used to refer to curriculum theory, as when someone says 'I study curriculum'; but it can also be used to refer to an alleged special facility to bridge the presumed gap between theory and practice.

This last use is very common in the United States, and, in one view, is what Schwabb meant when he referred to curriculum as 'the art of the practical'.[1] Whether Schwabb did mean this is not at all clear to me, but what is clear is that there are some people who understand curriculum experts to be people who are good at putting the ideas of theorists across to practitioners. On the face of it, this sounds well enough, but on closer inspection it is less satisfactory. Without anticipating the discussion of theory and its relation to practice in Chapter 20 too much, let me just say here (i) that it is not clear that the idea of a general facility or skill of putting theory into practice makes sense, and (ii) that, if it does, it is still not clear why the skill should be found among a specialist group of middlemen rather than among theoreticians or practitioners themselves. (On skills, see Chapter 13.) What sense can be made of the idea that there are on the one hand educational theorists, who are wise, clever, and profound in their abstract way, and, on the other hand, practical folk who can cope with children, such that a special art is needed to communicate the wisdom of the former to the latter?

Imagine that I am a good educational theorist: I have clearly worked out my aims and have articulated them with the clarity of a good philosopher. As a result of my understanding, I come up with a proposal of the form 'We ought to do x in schools'. Granted that some teachers may not be adept at the kind of theorizing that I engage in, or may simply lack the time that I can devote to it, surely that does not mean that my ideas are not communicable and comprehensible to them? If it does mean that, then what exactly would the middleman do? It is sometimes suggested that he is needed to temper theory with practice or practical wisdom. But this, depending on what precisely it means, is either something to be strongly resisted or else something that each practitioner should do for themselves. Suppose for example, that theoreticians conclude that we should do x in the school, but practical people are aware that there is no money to do x. If 'tempering theory with practice' means being 'realistic' in the sense of ignoring the question of what we ought to do because it is in practical terms difficult or politically awkward, then obviously such 'tempering' should be resisted. It is part of our job as educationalists to insist on what ought to be done from an educational perspective and to argue against political obstacles; whether we win or lose such battles is a different problem and irrelevant to the question of what we should be doing. The point here is that we cannot formally approve of cutting the coat of our ideals according to the cloth of politicians.

On the other hand, if 'tempering theory with practice' means that a theoretical prescription, which will by its nature be general in form, will need modifications and adaptations in particular situations – well, every teacher (and every theorist) knows that; but particular modifications clearly have to be worked out by the people on the spot, the people who know the particular situation, rather than by some outside middleman. Besides, what would it mean to say that one was blessed with the art of modifying things in general? How does one acquire it? Is it not clear that one gains the ability to modify particular kinds of thing by knowing one's particular territory? And is it not equally clear that individual teachers should have this ability to interpret educational theory in the context of their own classrooms?

What happens in fact is that certain individuals become semi-professional curriculum developers, designers, implementers, evaluators, etc. – that is to say they become practiced in going through various hoops typically associated with drawing up a new curriculum, designing it, implementing it, and so forth. For example, they become familiar with the idea of setting out aims in terms of various observable objectives or with the idea of testing the necessary resources for a particular curriculum proposal. But such people are not necessarily blessed with either the understanding of the theorist or the practical knowledge of the classroom teacher.

In short, I find it very difficult to see a plausible role for the curriculum expert as an identifiable middleman with a unique role to play. And I see more danger than advantage in leaving curriculum planning, design, and change to a group of specialists, rather than insisting that curriculum should be in the hands of teachers, provided that they first get to grips with theoretical understanding of their enterprise.

Means and Ends

And so we come to a most worrying tendency: the widespread acceptance of the idea that one can coherently pursue other curriculum questions independently of discerning one's aim or ends, combined with the more particular view that curriculum is a form of applied science.

Curriculum as an area of study started out by reference to some key questions, most famously enunciated by Ralph Tyler.[2] Since then it has become more ossified (as tends to be the way with ideas) and the domain is generally seen as divisible into the areas of development, design, implementation, and evaluation. The last two of these are fairly straightforward, though it should be noted that evaluation is concerned with the efficacy of a program rather than with its educational worth. Evaluators are not in the business of estimating the educational success or value of curriculum change or practice, but in that of assessing the tendency of a given program to be adopted as intended and to attain the ends that it was designed to have, whatever they may be. Development and design are not always clearly distinguished, but design is primarily concerned with the manner in which a curriculum should be set out or presented to would-be users. Development is concerned either with improving one's own design (on an individual, school, or district level) or with improving the manner of adoption in schools: that is to say, with looking at ways in which one's school might better adapt to more appropriate curricula. In this latter sense it evidently shades into implementation.

But the crucial thing to note, and, I suggest, to be seriously worried about, is the extent to which these various branches of curriculum are pursued and studied independently of each other, independently of serious philosophical consideration of aims, and in the mode of the natural sciences. I must of course stress that there are honorable exceptions to the tendency that I draw attention to. For example, Denis Lawton writes about curriculum with some concern for the integration of various aspects, and ties up all that he has to say with some clearly enunciated arguments about content and aims. David Hamilton, to take another example, argues specifically for a humanistic, informal, model of curriculum development and research. The late Lawrence Stenhouse specifically repudiated the idea of behavioral objectives, which can serve like a millstone around the neck of curriculum.[3] Nonetheless, although one could cite other exceptions too, the dominant trend in curriculum is undoubtedly towards a scientific view of the enterprise, such that curriculum specialists are deemed to be working on means to ends that have been determined by others, and research into those means is seen as a scientific business.

What this means in effect is, first, that implementers carry out research into how various programs can most successfully be adopted without being concerned about evaluating the program. Evaluators, by the same token, tell us about the principles that govern those curricula that successfully meet their objectives, but ignore questions of implementation. Both are likely to proceed without direct reference to the branch of design.

One might at this point raise the objection that this just is an age of specialism. Why, it may be asked, should designers be expected to understand about implementation and vice versa? This brings me to my second more urgent point: what one cannot reasonably do is proceed in any one of these branches of curriculum without a very firm and clear grasp of educational ends. It simply does not make sense to claim to have expertise in designing curricula without reference to some particular idea of educational success. More generally, one cannot say that x is a good principle in the abstract, because it can only be a good principle in the light of certain ends. To this we may add a quite distinct point, which is that it is far from clear why so many people take it for granted that there are significant *general* principles of design, implementation, and such like. Surely the best way to design a science curriculum for ten year olds may be in many important respects quite different from the best way to design an English curriculum for sixteen year olds?

In general curriculum wallahs seem to take far too little account of the specifically educational nature of their sphere of interest, of the nature of the particular subject matter on any given occasion, and of the multifarious particularities of any given teaching situation. This is a point to which I shall return in Chapter 19.

For the moment this brings us to my third and most serious objection, namely the tendency of many curriculum persons to be wedded, explicitly or implicitly, to an applied science view of the field. The ends are variously presumed to be given, unproblematic, the product of democratic consensus, self-evident, or, paradoxically, too complex for anyone but absent-minded philosophers to worry about. What they are not is firmly grasped, stated and connected to research, argument, and prescription pertaining to means. Consequently, implicit in much of the curriculum work is a set of very dubious and ill-thought-out objectives or end states. Notions such as intelligence, imagination, understanding – specifically human attributes – are either ignored or travestied by operational definitions couched in purely observable terms, despite the indisputable fact that something like understanding is not something that one can directly observe. Education itself and mind are more or less ignored. Instead we are presumed to be creatures with a brain, capable of being instructed rather than taught, assessable by reference only to such things as time on task. The world is seen as comprising only scientifically demonstrable means to unquestioned ends.

Values are central to the curriculum business and values are primarily a matter for philosophical inquiry. This is not, as is often wrongly supposed, because they are non-factual or necessarily part of the subject matter of philosophy. (Whether, to what extent, and in what way value judgments are or are not related to factual propositions is one of the issues that needs careful consideration. And there are plenty of other disciplines besides philosophy that may have an interest in values; for example, sociology.) The reason that philosophers are needed at some point in any serious discussion of values is that many of the crucial questions in the area are conceptual. That is to say, the first main problem we face in arguing about aims is in getting clear what people mean by such claims as that the aim of education is to produce a critical thinker, a happy person, or whatever.

It is argued by some that settling our values is a forlorn hope, since value judgments are relative. But at best any such claim would have to substantiate itself by philosophical means. At worst (and I believe this to be the case) the claim is false and based on a confusion between 'arbitrary' and 'not empirically demonstrated'. This is not the place to pursue this particular issue (but see Chapter 15). Suffice it to say that certain values seem undeniable, and are not in fact disputed, many if not all of them being conceptually tied up with what it is to be human and what morality is all about (Chapter 10). Furthermore, certain more specific values are conceptually linked to the nature of education.[4]

Where does this leave us? Curriculum is very often instituted as a distinctive subject or discipline. Within it there are subdivisions. It is not clear how wise or well-founded this is, but if it is going to be done it should start with the question of what we ought to learn. Everything else must then be pursued in the light of some specific answer to that question. Having outlined my own answer to that question in Chapter 7, we can now proceed to look in more detail at some of the subject matter I have argued for, beginning with religion.

Notes

1 Joseph Schwabb, 'The Practical: A Language for the Curriculum', *School Review*, 78 (1), 1969.
2 Ralph Tyler, *Basic Principles of Curriculum and Instruction* (University of Chicago Press, 1949).
3 Denis Lawton, *Class, Culture and the Curriculum* (Routledge & Kegan Paul, 1975); David Hamilton, *Curriculum Evaluation* (Open Books, 1976); Laurence Stenhouse, *An Introduction to Curriculum Research and Development* (Heinemann, 1975).
4 See further on these important issues John Wilson, *What Philosophy Can Do* (op. cit.); Robin Barrow, *The Philosophy of Schooling* (Wheatsheaf, 1981).

Further Reading

Robin Barrow, *Giving Teaching Back to Teachers* (Wheatsheaf, 1984) offers a full analysis and critique of the field of curriculum theory, while Kieran Egan, *Education and Psychology* (Teachers College Press, 1983) is pertinent to critical consideration of the contribution of psychology to curriculum.

Useful introductions to curriculum study are provided by Hugh Sockett, *Designing the Curriculum* (Open Books, 1976), D. Jenkins & M. Shipman, *Curriculum: An Introduction* (Open Books, 1976), and other volumes in Open Books' Curriculum Studies series.

Examples of the kind of curriculum theorizing criticized here are provided by David Pratt, *Curriculum: Design and Development* (Harcourt Brace Jovanovich, 1980) and D. Tanner & L.N. Tanner, *Curriculum Development: Theory and Practice* (Macmillan, 1980).

More recent works of interest include A. Moore, *Understanding the School Curriculum: Theory, Politics and Principles* (Bloomsbury Academic, 2015), and M.J. Reiss, 'The Curriculum and Subject Knowledge', in *Education, Philosophy and Well-being: New Perspectives on the Work of John White* (op. cit.)

Questions

What do you understand by the claim that "something that explains everything, explains nothing?"

What is your understanding of the argument in the text against the idea of curriculum experts as 'middlemen' between teachers and educational theorists?

Do you agree that the question of what should be studied is the central or primary question in respect of the curriculum? Why or why not?

9   Religion and Religious Education

There can be no denying the enormous significance of religion throughout history. Millions have died and continue to die in the name of religion, sometimes in conflicts between believers and non-believers, but generally in savage wars between religions, and sometimes in conflicts and disputes between different sects within the same religion. Religion has inspired people to savagery and cruelty from the time of the Roman persecution of Christians, through the wars of the Crusades and the years of the Inquisition, up to and including recent events in such places as the Balkans, not to mention ongoing hostilities, particularly in the Middle East. Of course, in many of these conflicts there are also other factors such as ethnic differences involved. But the fact remains that religion has been and remains a significant cause of war, terrorism, and cruelty, and when it stops short of violence in many cases it nonetheless breeds intolerance and fanaticism.

And yet most of the world's major religions are notable for preaching tolerance and love, and in many instances they also exhibit it. In addition, religion has undoubtedly provided genuine solace and comfort, as well as inspiration, to millions of people. It may also be argued that religious faith provides a welcome antidote to our more egregious materialistic, commercial, and consumerist tendencies.

Religion has also played a most important role in education. For centuries, the provision of education across cultures was predominantly provided by religious orders; it was for instance not so long ago that prestigious universities such as Oxford were primarily concerned to prepare people for the priesthood. It is true that in the Western world faith schools are now relatively few, but those that remain still give rise to debate about whether they should be accepted and if so on what terms. For example, should a university which is a religious foundation that regards homosexuality and pre-marital sex as objectionable be allowed to require its students to sign some kind of pledge condemning such activities? Conversely, should the legal profession be allowed to refuse to accept individuals whose qualifications were obtained at such an institution?[1] Should we have any concern about an increase in Madrasah schools in nominally Christian or secular societies? Occasionally, but nonetheless ferociously, there are conflicts over whether creationism

DOI: 10.4324/9781003120476-9

should be taught. There are severe disagreements about dress codes and in particular the wearing of religious symbols. Nor should we forget the recent spate of accusations of widespread child-abuse and subsequent cover-up by priests and others involved in various forms of child-care provided by religious organizations. Given all the above, it is surely rather surprising that by and large in many parts of the Western world there is effectively no longer any such thing as religious education. Indeed, for the most part there is a distinct sense that religion is a topic best avoided.

What is Religion?

I recognize that discussing religion can prove a sensitive issue. It is very easy to misunderstand or be misunderstood. So let me preface the remainder of this chapter by stressing that I do not intend to disparage any particular religion in what follows, nor to denigrate those who have a faith. My argument is simply that religious belief must be a matter of *faith*; nobody can reasonably claim that they *know* their religious beliefs to be true. This is not a particularly shocking claim, since religions themselves tend to stress that commitment is a matter of faith rather than knowledge. But it is a very important claim, since most of the bad or evil things done in the name of religion stem from the assumption that the religious believer is committed to an established *truth*, as distinct from a tentative, if deeply held, *belief.*

I should also note that most of my examples and the language I use betray a Christian background because that is the faith I was brought up in and with which I am most familiar (although I am no longer a believer). But my argument is meant to apply to all religions and not to Christianity alone.

Reference to 'all religions' raises the question with which it is anyway appropriate to start: What is religion? What counts as a *bona fide* religion as distinct from various others sets of beliefs? Are witchcraft, communism, or fascism religions, for example?

Let us start by distinguishing religion from the broader concept of spirituality. Many people may feel a sense of awe at the universe and believe perhaps that there must be some unknown unseen spirit or power that lies behind the whole thing. But so long as this power remains unconceptualized, so long as it has no specific form or attributes, it does not count as a religion. And indeed the question that surely needs addressing is not whether we do or do not sense that "there are more things in heaven and earth... than are dreamt of in [our] philosophy",[2] but whether there is good reason to commit oneself to some particular faith involving a set of specific beliefs and rituals, and if so, whether the reasons are strong enough to make us at least metaphorically stand and fight for its truth as we would fight for the truth of various scientific or historical claims.

The *Shorter Oxford English Dictionary* defines 'religion' as 'recognition on the part of man of some higher unseen power as having control over his destiny, and as being entitled to obedience, reverence and worship'. (Of course, 'man' here signifies 'humans'.) As we have noted before, a dictionary definition is not the same as analysis of a concept, but in this case it is not a bad place to start. The important difference between this definition and the sense of spirituality that I referred to above is the notion that this power or spirit has some kind of interest in and control over us, and that some form of recognition is owing to it on our part. The phrase 'control over [our] destiny' might be said to prejudge the complex issue of whether humans have free will; since this is not the place to go into that vexed question, I will rephrase it in these more open terms: 'having the ability, if it chooses, to exercise its power over us'. But we need to go further than the definition as it stands, in that any religion surely attributes certain specific characteristics to this unseen power. However mysterious the power or the god may be, it will be thought of as, for example, jealous, omnipotent, loving, vengeful, forgiving, or unforgiving.

So any particular commitment to a set of beliefs, if it is to count as a religion, should involve: a characterization of God in terms of some specific attributes; the belief that He (She or It) can exercise power over us; and commitment to a set of rituals that are presumed to please It. Such a conception, general as it is, has the merit of allowing that major faiths such as Judaism, Islam, Christianity, and Hinduism are indeed all religions. (Whether Buddhism should be so classified depends upon whether Buddhism is taken to involve the claim that there is no God, as some maintain, or that it merely involves rejecting various crude notions of God, as others argue.)

Attempts to Prove the Existence of God by Logical Reasoning

At this point I reiterate that the argument I am about to advance is not designed to establish that no religion is true. It is designed to show that no particular religion can be *known* to be true. You may of course have religious belief, and it is possible that your belief is true. But *knowledge* is widely understood to be defined in terms of three conditions, which, taken together, are both *necessary* and *sufficient*; to know is to have a *belief*, that is *true*, and that can be shown to be true or *justified*. The argument is that you cannot have *justified* true belief in a religion, because there is no agreed way to justify your belief. Needless to say, there are and have been many who would dispute this and argue that they can justify their beliefs, in the sense of show them to be *true* rather than simply show them to be *explicable*. First, and probably most interestingly from a philosophical point of view, there have been attempts to demonstrate the existence of God by logical reasoning. I will briefly describe three such attempts.

The first, often referred to as the Ontological Argument (or the argument from being), is particularly associated with St Anselm.[3] It goes like this:

1   God is by definition the most perfect being imaginable.
2   An actually existing being is more perfect than an imaginary one.
3   Therefore God must exist.

Ingenious no doubt, but surely quite unconvincing. While in particular instances, such as a real mother versus an imaginary mother, the real is certainly the better of the two, it is hard to even make sense of the general claim. What on earth does it mean to say that an actual horse is more perfect than an imaginary one? (Plato, for one, would argue the exact opposite: no actual horse is a perfect horse; only the Idea of a horse can be perfect.) But perhaps even more significant is the fact that the first premise seems already to smuggle in the conclusion, since it already presumes the existence of God (who is the most perfect being).

The Teleogical Argument (or the argument from design) suggests that the world seems so organized as to suggest an organizer, so well designed as to suggest a designer. An analogy is often drawn with a person living far from civilization who for the first time comes across a watch; this is presumed to be an old-fashioned pre-digital era watch, consisting of moving interlocking parts. Studying the watch the person in question appreciates that this is not a random set of metal bits, but a set of parts each of which has its function and all of which work together in harmony to fulfill a purpose. Seeing that the watch has a design, the conclusion is drawn that there must have been a designer.

But as a matter of fact, it is incorrect to assume that wherever we see a pattern or design there must have been a designer. Think of the quite common case in which we detect a design in a play, garden, or painting, which was not consciously intended by the author, gardener, or artist. Similarly, we can detect or impose pattern and design on what we see in circumstances where there was no designer of any kind. I therefore reject the assumption that the world, awe inspiring as it is and following rules of cause and effect and so forth as it does, *necessitates* a designer. Such a world can surely be equally well explained in terms of science; is not evolution, for instance, an example precisely of a theory that explains why aspects of our world take the form or design that they do? While it is true that the universe and our world could be as they are by the design of some being, there is no necessity for that to be so; consequently, this argument does not prove the existence of a designer.

Thirdly there is the so-called First Cause Argument (sometimes referred to as the Unmoved Mover) which goes as follows: everything must have a cause, yet this must stop somewhere if we are to avoid infinite regress, so we posit a First Cause that is itself without cause. But this simply contradicts itself: on the one hand the premise is that everything must have a cause; on the other hand, the conclusion is that something or somebody doesn't need a cause.

I find these attempts to establish the existence of God by logical means interesting but quite unsuccessful. But there is one more point to be made about them. Though they happen to have been advanced at one time or another by Christian thinkers, none of these arguments would establish the existence of a specifically Christian God. Even if the argument did prove the existence of the perfect non-imaginary being, the designer, or the First

Cause, none of these entities would have any defining characteristics. Consequently, the arguments would not serve to establish the truth of any *particular* religion even if they were in themselves valid.

Revelation and Authority

It is doubtful whether many believers base their faith on logical reasoning anyway. A few would claim that they saw the light or found the truth by revelation. The obvious problem with this is that one person's revelation is another person's delusion. In other words, I do not need to challenge or deny your claim that you heard the voice of God in your hour of greatest need; I fully accept that you had an experience, which you interpret as hearing the voice of God, and this perhaps fully *explains* your faith. But it doesn't *justify* it in the sense of show your interpretation to be true.

I would hazard the view that in fact the vast majority of believers come by their faith through some form of socialization and in response to authority. That is to say, they hold to the faith in which they were uncritically immersed when young, guided if not propelled by the faith of authority figures such as parents and priests. Once again this explains the reason many people adhere to their faith, but it has nothing to do with establishing the truth of the faith in question. Indeed, the very obvious observation that the majority of Muslims grew up among Muslims, and likewise Catholics among Catholics, Jews among Jews, etc., should surely alert us to the possibility that religious faith is essentially a culturally induced set of beliefs. But following the crowd or peer-group pressure and uncritically accepting the tenets of one's social environment are not appropriate ways to find the truth about anything.

When it comes to the question of authority, we need to distinguish between being *in* authority and being *an* authority. The two may sometimes coincide, as when a person who has expertise in medicine (i.e., is *an* authority on medical matters) takes charge of a medical laboratory (i.e., is placed *in* authority), but often they are not linked. An authority on a subject deserves some respect when talking about that subject. But, as we have already seen (Chapter 6), theologians, who are indeed authorities on their various religions, do not have any more ability than the rest of us to determine the truth or otherwise of their faith. Their expertise lies in understanding the nature of a given religion and not in establishing its truth or falsity. And being in authority does not in itself constitute any grounds for having one's opinions taken seriously.

Pascal's Wager

There is another famous but rather bizarre attempt to provide good reason to believe in God provided by the French thinker Blaise Pascal. Commonly known as Pascal's wager, it goes like this:

If I put my faith in God and He in fact exists, that is obviously to my advantage; and if it turns out that He does not exist, I haven't lost a lot by believing. On the other hand, if I repudiate the faith, I don't gain a great deal if I am right, but [assuming the existence of something like a Hell] I have an awful lot to lose if I am wrong.[4]

Sadly, there is a glaring flaw in this argument (quite apart from the fact that there is something a little awkward about committing to a faith on such self-interested terms). The flaw lies in the fact that this reasoning would at best give one a reason for adopting the true faith. But if we include all minor sects throughout history there are literally millions of faiths. If we are to reap the benefits of Pascal's wager it is no good simply adopting a faith (in Pascal's case Catholicism); we must adopt the right or the true faith. After all, if Islam is actually true, Allah is not going to be particularly pleased that Pascal turned to the Catholic Church. And, given the multiplicity of religions, the chance of getting it right is literally in the range of one in a million or more.

Historical Evidence

Some have argued that history can provide sufficient evidence to establish the truth of a religion, but this too fails to stand up. It may well be the case that Jesus, Mohammed, and other key religious figures were historical figures. But establishing that Jesus existed, even that he had disciples, cared for the poor and died on the cross, unfortunately does nothing to establish that he was the Son of God.

The historical record has other problems too. Sometimes the authenticity of evidence is itself disputed, as the Turin shroud, believed to have covered Christ after the crucifixion and to show the outline of his body, has sometimes been dated as contemporary with Christ and sometimes as being of a far later date. And of course even in the former case it is not thereby proven that the shroud was Christ's, nor, if it was, does it establish that he was the Son of God. Many of the relics (such as the bones of Saints or pieces of the cross) are, to put it politely, of doubtful provenance. And then there is the question of what is to count as evidence even accepting its historical authenticity. The Dead Sea Scrolls are undoubtedly ancient and are certainly evidence of near contemporary belief in Jesus as the Son of God, but that does not prove that such belief was true.

Religious people take their sacred texts very seriously of course. But when one considers their origins, awkward questions arise. *The Book of Mormon* provides perhaps one of the more egregious examples. According to the orthodox view among members of the Church of the Latter-Day Saints, this book, published by Joseph Smith in 1830, consists of the writings of ancient prophets living on the American continent between 2,200 BC and AD 421. Unlike some other sacred texts, which can at least be traced to near contemporary sources, there is no evidence whatsoever that these texts ever existed before their appearance in 1830. Smith maintained that an angel revealed to him the whereabouts of some golden plates containing writing in unknown characters (which he referred to as 'reformed Egyptian'), and instructed him to translate them, which he duly did and thus produced the Book. Eleven contemporaries of Smith avowed that they had at one time or another seen the plates in question. Apart from that questionable testimony, there is absolutely no evidence that the plates existed. Even if they did, there is no reason to suppose that an angel produced them, or that Smith in truth 'translated' a language with which he was wholly unfamiliar (assuming it existed).

That example may be extreme, but the Christian Bible presents two rather different conceptions of God in the Old and New Testament. The gospels, though they may be authentic in the sense that they were written at various times not long after Christ's death, and in the sense that they are written by people who believed what they wrote to be true, are nonetheless problematic, besides being in some respects incompatible with each other. Most awkward is probably the fact that the four gospels were selected out of a much larger number of gospels known to have existed at the time, including the fairly recently discovered gospel of Judas (Jesus' betrayer) – a reminder that all our putative evidence is filtered through human selection; and humans are prone to error. Add the fact that, though there are important and interesting overlaps, fundamentally the sacred texts of the various religions are in competition with each other, and add the hundreds if not thousands of schisms within each major religion, each one of which represents a disagreement about what is true, and it becomes pretty clear that one cannot prove the truth of one's religion by an appeal to history, however much historical evidence there may be relating to the progress of a faith.

Death by a Thousand Qualifications

My conclusion at this point is that there is no way of arriving at proof or demonstration of the truth of religion in general or, rather more importantly, of any particular religion. Let us therefore now try a different approach. If it is rational to adopt a particular religious faith then the key concepts of the faith must be comprehensible. To say that I believe in 'wadgereegee' when I have no idea what 'wadgereegee' means would be nonsensical, as, more prosaically, it would be meaningless for me to claim commitment to identity politics, if I have no understanding of what constitutes identity politics.

Take, then, the doctrine of the Trinity or the belief that 'God is Three Persons in one'. Most Christian believers will know that this refers to a belief in God the Father, God the Son (Jesus Christ), and the Holy Ghost, but does that amount to a real understanding of the Trinity? What constitutes the Holy Ghost? In what sense is Jesus the 'son' of God? And what does it mean to say that they are three persons in one? We know all of the words, but many of us would have to admit that we do not have any conception, any true understanding, of what the words signify. Or again one might question how many people have anything like a clear idea of 'transubstantiation', yet this term refers to a belief that marks a crucial distinction between Catholics and Protestants. The latter believe that the wine and the wafer (bread) that are taken during communion *represent* the blood and body of Christ. But the former believe that they actually turn into (*transubstantiate*) His blood and body. Once again, we understand the words, but can we really claim to comprehend what they mean? In what sense do the wine and wafer become His blood and body and why should we presume that they do, since to our senses they manifestly do not?

At this point, it is helpful to refer to a parable devised by Anthony Flew.[5] He asks us to imagine two men entering a hitherto unexplored jungle. They trek deep into the wild and untamed forest until suddenly and unexpectedly they come across an area of what appears to be carefully cultivated land: neatly ordered flower beds, well-pruned bushes, and recently mowed grass. "Goodness me", remarks one explorer, "we are obviously not alone here; there must be a gardener, since, look, this grass was cut very recently". "Well", replies the other, "that could be so, I suppose, but it's odd that we have not seen him or indeed any sign of him on our journey here".

So they remain by the garden for a week or so, but still there is no sign of a gardener. The second explorer, the skeptical one, concludes that there clearly is no gardener. But the other, the believer, concludes that there is one, but he must be invisible. The skeptic then suggests that they erect an electrified fence around the garden, which will give a shock and set off an alarm if the invisible gardener tries to climb over it. They erect it, wait for a week or so without any sound from the alarm, whereupon the skeptic is ready to declare his position obviously proven, but the believer says that the gardener is incorporeal and impervious to shock. So next they place dogs in the garden to catch the scent of the invisible gardener.

You can probably see where this is going: the skeptic proposes more and more tests to see whether there is a gardener, but each time the test fails to provide evidence of one the believer counters that the gardener is, variously, incorporeal, intangible, without odor, completely silent, and able to move through physical obstacles, as well as invisible. Flew calls this "death by a thousand qualifications", by which he means that by the time one has qualified the gardener with negative characteristics so many times, it is not clear what you have left. What *is* an invisible, intangible, impermeable, and (we may perhaps now add) eternal, all-knowing, all-seeing being? Is it really possible to conceive of one, as opposed to paying uncritical lip-service to the description or the mere labeling of one?

Perhaps, notwithstanding the above, some believers nonetheless could claim that they do have a concept of God because they have some kind of an image of Him in mind. This may well be true, but the problem is that it is highly likely that our image will simply be an idealized portrait of our own kind. As long ago as the sixth century BC, a Greek named Xenophanes observed that, "Ethiopians imagine their gods as black and snubnosed [i.e., like themselves], Thracians as blue eyed and red haired. But if horses or lions... could draw... as men do, horses would draw gods shaped like horses and lions like lions". Since this seems as true today as it was then, we surely cannot equate having a mental image of God with having a convincing conception.

In none of the above do I deny the mystery of the universe or the possibility that there is some force or power having some kind of influence on the world in general, and humans in particular. I do not categorically deny that there is a God, and incidentally I recognize the enormous comfort that having a faith may provide for people, even agreeing with Voltaire that "if God did not exist, it would be necessary to invent him" because psychologically a lot of people seem to need some such belief.[6] I do not even argue that all religions are false, although it is very important to note that 99% of all proclaimed faiths must be false, since if a given religion is indeed true, others, being at odds with it one way or another, cannot be.

My argument is simply that since no logical argument, no piling up of historical data, no appeal to authority or personal revelation can provide good reason to conclude that a given religion embodies the truth, and since some of the central concepts in religion seem to be literally inconceivable, by which I mean impossible to fully conceptualize, it follows that no particular religion can be *known* to be true. Religious commitment can only reasonably be seen as matter of *faith* in a fundamentally unverifiable set of beliefs. A conclusion, as I mentioned at the outset, that should not cause any offense since it is a fairly common view even among the religious. St Anselm, for instance, remarked "Credo, ut intellegam" ("I believe in order that I may come to understand"), echoing a viewpoint earlier put forward by St Augustine in the form of a command: "Believe in order that you may come to understand".[7]

Religion and the School

The preceding discussion has implications for education. Here, as we have seen, is an enormously powerful phenomenon that effects and in many cases directs people's entire lives, and yet in recent years in many jurisdictions the effective school policy is to ignore religion as a topic for discussion. There are exceptions, but by and large, partly as a consequence of emphasis on diversity, which seems sometimes to imply that it is rather bad form to draw attention to, let alone discuss, the merits and demerits of differing viewpoints, religion is tacitly ignored. But with large portions of the globe riven with religious rivalry and warfare, it seems extraordinary that so little attention is paid to the subject.

At this juncture it is pertinent to recall the distinction between training and education introduced in Chapter 2. At the elementary level schools do sometimes attempt to initiate children into the basic beliefs and rituals of the religion of the community. However, this is not always easy or straightforward in the multicultural settings to be found in so many communities today, and often amounts to little more than a version of 'show and tell', with children from different religious backgrounds providing examples and illustrations of their faith. In such circumstances, the family is likely to be the main influence. Whether provided by the community at large, the school, or the family, such initiation into the basic tenets of a given religion would constitute a form of religious training, and seems entirely acceptable. Why should one not introduce one's children to one's beliefs on this matter as one introduces them to one's ideas respecting good manners, politics, or social justice? Indeed, how could one avoid doing so to some extent?

Nor do I see any serious objection to the existence of schools designed to embody a particular faith, for the children of those who wish to introduce their children to an understanding of their faith. But there must surely be one big proviso: though certain religious values, beliefs, and rituals may be introduced and explained, the instruction should be, as in all teaching, critical, open, and regarded as provisional. The ultimate aim should be that on leaving school students should be in a position to consider and assess their religious beliefs for themselves. One thing that would be quite unacceptable would be to deliberately instill unyielding commitment to a particular set of religious beliefs or to indoctrinate students (see Chapter 11).

Having a religious *faith* is neither a necessary nor sufficient criterion of being educated, since clearly many religious individuals are not particularly well educated and many non-religious people are well educated. But, in line with the argument that educated people are those who have understanding of certain fundamental types of understanding and inquiry (Chapter 7), I would conclude that educated people should most certainly have understanding of religion in the broadest sense as a cultural, historical, and artistic phenomenon, along with a basic grasp of the philosophy of religion such as has been introduced in this chapter. Why? Because the subject matter is important, thought provoking, and illuminating, and because having some understanding of religion (as distinct from a particular faith) provides something of an antidote to fanaticism, dogmatism, and complacency. To have no awareness of the place of religion in history, to be ignorant of what religion can do for good and ill, to fail to distinguish between the verifiable claims of science and the unverifiable claims of religion, or to embrace uncritically a religious ideology devised by others, is to be lacking understanding of one of the major factors affecting human life. Understanding religion is simply one of the most worthwhile and useful of human endeavors. There is no need to revert to old-fashioned bible classes or even classes in religious education. But there is every reason to want other subjects, such as history, literature, and philosophy in particular, to ensure that the religious dimension is recognized as and when appropriate. Sadly, this is not happening to any great extent as things currently stand.

Notes

1   Such a case arose in connection with Trinity Western University in British Columbia, Canada, in 2018.
2   The quotation is from Shakespeare's *Hamlet*. Act 1. Scene 5.
3   St Anselm (1033–1109).
4   Blaise Pascal (1623–62). I have combined passages from sections 418 and 233 of *Les Pensees*.
5   Antony Flew, 'Theology and Falsification: A Symposium' in Antony Flew & Alasdair MacIntyre (eds.), *New Essays in Philosophical Theology* (SCM, 1955). Pp. 96 ff.
6   Voltaire (1694–1778). *Epitres*, no 96.
7   St Augustine (354–430).

Further Reading

Richard Holloway, *A Little History of Religion* (Yale, 2016) provides a useful introduction to the topic.

John Hick (ed.), *The Existence of God* (Macmillan, 1964) and John Hick & Arthur McGill (eds.), *The Many-Faced Argument* (Macmillan, 1968) provide a variety of useful papers on attempts to establish the existence of God logically.

On the gospels, see Elaine Pagel, *The Gnostic Gospels* (Random House, 1979) and Rodolphe Kassar, Maria Meyer, & Gregor Want (eds.), *The Gospel of Judas* (National Geographic, 2006).

Antony Flew spent most of his career arguing against religion in books such as *God and Philosophy* (Hutchinson, 1966) and Terry Miethe & Antony Flew (eds.), *Does God Exist?* (Harper, 1991). But just before he died, in a book written "with Roy Abraham Varghese", entitled *There is a God: How the World's Most Notorious Atheist Changed His Mind* (Harper Collins, 2007), as the title implies, he seemed to recant, though there has been some questioning of the extent to which the book authentically represents Flew's final thoughts.

Richard Dawkins, *The God Delusion* (Houghton Mifflin, 2006) will be a familiar title to many readers; less well known, perhaps, will be a response in Alistair McGrath, *The Dawkins Delusion* (SPCK, 2007).

Karen Armstrong, *The Case for God* (Alfred A. Knopf, 2009) is a strong counter argument to the view expressed in this chapter.

Alexander Waugh, *God* (Review, 2002) is entertaining and interesting.

On religious education, see Michael Hand, *Is Religious Education Possible?* (Bloomsbury Academic, 2017), and Richard Pring, *Challenges for Religious Education: Is There a Disconnect between Faith and Reason?* (Routledge, 2019).

Questions

What is the central argument of this chapter?

Are you convinced by it? If not, why not?

10 Morality and Moral Education

Morality is concerned with conduct that we ought to engage in for its own sake. To behave morally or ethically[1] is to behave in accordance with certain principles regardless of such extrinsic factors as whether it is profitable, enjoyable or useful to do so. Moral rules tend to coincide with legal rules because generally speaking societies want their legal system to be moral, but we need to remember that morality and legality do not *necessarily* march hand in hand. There can be bad or immoral laws. Similarly, while moral rules may happen to coincide with what is deemed politically correct, what is economically productive, what is socially acceptable, or what is regarded as natural, they do not necessarily do so. It is logically possible, and often the case in practice, that what we ought morally to do in a given situation is neither legally required nor in accordance with any other of the above types of value.

Unfortunately, there is not universal agreement either within or between societies, nor across time, as to what the moral rules are. Some think abortion morally wrong, others do not; some think whistleblowers are behaving wrongly, while others think they are doing the right thing. Awareness of this fact leads many people to conclude that moral rules are no more than conventions, adopted simply in accordance with the predilections of societies or individuals. But this, I shall argue, is not the case. There are certain criteria that a proposed rule must take account of if it is to count as a *bona fide* moral rule.

Four Distinct Features of Moral Discourse

The ethical or moral theory known as *emotivism* argues that moral language is purely emotive. That is to say, when we make judgments that this is right or that is wrong, or commend some actions as morally good and criticize others as bad, though we may think we are making some kind of factual statement such as that snow is white, in fact all we are doing is emoting or expressing our emotional attitude. Thus, the statement "Slavery is evil" is simply a way of expressing one's distaste for slavery, essentially equivalent to exclaiming, "slavery – ugh!".[2]

It is obviously correct to say that if I think that kindness is morally good then I necessarily approve of it, and others may legitimately infer my

DOI: 10.4324/9781003120476-10

positive emotional attitude from my saying as much. Equally, when I condemn bullying I am certainly signaling my distaste for it. But that is surely only part of what I am doing. There must be more to it than that, if only because there is a clear difference between the implications of saying, "I detest hip-hop" and the implications of saying, "I think bullying is wrong". Both involve revealing my emotional attitude, but the latter, being a moral judgment, involves more. One clear difference between the two statements is that the latter implies that I think other people ought to agree with me and object to bullying, whereas my dislike of hip-hop carries no suggestion that other people ought to agree with me.

This brings us to *prescriptivism*, a theory that holds that moral claims such as that "Cheating is wrong" are disguised imperatives: they imply a command or an order along the lines of "I abhor cheating; do thou likewise" (or, less poetically, "so should you"). More specifically the theory holds that your judgment can only count as a moral one if you are prepared to *universalize* it. Many commands or orders such as "Close the door" are particular and imply nothing about other occasions or other people, but if I am making a moral claim, such as "You ought not to play your trumpet late at night", then it is to be presumed that I and others should also refrain from making a loud noise at night. This suggestion owes a lot to the German philosopher Immanuel Kant's *Categorical Imperative*, which in one of its formulations reads "Act only on that maxim that you can will as a universal law". Moral prescriptions, that is to say, necessarily apply equally to all people in similar situations.[3]

Prescriptivism, like emotivism, makes a valid point but is far from being the whole truth about moral discourse. It is true that if you believe that something is morally wrong, then part of what you mean is that nobody should do it and that you are implicitly making the demand that they should not. But equally clearly the claim that nobody should engage in a certain activity is not always a moral claim; for example, I don't think anybody should plunge into a vat of boiling water, but that is not a moral judgment; it is simply the view that it would be a crazy thing to do.

Emotivism of course involves the denial that there is such a thing as objective moral truth, in the sense of judgments about the rightness and wrongness of actions that just are true, and therefore true whether particular individuals recognize the fact or not. Prescriptivism does not explicitly deny this, but clearly implies such denial, since its assumption is that provided that I can sincerely universalize my judgment then it is a moral judgment, regardless of the question of whether we can establish its truth or falsity.

For the prescriptivist, a universalizable command is what a moral judgment is.

Intuitionism, by contrast, is a theory that holds to the view that moral judgments can be objectively true. It concedes that they cannot be proved to be true empirically or by any form of demonstration, but maintains that the truth or otherwise of a moral claim can be, indeed has to be, recognized intuitively. Just as, though we cannot prove that a new acquaintance is a poseur and a fraud, we can intuit it, so we can intuit the truth or falsity of moral claims. To the objection that intuitions notoriously differ and that we have no way of discerning between one intuition and another, the intuitionist responds by drawing an analogy with physical sight: just as some are physically blind, so some are morally blind. In neither case need we deny the sight or insight of those who have sound eyesight or sound moral intuition. This is somewhat unsatisfactory given the range of different moral intuitions that there seem to be; nonetheless I think it difficult to deny that at some stage in moral discussion one has to make reference to intuition and make some such observation as "Well, if you can't see that that is wrong, there's nothing more to be said".[4]

From this brief survey of three ethical theories, we come to the conclusion that at least part of what distinguishes moral discourse is (i) that it is necessarily emotive, (ii) that it is necessarily prescriptive, (iii) that its claims cannot be verified in the same way as other factual or empirical claims, and (iv) that it may ultimately have to rely on intuition. This brings us to the notion of *relativism*, which, though persistently popular in one form or another, is potentially dangerously misleading.

In his *Ethics* Aristotle observed that "Fire burns the same in Greece and Persia, while the idea of right and wrong varies from place to place",[5] and, we may add, from historical period to historical period. In other words, different people have different ideas about what is and isn't morally acceptable. The view that there is nothing objective or as we might say factual about the rightness or wrongness of actions is explicitly maintained by a character named Thrasymachus in Plato's *Republic*: Thrasymachus' view is that "Justice is simply the interest of the stronger". Actually, this claim as stated is ambiguous. He might mean that it is objectively the case that it is right that the strong should get their way. But it is generally assumed that his view is the cynical one that there is no such thing as objective morality or a question of a moral judgment being correct or incorrect; rather, the powerful invent rules that are in their own interests and try to legitimize them by calling them moral imperatives. So the idea that moral values are simply the preferred values of a given society or particular individuals, and have no more claim to be objective or true than the opinion that strawberries are the nicest fruit, was alive and kicking in Ancient Greece, and it has always had its supporters, not least today.

Moral Relativism

Why is moral relativism apparently so tempting? One reason is obviously that different cultures often have different moral views. Secondly, it is an historical fact that moral views change over time, as, for example, slavery was once regarded as acceptable. Thirdly, there is the point, agreed by both those who believe that moral values are just a matter of preference or opinion and intuitionists who think they can be true or false, that they certainly can't be tested and proven in the way that empirical claims about the world can be. To put it simply: there is no demonstrable proof to support a claim such as that kindness is good.

Yet, there are some considerations that should stop us from too hastily drawing the conclusion that what is morally desirable is just a matter of opinion. In the first place there is the interesting fact that all societies seem to have a moral sense. That is to say, regardless of their specific values, all societies have a sense of shame or guilt; they all make a clear distinction between mere matters of taste or opinion ("You like detective novels, I don't") and matters where difference of opinion is not to be tolerated.

Secondly, despite the fact that there are some differences between the moral values of different cultures, there are also quite a lot of similarities, both at any given time and throughout history. Today, for example, although admittedly some forms of slavery do persist (depending on how we define 'slavery'), it remains true that all societies formally indict slavery as immoral. Historically, every society with which I am familiar has felt it right that the dead should be honored, although they often differ in their view of how to honor them, some thinking it appropriate to bury the dead, some to burn them, and (if Herodotus is to be believed) some to eat them.[6] This example reminds us that sometimes apparent differences of value actually arise from different physical circumstances, as for instance when a society embraces the view that the dead should be quickly cremated because of extreme hot weather. Different practices that are regarded as moral differences may in fact differ because of different empirical factors (whether geographical, technical, or simply other nonmoral beliefs such as religious beliefs) rather than because of different moral values. Not all arguments about abortion, for example, hinge directly on different moral viewpoints: for some the argument hinges rather on religious beliefs or on a view of what constitutes a viable human being.

So, at least sometimes different practices in the moral sphere come about because of different factual or empirical conditions, and sometimes different actions may be morally required by different circumstances. Killing provides an obvious example. Killing in our society is regarded as in itself a bad thing; it is immoral to kill another human, so much so that in most Western societies the death penalty is taboo even for heinous crimes. Yet, with few exceptions, people would agree that there may be circumstances, such as defending one's family from a serial murderer, in which killing would be justified.

The above comments make it clear that in the moral sphere things are by no means always cut and dried or easy to determine. And there certainly are some genuine moral dilemmas, which is to say problems that cannot be resolved by reason. There is for example surely no 'correct' answer, on any moral theory, to the question of how many other lives saved might justify killing a known terrorist. But does it follow that ultimately moral claims are just the product of preferred values where questions of truth and falsity, correct and incorrect, or reasonable and unreasonable do not arise? Surely not. Surely some putative moral claims are simply not coherent and others, though coherent, are untenable.

In the first place, the moral sphere, like any other, has its limits: not everything is a moral issue or has a moral dimension and some potential moral suggestions can be ruled out as simply failing to understand the nature of morality. Somebody who proposed that we all have a moral duty to paint everything purple might reasonably be dismissed as simply having no idea of what is meant by morality. Less absurd but equally unacceptable would be the suggestion that we have a moral duty to make as much money as possible. It is not a question of whether making money is good or bad; it is a question of appreciating that whatever morality does or doesn't entail, it is clearly a misunderstanding to think that failing to make a lot of money is a specifically moral failing.

Secondly, intuition surely does have a part to play in this: the suggestion that there is nothing morally wrong with the *gratuitous* infliction of extreme pain is surely something that we all intuitively reject as unacceptable. Conceivably some people may not care about the issue, and some psychopaths may be blind to it, but surely nobody could conclude that it was morally acceptable. Thirdly, there are certain claims that don't make sense, as for example the claim that one can break promises when one feels like it. To take that position betrays a misunderstanding of the very nature of promise keeping; it is an enterprise that only makes sense on the assumption that one should keep a promise. Of course most of us have on more than one occasion broken a promise, but that, whether justifiable or not, is irrelevant to the point that thinking it morally acceptable to break a promise, not in certain specified circumstances, but simply when you feel like it, makes promising a redundant exercise.

At this point it seems appropriate to conclude that, while there are reasons to reject the bald claim that moral values are simply matters of opinion and thus relative (i.e., legitimately differing from place to place, time to time, and individual to individual purely according to varying taste), there are nonetheless few, if any, hard and fast rules that are clear and absolute in the sense of applying to all people at all times without exception. That being the case, it will be useful to introduce a distinction perhaps not sufficiently stressed by moral philosophers, namely the distinction between something being wrong and something being unjustifiable; for surely even if we cannot always prove that an action or a course of conduct is wrong (or right), we often can show it to be unjustified (or justified), inasmuch as it is unreasonable (or reasonable). I may not be able to provide demonstrable proof that bullying is wrong in the way that I can provide proof that physical violence hurts its victims, but I can surely point out that you cannot justify your bullying by any process of reasoning that carries conviction.

Five Fundamental Moral Principles

One's response to the claim that morality is relative depends, as so often, upon how one interprets the claim. If the suggestion is that morality can be defined in any way you choose, that any code of conduct, no matter what its details, is moral if designated as such by a given culture or individual, or that every society's view of what is moral is in all respects equally true or valid, then the claim is false. The mere fact that a society believes that telling lies is morally acceptable or that unkindness is acceptable does not make it so. And we can surely say that the abolition of slavery was a moral advance, while the use of chemical weapons on innocent civilians is morally retrograde.

But if moral relativism is taken to mean that, *within limits*, different codes of behavior may be equally moral, then it is true. The limits in question are set by differing material circumstances, different non-moral beliefs, and certain basic principles which any code of conduct that is to count as moral must recognize. Thus, the rather different codes of conduct that prevail in the United States and Sweden cannot perhaps be judged as more or less moral than each other; but that admission does not prevent us from legitimately concluding that, whatever their faults, both are morally preferable to the code of Nazi Germany between 1930 and 1945.[7] That is essentially because the Nazi code of conduct offended against every one of five principles which, I now suggest, are fundamental to any code of conduct that can count as a *moral* code. These five principles are the principles of freedom, fairness, respect for persons, truth, and happiness.

The value of *freedom* to some degree and in some respects is presupposed by the very idea of moral behavior, for my actions can only count as moral if, among other things, I undertake them freely or by my own choice. It is no doubt a good thing if I refrain from killing my neighbor whatever the circumstances; but I deserve no moral praise if I refrain only because I am forcibly restrained by others. Part of the meaning of genuinely moral behavior is freely chosen behavior. Obviously, this is not to say that we should be free to do anything we choose or to deny that there may be a number of legitimate checks on our freedom. But it is to say that in and of itself, and other things being equal, freedom is a moral necessity, and hence a moral good.

Similarly, *fairness* by which I mean treating others impartially or without special favor, would seem to be built into the very notion of moral conduct. Being fair does not necessarily imply treating people the same; fairness, for example, when distributing food and milk to a group, might involve giving more milk to babies and nursing mothers and more meat to full-grown men. But fairness requires that one gives equal consideration to the claims of every individual (and of course that one does not favor oneself above others). No system of conduct that involves giving preference to some on non-moral grounds such as one's liking for them, their shared religion or ethnicity, or their promise of support, can count as moral.

It is arguable that fairness in the sense of impartial treatment is barely distinguishable from what, following Kant, I am calling the principle of *respect for persons*. Nonetheless, I list it separately because fairness only requires that one does not treat people differently for reasons that cannot be justified. The notion of respect for persons makes the further point that any genuinely moral perspective must recognize that all human beings deserve to be recognized equally as ends in themselves, and that no individual can legitimately be regarded as simply a means to one's own or other people's ends.

The value of *truth*, like those of freedom and fairness, is surely built into the very idea of moral conduct. As a matter of fact, it is presupposed by any sincere attempt to understand anything: how could one claim to be sincere in one's desire to understand planetary motions if one did not care whether what one was told was true or false? And if we do care that the answers we receive should be true, that is presumably because we value the truth. If we are trying to formulate a theory of right conduct or how we ought to live our lives, it would seem contradictory to not care whether our conclusions are correct or incorrect. This principle, like the preceding three, is what is often called a high-order principle, meaning that it is very general and does not in itself tell us what specific rules concerning truth we should follow. But it is still very important in that it gives us the ground-rule that both telling the truth and pursuing the truth are in themselves morally good, even while we acknowledge that the demands of one or more of the other basic principles, as well as particular circumstances, will sometimes cause us to qualify our commitment. In other words, there may be occasions on which it is right to lie (to a terrorist, perhaps) or when the pursuit of truth should be set aside (when ordered to devise a new chemical weapon, perhaps), but that does not alter the fact that in general and in default of argument based on particular circumstances truth should be sacrosanct.

The final principle I have designated as the principle of *happiness*. Actually, deciding how to label it is not easy. Some, perhaps thinking that 'happiness' has irrelevant connotations of jumping for joy, have suggested alternatives such as 'contentment', 'flourishing', 'well-being', or even negative formulations such as 'absence of pain'. However, I will stick with 'happiness'. John Stuart Mill famously thought that he could prove happiness was the supreme moral value. In outline, he argued that everybody desires happiness, and that this is pretty persuasive evidence that it is desirable. The immediate response of critics is that Mill is playing on the ambiguity of the word 'desirable', which can be used both descriptively (i.e., something is desired) and normatively (i.e., ought to be desired). To this it might be countered that Mill is simply pointing out that if there is one thing that everybody agrees they ultimately value for its own sake, then it is a pretty good candidate for being the ultimate value. Personally, I find this argument quite persuasive, but I cannot say that that is generally agreed.[8] What I suggest we can say is that the idea of people being happy is central to the idea of a morally good society. There is an implicit contradiction in "This is a moral community, though nobody is happy". A society characterized by people in a state of happiness is precisely what we hope a moral society would be. Happiness is the very object of morality.[9]

But if the reader is unconvinced by this attempt to argue that commitment to the idea of people's happiness is built into the idea of morality, I shall simply have to fall back on to the notion of intuition: one just does sense or intuit that a happy society is morally desirable. There seems to be something logically odd about valuing unhappiness or even not caring about whether people are happy or not.

Now of course, as already indicated, adherence to the above principles does not immediately yield specific rules of conduct and it does not solve all moral problems; the principles themselves may be in conflict, and, even when they are not, there are many other considerations to take into account before one can draw specific conclusions about whether a parti-cular freedom should be protected, whether a particular lie is justified, whether a particular distribution is fair, what rules will contribute to overall happiness, and so on. But what I have tried to do is indicate that there are at least these five basic principles or values which any moral argument or discussion has to take into account, and that any moral debate or provision that ignores giving consideration to these principles cannot be considered as truly engaging with the moral sphere.

Morality and Religion

Some readers may be puzzled that in the previous section I did not con-sider the idea of grounding certain moral principles in religion, since it is undeniable that many individuals do in fact derive their moral views from their religion. On this point, it needs to be clearly stated that while it may *contingently* be the case that many people derive their morality from their religion, there is no *logically necessary* connection between the two. People with widely divergent religious beliefs can be equally moral; one can be moral without having any religious beliefs, and one can, alas, be religious and behave immorally, as we know from many recent and disturbing accounts of priestly behavior in regard to child-care generally and sex in particular. Furthermore, to behave in a certain way, even if it conforms with what we regard as moral, does not count as moral behavior if it is engaged in merely as a religious duty or on the grounds that such behavior is mandated by the faith; it must be engaged in freely, because one sees it as desirable for its own sake, if it is to count as moral.

The Language of Rights

It is very common these days to hear moral debate conducted in terms of appeal to various 'rights'. But there is a danger that in so doing we fail to engage in any true reasoning or debate. For, if I have a moral right to x, there must be a framework of some sort that gives rise to the right. A legal right, for instance, only exists if the law establishes the right. In the same way a moral right must be established by reference to moral argument. Admittedly, there are some fairly uncontentious claims to a moral right; for example, it is widely agreed that we have a right to fair treatment and a right to free expression (though precisely what the latter amounts to may require further examination. See Chapter 14). But these can only be regarded as rights because we have set out the argument for them. Given the open-ended nature of much moral discourse, the danger is that in too hastily invoking the language of rights we simply beg the question at issue. Thus, claiming that abortion must be wrong simply because it is counter to the 'right to life' is not to advance the argument, but merely a way of asserting one's personal conviction that it is morally wrong; similarly, to counter that position by referring to the 'right to choose' is merely to assert a contrary position. Some seek to provide a framework by appealing to 'natural', 'human', or 'universal' rights, but simply to invoke such phrases does not in itself make any difference. To provide a legitimate framework that establishes a proposed right as natural, human, or universal still requires reasoning to support the contention that the right in question is indeed mandated by nature (whatever that means) or by our being human.

So, appeals to 'rights' is a poor way to conduct moral debate, involving no more than assertion and counter-assertion of moral standpoints. What is needed is reasoning to establish that it is a right. The contemporary tendency to discuss moral issues by referring to various putative rights effectively bypasses genuine argument and debate.

Morality and Education

There is no direct logical connection between education and morality, however we define the latter. It makes perfectly good sense to say that a person is well educated but immoral, or conversely that they are very moral though lacking in education, and it is contingently a matter of fact that some educated people are not particularly good people (and vice versa). An educated person, then, is not necessarily particularly moral, and one does not have to be well educated to be moral. It follows that if we wish to promote moral behavior we are going to have to do more than simply educate people well.

"Why are the children of morally good people often bad people?" was a question that exercised Plato. Carpenters and plumbers can teach their children their trade, why can't good people do the same? But the question is not well-founded. In the first place not all carpenters' children do learn to become good carpenters. In the second place the majority of children of virtuous parents do grow up to be morally decent; there is no reason to conclude that generally speaking we are producing a generation of immoral citizens. In the third place teaching one's children to be something such as a carpenter is a matter of developing skills, which is rather different from developing a certain kind of character, such as moral character.

Furthermore, in so far as we are concerned about a lack of moral development in children, it is a wider social problem rather than an educational one. Those individuals who are indeed lacking in moral sense are very likely that way for reasons that have nothing to do with their schooling. In extreme cases we may be dealing with genetic defects; in others we may be referring to individuals whose problem lies in learning disabilities rather than specifically moral failings. But for the most part moral delinquency is surely the result of wider social problems. Such things as dysfunctional families, poverty, drug culture, and a general lack of purpose and opportunity are far more likely to lead to moral inadequacy than anything that does or does not occur in a school context. There is a regrettable tendency for critics to lay the blame for all social problems at the door of the school. But, generally speaking, schools (let alone education) cannot be held responsible for the existence of bullying, stealing, knifings, obesity, smoking, drugs, or sexual problems. On the contrary, schools clearly do their best to combat these and similar problems, and, in so far as they are not entirely successful, we must lay the blame at the door of parents and society generally.

Nonetheless, society does want to develop a standard of moral conduct in its citizens, and reasonably enough expects its schools to play their part in modeling, promoting, shaping, and developing moral values. And, while the extent of moral turpitude in society may sometimes be exaggerated, there is perhaps room for concern about the extent of moral complacency or even apathy. The problem is not so much one of combating immorality as promoting a more active concern for moral issues on an everyday level. Are we doing enough to bring up a generation of people who care about treating people well, being kind and fair, being honest and so forth?

Discussion of morality tends to be around big issues such as abortion, assisted dying, transgender rights, or the relationship between morality and religion. This is partly because these are contentious issues about which people feel strongly, and partly because philosophers tend to focus on overarching moral theories or the basic question of validating moral claims. There has been relatively little attention paid to discussion concerning everyday decent behavior. But when as citizens we worry about moral education, we are for the most part not concerned with a philosophical grasp of the subject or even a clear stance on issues such as the toppling of statues or the rights of the LGBTQ+ community. We are concerned primarily about such things as everyday integrity, honesty, and lack of hypocrisy. And surely what we should look to schools to provide is not so much a magic way to end all crime as to reinvigorate a general sense of trust and trustworthy behavior. It is the sense that politicians, bankers, the CEOs of global enterprises, pharmaceutical companies and the like seem now to routinely mislead, lie, bribe, and otherwise break the law and act unethically that both angers us and sometimes filters down so that we feel less inclined to behave morally ourselves. (If a senior government advisor can flout health rules to suit himself during a pandemic, why should I obey these or any other restrictive rules?[10]) Schooling and education cannot completely solve this problem either, but they can contribute to the fight against this moral malaise. Schools as institutions can concentrate on ensuring a social environment that values and protects moral decency, and the study of subjects such as history, philosophy, and literature can emphasize the moral dimension, while all subjects can be taught in such a way as to illustrate the supreme importance of truth, honesty, and concern for the common good.

Values Clarification

Here it is worth referring to an approach generally referred to as '*Values Clarification*', particularly associated with Louis Raths.[11] Though devotees of this approach may differ in their detailed approach, the essential idea is to engage students in direct discussion of values. The assumption is that as a result of thinking about their values, students will come to a clearer understanding of and stronger commitment to those values. However, limited empirical studies of such programs offer largely negative conclusions. It seems that student interest in discussing values is not sustained over time for long; that the approach is insensitive to the sensitivity of the students (for example, some children feel embarrassed talking about friendship, some feel that their privacy is being encroached upon, some do not want to expose their cultural differences); that there is a failure to distinguish between different types of values, despite the fact, as was stressed at the beginning of this chapter, that there are many kinds of value besides moral value, and a discussion about what kind of music one values is something entirely different from a discussion about whether to report the wrongdoing of a friend; that there is a failure to distinguish between explanation and justification, yet it is vital to understand that the statement "I am punishing this child because she hit another child" is quite distinct in kind from "I am punishing this child because I am angry with her", the former giving a reason that is designed to justify the action, the latter a reason that merely explains it; and finally that there is a failure to evaluate responses – in other words, students are encouraged to give their reasons but no attempt is made to distinguish the sensible from the silly, the plausible from the implausible.

Now criticisms such as these, insofar as they are valid, could be met by improving the approach to talking about values. It would not be difficult, for instance, for the teacher to start commenting on the quality of individual contributions, for the difference between explanation and justification to be explained, for the distinction between different kinds of value to be introduced, and so on. But even a serious rational debate about moral values as distinct from other values, though it may have its intrinsic value, is not going to solve the problem of moral complacency, because there is no logical connection between studying morality and being moral, and there is no convincing empirical evidence that such study tends contingently to result in more moral behavior.

Conclusion

Drawing on the distinction between training, socializing, and education introduced in Chapter 2, I would conclude that one thing we can reasonably do is what on the whole we are doing: namely, *training* children to behave in certain ways from a young age by modeling the required behavior, encouraging it, demanding it, praising it, and blaming its lack. For as many have observed, following Aristotle, we become virtuous by practicing virtue. Moral *education*, by contrast, would involve studying the subject of morality, which in turn would mean the history and philosophy of moral attitudes and theory and contemporary empirical data pertaining to moral questions.

Sadly, there is plenty of evidence that moral philosophers, though they may have a better intellectual understanding of the subject than others, are not necessarily any more moral as persons. Conversely, many highly moral people have never studied any kind of philosophy, let alone moral philosophy. But there is a counter-consideration. I argued in Chapter 6 that philosophy is one of three distinct forms of knowledge or types of inquiry, and that as such it should be studied in schools. One way to introduce philosophy would be in the shape of moral philosophy, which would probably have more appeal than, say, the study of epistemology or ontology. I would conclude, therefore, while recognizing that the study would not necessarily make any difference to the moral quality of society, the secondary school curriculum should include the study of moral philosophy, while other subjects as diverse as science, literature, and history should always be mindful of a moral dimension. Is it acceptable for a physicist working on nuclear research to simply ignore questions about when the use of nuclear weapons is morally justified? Historical study should include consideration of the rightness and wrongness of actions. Consideration of the moral quality of the actions of characters should be integral to the study of literature. The study of religion should not avoid the question of the moral acceptability of the Church's actions or indeed the virtues of its moral teaching.

Finally, there is the matter of morally acceptable teaching. In Chapter 6, it was argued that since education is a normative term, teachers should only employ morally acceptable ways of engaging with their students. There are some practices such as torture, bribery, and seduction that this so obviously rules out that we do not need to discuss them in any detail. Other practices such as punishment deserve more careful consideration. 'Punishment' is a word with which many are uncomfortable, but it is not inherently morally unacceptable, as some would maintain. It is important therefore to distinguish between different forms of punishment and to consider in what circumstances what form of punishment might be appropriate. It would be widely agreed today, for example, that the form of punishment should not be intrinsically degrading or humiliating and that it should be reserved for bad behavior of one sort or another and not used in respect of academic shortcomings. Persistent failure to produce homework is more obviously a punishable offense than providing poor homework. Those who would like to pursue this particular topic more fully should follow the references in the Further Reading section.

But there is one practice that is sometimes hard to detect which can nonetheless be a real and present danger to education. I am referring to indoctrination, which will be the subject of the next chapter.

Notes

1 I use the terms 'moral philosophy' and 'ethics' interchangeably.
2 Emotivism is particularly associated with the early work of A.J. Ayer, *Language, Truth and Logic* (Gollancz, 1936).
3 On prescriptivism, see R.M. Hare, *The Language of Morals* (Clarendon Press, 1952). See also, Immanuel Kant, *Groundwork of the Metaphysic of Morals*, translated and analyzed by H.J. Paton as, *The Moral Law* (Hutchinson, 1948).
4 On intuitionism, see W.D. Ross, *Foundations of Ethics* (Clarendon Press, 1939). On this section generally, see also Geoffrey Warnock, *Contemporary Moral Philosophy* (Macmillan, 1967).
5 Aristotle, *Nicomachean Ethics* (Penguin, 1955) Bk 5, 1134b.
6 Herodotus, *Histories* (Penguin, 1954) 3.38.
7 It has been suggested that authors of my generation should cease to make extensive use of the Nazi regime as an example. I cannot concur given the enormity of that regime's inhumanity. Furthermore, the example apparently needs to be brought to the attention of the young: according to a report in the *Guardian* of September 16, 2020, 23% of Americans between the ages of 18 and 39 believe that the Holocaust is a myth or a gross exaggeration. 63% did not know that over 6 million were killed. On the positive side, 64% believe that some form of education relating to it should be compulsory.
8 John Stuart Mill, *Utilitarianism; On Liberty; Representative Government* (Dent, 1968).
9 See further, Geoffrey Warnock, *The Object of Morality* (Methuen, 1971).
10 The reference is to Dominic Cummings, unelected advisor to UK Prime Minister Boris Johnson. He both broke his own rules on lockdown during the Covid-19 pandemic and then apparently lied about the matter. There was great indignation expressed throughout the land, but, as so often, there were no repercussions and life went on as before.
11 Louis Raths & S.B. Simon, *Values and Teaching* (Merrill, 1966).

Further Reading

I have dealt with this topic more fully in Robin Barrow, *An Introduction to Moral Philosophy and Moral Education* (Routledge, 2007).

For an excellent standard introduction to moral philosophy along traditional historical lines, see John Hospers, *Human Conduct* (Hart-Davis, 1970). See also, David E. Cooper, *Illusions of Equality* (Routledge & Kegan Paul, 1980).

On rights, see Mary Ann Glendon, *Rights Talk: The Impoverishment of Political Discourse* (Macmillan, 1991), Michael Ignatieff, *The Rights Revolution* (Anansi, 2000), Stephen Hopgood, *The End Times of Human Rights* (Cornell University Press, 2013), and Colin Wringe, *Children's Rights* (Routledge & Kegan Paul, 1981).

On moral education, see Roger Straughan, *Can We Teach Children to Be Good?* (Allen & Unwin, 1983), papers by David Carr, Stefaan Cuypers, and Harvey Siegel in D.J. Ruyter & S. Miedema (eds.), *Moral Education and Development* (SensePublishers, 2011), and Michael Hand, *A Theory of Moral Education* (Routledge, 2018).

On punishment see Chapter 2 of Kenneth Strike & Jonas F. Soltis, *The Ethics of Teaching* (Teachers College Press, 2009), Harold Loukes, John Wilson, & Barbara Cowell, *Education: An Introduction* (Martin Robertson, 1983), or John Wilson & Barbara Cowell, *Children and Discipline* (Cassell, 1990).

Of interest is Cathy Gere, *Pain, Pleasure and the Greater Good: From the Panopticon to the Skinner Box and Beyond* (University of Chicago Press, 2017).

Questions

In what sense is moral relativism true and in what sense is it false according to the argument here? Do you agree?

How convinced are you that the five principles proposed here are essential to anything that might count as a moral theory?

What would you propose in the name of moral education, and why?

11 Indoctrination

To 'indoctrinate' originally meant simply to 'teach' or 'instruct'. But today it is generally regarded as a normative term with strong negative overtones. To indoctrinate now implies something like taking over, closing, or controlling the minds of others. Indoctrinated people hold unwaveringly to their views, and we associate them particularly with political and religious extremists. Furthermore, indoctrination seems to be a fairly common phenomenon. We need only look to North Korea, so-called 're-education' camps for the Uighur in China, or the populist nationalism incessantly and insistently instilled around the world. Terrorists who believe unwaveringly that they are justified by their cause, people who are willing to bring death to their own supporters in their unyielding conviction that they alone have access to the truth, people who are incapable of critically examining their religious beliefs, those who cannot see beyond 'my country, right or wrong', and those who do not pause to question as they carry out hideous atrocities on fellow humans in the name of some creed, faith, or ideology – all testify to the reality of indoctrination. Nor is indoctrination only to be found in foreign terrorist cells. Some religious and political fanatics in the West appear to be as thoroughly indoctrinated as members of Al-Qaeda or Isis. But what exactly turns religious instruction or political teaching into indoctrination in this negative sense? What is the difference between being committed and being indoctrinated? Is teaching children to salute the flag and believe in the greatness of the nation indoctrination? What are the defining characteristics of indoctrination?

Indoctrination clearly involves causing people to hold certain beliefs. If a teacher has responsibility for a particular child for a year and by the end of that year she has not imparted any beliefs of any sort, then whatever she has been doing or trying to do she has not succeeded in indoctrinating him. Indoctrination is therefore to be distinguished from conditioning. To condition someone is to cause him to behave in certain ways and does not necessarily involve any reference to beliefs at all. We talk of conditioning rats to respond in specific ways to various stimuli, but we do not talk of indoctrinating rats, because we assume that rats do not have beliefs.

But equally clearly the fact that a teacher has imparted certain beliefs to children is not a sufficient indication that he has indoctrinated them. If I

DOI: 10.4324/9781003120476-11

cause you to believe that there is a world energy crisis, it does not automatically follow that I have indoctrinated you. It is a *necessary* condition of indoctrination that beliefs should be imparted, but it is not a *sufficient* condition.

What other conditions necessarily have to be present, then, for one to conclude that indoctrination is going on? What does the concept of indoctrination involve besides the imparting of beliefs? What distinguishes it from other teaching activities whereby children come to hold certain beliefs?

Let us start with a paradigm case of indoctrination. By a paradigm case is meant an uncontentious example, an example that virtually everybody would concede is an example of indoctrination, notwithstanding the fact that different people have different views as to what is essential to the concept. By separating the various strands involved in the example and considering each one in turn it may become easier to form a judgment as to which of them are *necessary* to indoctrination and which of them merely *contingent*.

Imagine a Catholic school in which all the teachers are committed Catholics and where all the children come from Catholic homes and have parents who want them to be brought up as Catholics. Imagine also that the teachers are determined to try to bring up the children as devout Catholics. They deliberately attempt to inculcate in their pupils an unshakable commitment to the truth of Catholicism and of the various claims or propositions associated with it. They thus bring up the pupils to believe in the unquestionable truth of such propositions as "The Pope is infallible", "One should not use artificial birth-control methods", and "God exists". They bring them up to believe in these and similar propositions in such a way that the pupils come to regard those who do not accept them as true propositions as being simply mistaken, and in such a way that no reasoning put forward that might cast doubt upon their assurance that Catholicism and the propositions related to it are incorrigible truths can cause them to reconsider their assumptions. They are, let us assume, drilled by their teachers in 'answers' that explain away any possible doubts about or objections to the claims of Catholicism. The techniques used by the teachers to evoke this commitment to Catholicism may be many and various: some of the propositions presented may be put forward with rational explanation, but others will be cultivated by means of the example set by the teachers, the use of praise and blame or the withholding of approval by the teachers, or simply the use of their authority to reinforce their insistence on the undeniable truth of the Catholic view of the world and our place in it.

It is difficult to conceive of anyone seriously doubting that these teachers are indoctrinating. But the question remains: why 'indoctrinating'? What is it about what is going on here that indicates that it is an example of indoctrination? Do all the features of this example have to be present for one to describe it as a case of indoctrination, or might one still regard these teachers as indoctrinators even if some of the details in the example were changed? To find an answer to these questions it is necessary to examine the various features of the example in isolation.

Content

One notable feature of this example is that the beliefs which the children are being brought to accept are of a particular sort. Catholicism is a doctrinal system of belief; that is, it consists of an interrelated set of ideas, based upon certain propositions or postulates that cannot be demonstrated to be unquestionably true, which taken together have repercussions for the way in which the believer views the world and for the way in which she lives her life.

In referring to a proposition as one that cannot be demonstrated to be unquestionably true, one is not necessarily denying that it is true. An unprovable proposition cannot be demonstrated to be unquestionably false either. The distinction is between propositions in relation to which, whether they are in fact true or not, there is no disagreement as to what sort of evidence would count to show whether they were true or false (provable propositions), and propositions in relation to which there is no such agreement (unprovable propositions). Thus, propositions such as "Metals expand when heated", "Trollope wrote *Can You Forgive Her?*", or "There is a planet made of green cheese" are all provable propositions. All are in principle verifiable or falsifiable, even though some or all of us may not in fact know for certain whether they are true or false. We all agree on the sort of evidence that would count in favor of or against the truth of such propositions, even if we do not actually have the evidence to hand.

As we saw in Chapter 9, fundamental religious beliefs are not like that. There is no agreement on how one could verify or falsify them. Belief in unprovable propositions such as "God exists" and "The meek shall inherit the earth" is dependent on faith. The situation is the same with a number of fundamental non-religious propositions such as "Economic considerations are the determinant of social change". There is no general agreement over what would count as evidence for or against these propositions or on how to interpret the supposed evidence. For me, as a non-Catholic, there is fairly strong historical evidence that the Pope is not infallible; but to a committed Catholic this evidence can be explained away; it doesn't count. For some the fact that there is suffering and misery in the world is a strong argument against any notion of an omnipotent and loving God; but the believer does not deny the existence of suffering, he merely denies that it counts as evidence against the existence of such a God, and he explains the evidence away at least to his own satisfaction. More generally, every piece of evidence produced by the religious skeptic against the notion that there is a God (we cannot see him, hear him, touch him, and so on) is dismissed by the believer as irrelevant, until it is not clear to the skeptic whether anything even in principle could be allowed by the believer to count as evidence against the existence of God. But if nothing could count as evidence in principle, what kind of a belief is it? Certainly not a belief that is demonstrably true or false. Similarly, one who is committed to an exclusively economic interpretation of social change simply interprets the history of social change in the light of that commitment. It is entirely unclear what would count as evidence against this interpretation. These propositions, which by their nature are neither verifiable nor falsifiable, serve rather as guiding principles for interpreting the world. In each case it seems that for one who is committed to the truth of the proposition nothing counts as evidence against it, whereas for those who are not so committed quite a lot of evidence counts against it. The situation is thus quite distinct from that in which two people disagree about whether metals do or do not expand when heated but would nonetheless agree in principle upon what would count as evidence for or against the proposition.

It will be seen from this that all political and religious systems of belief are doctrinal, at least in so far as it is agreed that fundamental political and religious axioms constitute propositions the truth or falsity of which there are no generally agreed criteria for establishing. It should be stressed that this is not to say that those who are committed to a specific doctrinal system, be it Marxism, liberal-democratism, Catholicism, or whatever, are wrong or ought not to be so committed; indeed it is difficult to imagine a person who is in no way committed to any doctrine. Nor is it to say that people who are committed to doctrines are altogether irrational. Given the basic assumptions of a specific doctrinal system, an adherent of that doctrine may behave, argue, and generally proceed in an entirely rational manner. All that is being said is (i) that propositions such as "There is an omnipotent God" are distinctive in that it is not clear how even in principle one could incontestably demonstrate their truth or falsehood; (ii) that a doctrinal system (or ideology) is a set of beliefs enjoining a particular way of looking at the world and a particular way of life on the believer that is based upon such unprovable propositions; and (iii) that Catholicism (along with other religions and political creeds) is an example of such a system.

It is arguable whether those philosophers who have claimed that *only* doctrines can be indoctrinated are correct. I have already argued that an etymological connection (such as that between 'indoctrinate' and 'doctrine') proves little (Chapter 6), and *prima facie* there is nothing conceptually odd about the idea of indoctrinating propositions that are simply false. But it is clear that, whether it is a matter of logical necessity or contingent fact, it is in respect of doctrine that indoctrination is usually to be feared. That is to say, we are more worried about teachers and parents instilling belief in doctrines than instilling belief in truths such as $2 \times 2 = 4$. Getting people to believe in falsehoods seems adequately characterized simply as 'lying' or 'talking nonsense'. For convenience, then, we may take indoctrination to involve the imparting of doctrinal beliefs. The next question is whether imparting belief in a doctrine is a sufficient condition of indoctrination. Is anybody who in any way contributes to the formation of belief in a doctrine by another person thereby indoctrinating her?

I shall argue that the answer to this question is 'No' and that there are three other necessary conditions of indoctrination.

Unshakable Commitment

Another striking feature of our paradigm case was that the teachers were concerned to implant an *unshakable commitment* to the truth of Catholicism. They were not concerned simply to present Catholicism and all it entails as a set of beliefs involving a particular view of the world and our place in it, and then to leave the children to decide for themselves whether they felt drawn to adopt this set of beliefs. The doctrines were presented as truths. And this surely provides us with another necessary condition of indoctrination. The most obvious hallmark of the indoctrinated person is that he has a particular viewpoint and he will not seriously open his mind to the possibility that that viewpoint might be mistaken. The indoctrinated person has a closed mind when it comes to the question of the truth or falsehood of the doctrines to which they are committed. If this condition (that to be indoctrinated involves having a closed mind) is not accepted as a necessary condition, we should have to accept the conclusion that we are all equally indoctrinated, since all of us in practice live our lives in accordance with some system of beliefs involving a way of interpreting the world. If we accept an analysis of what it is to be indoctrinated that leads to the conclusion that we are all inevitably indoctrinated, there is not much point in troubling ourselves further about the concept. But if to be indoctrinated is to have a closed mind, then to indoctrinate must involve causing someone to have an unshakable commitment to the truth of the beliefs in question.

In other words, the claim here is that if the pupils had left school believing in Catholicism, but they were nonetheless aware that its truth was not incontrovertibly established, and were quite willing to engage in discussion on the question of whether it was true and how one would set about establishing its truth or falsehood, we should not regard them as having been indoctrinated. It is still of course possible that their teachers may have been *trying* to indoctrinate them and simply have failed. But in so far as the pupils, while being devout Catholics, do not regard the doctrines as having the status of incorrigible truths, the teachers have failed to indoctrinate them. And if the teachers have failed, the students manifestly have not been indoctrinated.

A second necessary condition, then, of indoctrination is that the indoctrinator should cause someone to have unshakable belief in what are in fact unprovable propositions.

Method

If the first two conditions are accepted, it follows logically that a third condition relating to the method whereby the beliefs are imparted must also be accepted as necessary to indoctrination. If only doctrines can be indoctrinated (content), and if for a person to be indoctrinated the doctrine has to be regarded as unquestionably true (unshakable commitment), then indoctrination must be a process of inculcating belief by non-rational methods.

For clearly, if the basis of a doctrinal system is a set of fundamental propositions that cannot be rationally demonstrated to be true, commitment of an unshakable sort to these propositions cannot be based on rational demonstration of their truth. Therefore, although none of the *particular* examples of non-rational techniques of persuasion listed in the paradigm example may be necessary to indoctrination, *some form* of non-rational persuasion designed to bring about unshakable belief is necessary.

Intention

The teachers in the paradigm example *intended* to implant unshakable belief. Is such an intention a necessary condition of indoctrination or merely a contingent feature of some examples of indoctrination? Surely it is not merely a contingent feature; it is not the case, in other words, that the indoctrinator *sometimes* happens to intend to promote conviction. Intention is logically necessary to the concept of indoctrination. The mere fact that unshakable belief has already been put forward as a criterion suggests that intention must come into the picture, for it seems very strange to talk about bringing about such belief without at the same time necessarily making reference to the intentions of the person engaged in bringing about the belief.

What causes difficulty in ready acceptance of intention as a necessary feature of indoctrination is the fact that it is not always obviously present. It is seldom the case, for example, that an indoctrinator will admit to having the intention to produce unshakable beliefs. Sometimes she will claim that her intention is anything but this; she will claim, let us say, that she wants her pupils to think for themselves, to make up their own minds on the issue in question, and that all her efforts subserve this end. We are faced here with a distinction between *avowed* intention (what the indoctrinator *says* he is trying to do) and the *real* intention (what the indoctrinator is in fact trying to do), and as far as the latter is concerned evidence concerning it is only to be drawn from observation of the particular teaching situation concerned. In the very nature of the case it is impossible to get clear about real as opposed to avowed intention by asking the teacher.

Consider an example, borrowed from J.P. White, of the distinction referred to. White considers the case of a teacher of Marxism or Catholicism whose avowed intention is to get his pupils to make up their own minds on these difficult matters, and he asks, on the supposition that the teacher is an indoctrinator,

> Is it conceivable, that his avowed intention is also his real intention? If so, then if any of his pupils questions a fundamental proposition of the doctrine, like 'There is a God' or 'The course of history is predetermined', he will not fob him off with specious argument or use non-rational techniques of persuasion to get him to believe the proposition, but will try to explore with the pupil whether there are any

good grounds for it. But if he is as open-minded as this, would we, seeing him from outside the system, say that he is indoctrinating?... If the teacher inside the system *is* an indoctrinator, it is therefore inconceivable that his avowed intention is also his real intention.[1]

In other words, the argument points inescapably to the conclusion that intention is logically tied to the concept of indoctrination. The nature of this intention is real intention, which may or may not coincide with avowed intention. If there is coincidence then no problems arise, but if there is a lack of coincidence then real intention, based upon general contextual evidence, takes precedence over avowed intention.

Indoctrination and the Teaching Situation

In the light of the above analysis let us now consider the extent to which indoctrination is, or could be, a significant element in the teaching that goes on day by day in our schools.

One thing is fairly clear. If a teacher's subject matter is of the hard fact variety or, more generally, if at no stage she finds herself trying to get across essentially disputatious propositions (doctrine), then on the content criterion there can be no possibility of her indoctrinating. Take mathematics, for example. Whether the content consists in the multiplication tables, how to solve quadratic equations, how to bisect a line, or Euclid's geometrical proofs, what is clear here is that nothing remotely resembling doctrine is involved. As far as the content and techniques of mathematics are concerned there is agreement among mathematicians as to the truth of statements like '$3 \times 2 = 6$' or the correctness of techniques in solving various types of equation. It would be very odd to say of someone who, as a result of attending classes in mathematics, could solve all kinds of differential equations that he had been well and truly indoctrinated.

Similar considerations apply to science teaching. The very nature of scientific activity precludes the possibility of indoctrination in science. Broadly speaking, scientific method consists in setting up a hypothesis designed to explain some phenomenon or other and then testing (by experiment) to see if predictions made on the basis of the hypothesis are correct or incorrect. If the predictions are shown to be incorrect then the original hypothesis is rejected; it will either be modified or abandoned altogether and the process of testing will be repeated with a new hypothesis. Clearly there is no room here for clinging on to a hypothesis through experimental thick and thin. If one allows nothing to count against a hypothesis, just as the teachers in the paradigm example allowed nothing to count against the truth of certain religious statements, then one would no longer be doing science. A good instance of this is provided by the celebrated Russian 'scientist' Lysenko. Lysenko held that acquired characteristics of an organism are subsequently inherited by succeeding generations. C.M.M. Begg in his *Introduction to Genetics* remarks of this theory that there was no "supporting evidence" for it and draws attention to the "difficulty of conceiving of a mechanism for such inheritance". Why, then, did Lysenko's views gain ground in Soviet Russia to the extent that he "became President of the Lenin Academy of Agricultural Sciences, and many 'orthodox' geneticists disappeared from the Soviet scene"? Begg answers as follows:

> Suffice it to say that Marxism ascribes to the environment an over-riding significance in determining the course of history. It is a short, if not necessary, step to extend this idea to cover the whole living kingdom, and see in external conditions not merely an agency which directs evolution by weeding out the unfit and preserving the fit, but an active force which moulds animals and plants directly in each generation, the modifications so acquired being passed on at any rate in part to the progeny. For this view there seems to be no factual basis.[2]

In other words, the very nature of scientific activity runs counter to the possibility of indoctrination being practiced in science. To teach Lysenko's theory as an unquestionable truth is to cease being scientific and to begin indoctrinating.

Of course, it might be that teachers of mathematics and science lay themselves open to the charge of indoctrinating, but this can never be so by virtue of the fact that they teach these particular disciplines. For example, a mathematician might claim that God is the supreme mathematician and that all mathematics stem from Him, or a scientist might claim that only science is worth doing and that arts subjects are a waste of time. In so far as the mathematician and scientist peddle these questionable doctrines they will run the danger of being labeled 'indoctrinators', but the important point to note here is that these doctrines have nothing to do with the nature of mathematics and science as such.

When one turns to other subjects that figure on the school curriculum the situation is rather different. Aspects of the teaching of literature, history, civics, ethics, or religion all seem to have to do with essentially contentious subject matter and, therefore, teachers of these subjects have to be on their guard if they do not wish to be classed as indoctrinators. I say 'on their guard' because the nature of the subject does not alone decide the issue. Analysis of indoctrination showed that intention to bring about unshakable belief and use of fundamentally non-rational means were also necessary conditions additional to the content condition. It follows, therefore, that the mere fact that a teacher is a teacher of history or of religion does not of itself settle the question as to whether or not she is an indoctrinator.

In this connection a particular problem faces the teacher of young children. It is often said that young children – let's say aged between five and eight – are not capable of appreciating the reason why of things. They are incapable, for example, of understanding the reasons for not being spiteful to members of their peer group, for not lying, or for not breaking promises. And it is claimed that because of these facts about young children their teachers cannot help being indoctrinators. But this is false. In the first place, even with young children one can give reasons up to a point: if the child asks why he should not steal one can offer an explanation in terms of considering other people's feelings. But even granting that such explanation might be meaningless to the child or that, in any case, one readily reaches a point at which it becomes meaningless (as, for example, if the child asks why he ought to respect other people's feelings), this still does not turn such teachers into indoctrinators. It is true that on these conditions they are trying to bring children to accept certain moral propositions by non-rational means; that is to say that in so far as rational explanation will be meaningless to the child they will have to resort to persuasive techniques such as setting an example or praise and blame. On the assumption that it is agreed that fundamental moral propositions are not known to be true or false or that they are essentially contentious, it does indeed follow that some of the necessary conditions for indoctrination are present. But they are not *all* present. So long as the teacher's intention is not to plant unshakable belief in the moral propositions in question she is not indoctrinating. She is merely influencing children towards the acceptance of certain patterns of belief and behavior. But to influence is not in itself to indoctrinate. Provided that children are ultimately brought to examine for themselves the various moral values that are adhered to within a society and which they have been initially brought to conform to, they have not been indoctrinated. The danger lies in forgetting that the measures adopted with young children are conceived of as temporary and in never actually coming to the age of rational debate.

The example of the teacher of the very young can be generalized. It does appear to suggest that all teachers of all subjects to all age groups (including mathematicians and scientists in so far as they will inevitably find themselves treating of more than just strict mathematics and science) need to have an overall awareness of just what it is they are trying to do, of their overall aims and particular objectives, if they sincerely wish to educate rather than indoctrinate. This will involve not only thinking about their methods of teaching, how they go about putting things over, but also thinking about the logical nature of the subject matter with which they deal.

Conclusion: What's Wrong with Indoctrination?

We have assumed that indoctrination involves doctrines but we have seen also that the presence of doctrines as subject matter in a teaching situation does not necessarily mean that indoctrination is taking place. In other words the presence of doctrinal subject matter is consonant with a situation being an *educational* situation. Thus it makes perfectly good sense to talk about religious education, political education, and any other kind of education involving doctrinal subject matter. When then does, say, political education become political indoctrination? On the analysis presented the answer must be when the teacher ceases to present the various views held by different people on the controversial political issue under discussion and becomes intent on getting his own views on the issue taken as gospel by his students, an intent which will, again as we have seen, necessarily involve the overriding of the rationality of those same students.

In that it necessarily involves lack of respect for an individual's rationality, indoctrination is morally unacceptable. The moral principle here appealed to was briefly referred to in Chapter 10 and finds its most forceful advocate in the work of Immanuel Kant. He stated the principle as follows:

> Now I say that man, and in general every rational being, *exists* as an end to himself, *not merely as a means* for arbitrary use by this or that will; he must in all his actions, whether they are directed to himself or to other rational beings, always be viewed *at the same time as an end.* [3]

Indoctrinators violate this principle in that essentially they treat their audience as means. People are to be *got to believe* the preferred doctrines and there is to be no detached consideration of them.

The preceding argument does not involve denying that we generally want students to share our values: to believe, for example, that certain works of art are superior, that science is valuable, that some conduct is morally unacceptable, or that the humanities matter. But we have to proceed by reasoning, trusting that students will come to see such things for themselves, and not by coercion or distortion. So it is not the natural desire to uphold and share our values that is at issue. It is determining to impose those values and beliefs so that they stick come what may that is reprehensible. That is what leads to the closed mind, that is what leads to fanaticism, and ultimately to the delusion that one is justified even in torturing and killing in the name of one's creed or ideology.

Notes

1 J.P. White, 'Indoctrination' in R.S. Peters (ed.), *The Concept of Education* (op. cit.) pp. 182–3.
2 C.M.M. Begg, *Introduction to Genetics* (Edinburgh University Press, 1959) pp. 229, 231. Though what is said in the text still seems to me correct, I am a little uneasy about uncritical acceptance of the orthodoxy that the theory of evolution put forward by Lamarck, to which Lysenko's views are closely related, is obviously false. The attempt of some contemporary Creationists to ban the teaching of evolution would be an alternative example.
3 H.J. Paton's translation of Kant's *Groundwork of the Metaphysic of Morals* (op. cit.) p. 95. Translator's italics.

Further Reading

The literature on indoctrination is extensive. Suggested texts are: papers by John Wilson and R. M. Hare in T.H.B. Hollins (ed.), *Aims in Education* (Manchester University Press, 1964), Antony Flew, 'What is Indoctrination?' in *Studies in Philosophy and Education*, 4 (1966); I.A. Snook, *Indoctrination and Education* (Routledge & Kegan Paul, 1972) and I.A. Snook (ed.), *Concepts of Indoctrination* (Routledge & Kegan Paul, 1972); Richard Bailey, 'Indoctrination' in *The Sage Handbook of Philosophy of Education* (op. cit.) and Harvey Siegel, *Education's Epistemology: Rationality, Diversity and Critical Thinking* (Oxford University Press, 2017).

See also William Hare's *Open-mindedness and Education* (McGill-Queen's University Press, 1979).

Questions

What are the four necessary conditions for indoctrination cited here? Are they all necessary in your view? Taken together are they sufficient?

Why is it claimed that teaching Lysenko's theory in the Soviet Union was an example of indoctrination?

Does the United States' preoccupation with the flag, the national anthem, the belief in American greatness etc. amount to indoctrination?

12 Rationality

A Rational Animal

It was Aristotle who first defined a human being as a rational animal, and he meant by this that humans were to be distinguished from other animals in that they had the ability to think, calculate or reason.[1] Other animals can respond to their environment; they can sense the heat from flames, for example, and withdraw from the fire. Instinctively they can seek shelter in appropriate places from bad weather or from enemies. Not only do they respond in a regular manner to specific signals, but they can also be conditioned by humans to respond to artificial signals. The wild animal senses its prey and automatically responds with the appropriate hunting behavior. The dog, taken over as a household pet, automatically responds to certain food-preparing activities on the part of the owner. In extreme cases, as in Pavlov's experiments, the animal is conditioned to respond to signals such as the ringing of a bell. But what animals cannot do is act purposively. They cannot decide to do this rather than that on certain grounds, they cannot work out what is going on, or reflect upon the possibility that the ringing bells may be part of some experiment on their behavior. Humans differ from other animals in that they are able to act purposively, to plan, choose ends and adopt means, and in that they are able to control their environment rather than simply respond to it. They are able to memorize, to imagine, foresee, to predict, to hypothesize. To use the imprecise term which in common language includes all such activities, humans have the capacity to think. (See Chapter 3.)

Theoretical and Practical Reason

Aristotle did not mean that we all have an equal ability to make rational choices, still less that we necessarily do so. The fact that all humans have the capacity to think does not mean that we are all equally good at thinking, just as while most of us have the ability to see, we do not all see equally well. Clearly, when people talk of aiming to promote rationality they mean that they want people to think well. And a great many educationalists do talk in these terms. T.H.B. Hollins, for instance, in his introduction to *Aims in*

DOI: 10.4324/9781003120476-12

Education: The Philosophic Approach, noted that all the contributors to the volume put forward as their "chief aim of education the developing of rationality in children". John McPeck in his *Critical Thinking* likewise provides testimony to the widespread interest in developing rationality, as do the many others who promote critical thinking as an aim of education (see Chapter 13). But if rationality is understood as good thinking and irrationality as bad thinking the question arises as to how we are to distinguish between the two.

The fact that rationality is inextricably tied up with the notion of thinking may lead one to assume that the proper application of the term is in the sphere of pure thought. Rationality may be seen as a quality reserved for academics and theoreticians. To be *really* rational, it might be said, one would have to be some kind of professional thinker. But this is surely not acceptable. It may be helpful for some purposes to make a distinction between theoretical reasoning, such as a philosophical argument or a historical dissertation, and practical reasoning, by which is meant thinking bound up with action (e.g., the sort of thinking involved in a game of chess or thinking about what to do in specific situations). But the thinking that goes on in each case is not in some mysterious way of a different type. Whether one's thinking is entirely abstract or geared to some activity, one is still thinking. And one can still do it well or badly. It seems quite clear that rationality and irrationality can be displayed in both theoretical and practical reasoning. An argument designed to elucidate the concept of education (or the concept of rationality, for that matter) may be more or less irrational; thinking directed towards deciding what to do in certain circumstances can be more or less irrational; and the thinking involved in playing a game of chess can be more or less irrational. If Aristotle can be judged as more rational than most people, that is not because he did more theorizing than most people. It does not have anything to do with either the *type* or the *amount* of thinking that he indulged in. We call a person rational or irrational in respect of the quality of their thinking *when* they think and in *whatever sphere* they think.

Nor is an individual's rationality to be identified with being right. A rational argument is not necessarily one that leads to the correct conclusion, and rational behavior is not necessarily behavior that is right or appropriate. There are vast areas of human experience, such as the spheres of religion, politics, morality, and aesthetics, where there is little or no agreement as to what the answers are, or indeed as to whether it makes any sense to talk of wrong and right answers. (Is there a right answer to the question "Was Beethoven a greater composer than Wagner?") If we do not know or agree on the answers to certain questions, then we are in no position to judge whether people are being rational about these questions if 'being rational' is synonymous with 'being right'.

It makes perfectly good sense to describe somebody's argument as rational, even if we do not happen to agree with the conclusion of the argument or if we are unsure as to whether the conclusion is acceptable or not. It is quite possible to watch a debate between two people and to feel that the person who is defending the point of view that one happens to hold oneself is arguing less rationally than her opponent. If we identified rationality with being right, it would not make sense to do this. We should be unable to judge the rationality or irrationality of an argument except in those cases where there was only one correct answer and we knew what it was. In complex cases, such as arguments for and against communism or comprehensive schools (where, even though one may have an opinion on the matter, one may nonetheless feel that the issue is too complex to admit of an indisputably right answer), one would not be able to distinguish between rational and irrational arguments. But these conclusions are incompatible with the way in which we use the word. We can distinguish between a rational argument for communism and an irrational argument for communism. And we can do this whether we believe in communism or not. We may quite reasonably distinguish between one argument as rational and another as irrational even if both arguments end with the same conclusion.

Rational Argument

A rational argument, then, is not an argument that necessarily ends with the right answer. To describe an argument as rational is to say something about the *process* of reasoning involved in it. It is not to say anything directly about the conclusion of the argument, except that the conclusion follows from the previous steps of the argument. Arguments proceed from certain premises towards a conclusion. To say that an argument is rational is to say that the chain of reasoning from premises to conclusion is valid. But of course the premises from which an argument starts may be false, dubious, or simply unproven hypotheses, and so it is that, although the conclusion may follow from the premises, and although the argument may itself be rational the conclusion may nevertheless be false or unproven. Conversely, we may believe that the conclusion of somebody's argument is a true or correct statement, but nonetheless feel that her argument is irrational, if we feel that the chain of reasoning presented does not in fact lead to the conclusion, or is at fault in some other way.

A rational argument is one that proceeds logically, that is to say, in which each step of the argument as given does indeed follow from the preceding step, and in which the reasons that are used to move from the premises to the conclusion are good reasons. An argument may fall short of being rational in a number of ways: it may refuse to take account of pertinent evidence that would upset it; it may lay stress on irrelevant evidence; it may appeal to emotion rather than reason; it may contain contradictions and inconsistencies; or it may contain illogical steps (e.g., all cats are four-legged; this is four-legged, therefore this is a cat). But whatever the precise way in which a particular argument is irrational, what it clearly means to describe it as such is to claim that it proceeds without respect for the notion of giving good reasons.

Hitler's argument that all the great works of art throughout history have been the product of the Aryan race and that therefore the Aryans are entitled to dominate other races is irrational, because there is simply no connection between the two propositions. The 'therefore' is quite inexplicable. The claim that the Aryans produced the great works of art, even if it were true, is not simply a weak reason for the conclusion: it is not recognizable as a reason at all. It seems no more relevant to the conclusion than the fact that Aryans do not come from Antarctica. But it is important to note that it is the lack of coherence in the reasoning that makes this particular – oversimplified – argument irrational. It is not the fact that the premise itself is nonsense. One might claim that the premise is also irrational, by which one would mean that the premise cannot be shown to be true by any rational argument. But there is a distinction to be made between an argument that is irrational, and an argument which, though it may be rational itself, is based upon an irrational premise. Hitler's argument happens to be culpable in both ways.

Rational Behavior and Feelings

Use of the terms 'rational' and 'irrational' in respect of other things besides argument confirms the suggestion that the essence of rationality is the giving or holding of good or relevant reasons. Irrational hatred, for example, is hatred that is based on no good reason; irrational jealousy is jealousy that has no proper grounds. This is not to say that irrational hatred or jealousy are inexplicable. In theory some kind of *explanation* can always be given as to why people feel hatred or jealousy. To describe these feelings in a particular person as irrational is to say that they are not based on anything that could be regarded as a good reason for hating someone or feeling jealous of them. No doubt a good psychoanalyst could give an account of *why* someone feels jealous, even in a situation where we should still want to describe the person's jealousy as irrational, because there are no good reasons for harboring the suspicions that cause the jealousy. But to explain that a man is prone to jealousy because he has an insecurity complex is not to say that his specific jealousy of a particular individual is well-founded. When people say that love is an irrational emotion, they mean that feelings of love do not necessarily arise in us for good reasons. People cannot help falling in love with other people who are in various ways most unsuitable objects for their affections, and who could not be said to be or to have done anything that constitutes a good reason for loving them. Falling in love is not an activity that takes note of the notion of giving good reasons at all, and that is why it seems appropriate to regard it as an irrational business.

More generally, rational behavior is behavior that can be rationally defended. If we refer to somebody's behavior as rational we do not necessarily imply that she has actually thought about what she is doing. Her behavior may be rational either in the sense that she has a rational account to give of why she is behaving in this way or in the sense that we feel that it is possible to give such an account, despite the fact that the agent acted without conscious reflection. But whichever is the case, for behavior to be correctly described as rational as with argument it must be based upon good reasons. Irrational behavior is behavior for which there is no good reason.

Unreasonable vs. Irrational

But now suppose that an employer turned down an applicant for a job because they didn't like the fact that she had tattoos. Suppose also that we hold the view that that is not a good or appropriate reason for turning her down. Yet it does not seem quite right to accuse the employer of being irrational. We don't think the reason good enough, but we cannot readily dismiss it as totally irrelevant. (The employer might for instance associate tattoos with drug taking, and might even have some experience to support this connection.) Some might therefore describe the employer's behavior in this instance as unreasonable rather than irrational. Is there any real distinction between these concepts?

It is clear that, if what is meant by irrational behavior (or argument or feeling) is behavior (argument or feeling) that is based on irrelevant reasons, then the concept of irrationality does not exhaust the ways in which behavior or the holding of a particular opinion may be regarded as ill-founded. For as well as behaving in certain ways or holding certain opinions for reasons that are irrelevant, people may (and very often do) act in certain ways or have certain views for reasons that are weak rather than irrelevant. In the minefield of sexual politics, for example, some positions, such as the view that one is whatever sex (or, as people incorrectly say, 'gender') one identifies with, might be thought to be unreasonable by some, but it is not clear that it is actually irrational.[2] It is irrational to assume that everybody hates you in the absence of any evidence for this assumption. But it may only be unreasonable to assume that your boss hates you on the evidence of his refusal to promote you. He *may* hate you, you *may* be right, but your opinion seems unreasonable because, in the absence of further information about the situation, the reason you produce for holding it looks weak.

The suggestion is, then, that a person is irrational in so far as he behaves or argues without concern for reasons or by reference to irrelevant reasons, whereas he is unreasonable in so far as his behavior or argument is backed by reasons that are not obviously irrelevant but which are nonetheless weak and insufficient to justify his argument or behavior. But now we come to the problems.

Can We Distinguish between the Rational, the Irrational, and the Unreasonable?

First of all, it may be pointed out that although in principle there obviously is a distinction between 'irrationality' and 'unreasonableness', in practice it may be exceedingly difficult to distinguish between them. Is it irrational or merely unreasonable (or neither) to deny any Russian involvement in hacking the Internet to interfere in Western politics? Are one's reasons for holding this view weak or palpably inadequate? Tied up with this is a second, more serious problem. Some people have argued that although the formal outline of 'irrational' and 'unreasonable' makes sense, not only can one sometimes not distinguish between them in practice, but one can never be sure that any behavior or argument is either. The paranoiac, for instance, may behave in ways that we regard as irrational, but surely, given his way of looking at things, his behavior may be entirely rational. Are we entitled to call a man irrational who shoots somebody on the grounds that the person is a member of a certain race? *We* may think that an absurd non-reason, but he has a view of life such that it constitutes a good reason. Do we not therefore either have to admit that a lot of so-called irrational behavior is not irrational, or else confess that by rational behavior we mean behavior that we regard as rational, which is to say behavior that we regard as backed by good reason – which means effectively behavior that we approve of?

It begins to look as if the cynic who claims that we call people who agree with us 'rational' and people who disagree with us 'irrational' may be right up to a point. Naturally we tend to use the word 'rational' to describe people who see things in a similar way to that in which we see them. How can I regard what does not for me constitute a good reason for a certain action as a good reason, just because somebody else thinks that it is?

But the cynic is talking about a tendency of ours in using the word, and she is not talking about the meaning of the term. 'Rational' does not *mean* 'seeing things my way', even if it may be difficult sometimes to attribute rationality to people who do not see things my way. In the same way, we tend to describe only those people whose actions in certain situations we admire as brave, but 'brave' does not mean simply 'actions that I admire'. What is true, however, and what those who are skeptical of the promotion of rationality as a feasible aim (or who see it as a covert way of maintaining the status quo) sometimes confuse with the generalization that 'being rational' is 'seeing things in the accepted manner', is that it may occasionally be very difficult to judge whether an individual is being rational or not.

In order to judge whether people are being rational we have to know what their premises are as well as observe their behavior and listen to their arguments. For it is only in the light of premises that we can assess reasons as good or relevant reasons. One's natural assumption, for instance, would be that a man was being irrational if he pounced on another man and beat him up simply because the latter had bent down to tie up his shoelace. But it might transpire that the first man had had considerable experience of some out of the way community where people kept knives tucked away in their shoes and that therefore, to him, the fact that the second man reached down to his shoes provided a very good reason for responding quickly and violently.

In the same way, to someone who has grasped no more about soccer than that there are two opposing teams trying to kick the ball into each other's net, it would seem quite irrational for a player to stop just as he was about to score, simply because somebody blows a whistle. It is only on the assumption that one recognizes and accepts the rules of soccer that the fact that the referee blows a whistle constitutes a relevant reason for ceasing to storm on towards the goal. It is therefore sometimes difficult to know whether a person's behavior is rational or not because one is in ignorance of the assumptions on which that behavior is based.

But the cynic may want to go further than this. She may point out that it is not only that we sometimes do not know the premises on which another man bases his behavior; very often we know another person's premises but do not share them. The premise of Christian Scientists might be that one should not interfere with what God ordains. The child of such parents is sick. God ordains it thus and therefore, the parents conclude, medical aid should not be provided. What are we to say about such parents? There is nothing faulty or irrational in their argument or behavior, if the premise is granted. Are we entitled to call them irrational simply because we do not share that premise? We may say that the premise is irrational, but here we would be on much trickier ground, for how are we to decide what count as good or relevant reasons either for holding or for rejecting this premise? But if we do not call these parents irrational, then one might have to accept that certain madmen, as we should conventionally term them, were not irrational either. A man might shoot me on the grounds that a pigeon flew by the window and nonetheless avoid the charge of irrationality by explaining that his premise is that God expects us to shoot whenever He causes a pigeon to fly by the window. Does this kind of consideration lead us to the conclusion that we cannot meaningfully distinguish between rationality and irrationality, let alone irrationality and unreasonableness, and that we either have to allow that everybody is equally rational or else concede that in picking out some people as more rational than others we are simply picking out those who see things our way and that there is no objectivity in this selection?

It does not. In the first place there is still room for distinguishing between rational and irrational argument or behavior, even if we ignore the question of what premises people hold. If a person contradicts herself, produces an incoherent argument, or appeals to considerations that are irrelevant on her own terms, she is being irrational and that is all there is to it. We can certainly distinguish between the relatively rational and the relatively irrational person, at least in many cases, because some – probably most – irrationality is displayed in people's inconsistency or lack of coherence given their own world-view. If I believe that it is important to use sun-screen in order to ward off skin cancer then I am being irrational in failing to use it. If I criticize the prime minister on the grounds that he changes some of his policies and refuse to criticize the leader of the opposition when he does the same thing, I am being irrational.

Second, despite what was said above about the difficulty of knowing in some cases what would count as relevant reasons for establishing or rejecting certain premises, there are surely some premises or some world-views that we simply will not accept as rational. It is of course quite true that in saying that it is irrational to base one's behavior on a premise such as "God expects us to shoot when pigeons fly by" or "The Aryan race is entitled to preferential treatment" one is appealing to others to adopt one's view of the sorts of thing that do not seem to be supported by anything that could count as good reasons. It is not clear how one could prove that it is not true that God expects us to shoot people when pigeons fly by. But we may still argue that it seems to us an irrational belief, since we cannot see anything remotely resembling a good reason for believing it.

Finally, and most importantly, a rational individual, being a conscious creature, must surely be one who has *respect* for the idea of giving good reasons. A person may adopt an idiosyncratic point of view, but, if she is rational, she must at least be the sort of person who attempts to produce reasons for that point of view and who takes notes of arguments against it. What seems to be forgotten by those who delight in raising bizarre examples about people who shoot on the strength of seeing a pigeon is that in practice, in nine cases out of ten, what indicates the irrationality of such madmen is not so much the holding of a peculiar premise as the fact that they cannot and will not consider alternatives or the problem of justifying their point of view.

Rationality and Education

Those who argue that education should aim to promote rationality are arguing that we should aim to promote in children a respect for the notion of giving good reasons, for thinking (and hence behaving) in a coherent manner and, as a natural consequence, for evaluating the arguments, ideas, and opinions of others by reference to their coherence rather than by reference to their emotive appeal, the status of the person arguing, or any other irrelevant consideration. It is perhaps true that to some extent this will in practice lead to the assumption or adoption of opinions, attitudes, and ways of behaving that are not idiosyncratic and that coincide with what we happen to regard as rational opinions and behavior. But this is not a necessary consequence and it is not the aim of those who advocate the development of rationality as an educational objective. For the aim of promoting rationality is not the same thing as promoting commitment to those opinions and judgments that we regard as rational.

In fact, to set up rationality as one of one's educational aims is automatically to oppose the practice of educating children in such a way that, as adults, they become unreflective individuals who act and think in response to the dictates of authority figures. Implicit in placing a value on it is the idea that people should act in a certain way or hold particular opinions because they see good reason to do so and not because they have been told to do so.

This is not to say that the aim is to deter people from taking any notice of what experts or authorities in any particular sphere may have to say. As was briefly mentioned in Chapter 9, there is a distinction to be made between being *in* authority and being *an* authority. To be in authority is to be in some position by virtue of which one has authority in the sense of a degree of power, as, for instance, a headmaster has authority over his school and parents have legal authority over their children. (There is also a distinction to be drawn between formally being in authority, and hence technically having authority, and actually having authority. A school principal might in fact lack authority, despite her position, because of her weak character, whereas one of her staff, though technically not in any position of authority, might actually have considerable authority with the children. But this distinction is not germane to our purpose here.) To be an authority in a particular sphere, on the other hand, is to be one who has knowledge and expertise in that sphere, as, for example, doctors are authorities in medicine. Clearly an individual might be in authority without being an authority in any sphere, and vice versa.

Generally speaking, it would be foolish to ignore what authorities, in the sense of experts, have to say in various spheres. In general, we should be well advised to take note of what the doctor, being an authority in medicine, has to say about our health (although even here it has to be remembered that authorities in a particular sphere often disagree and the mere fact that somebody is an authority does not automatically make them right). But to give particular attention to what *an* authority says is one thing; to give particular attention to what those *in* authority say is quite another. The aim of those who advocate rationality is not to do away with any concern for what authorities in various spheres have to say, so much as to deter people from assuming that the fact that somebody or some group has authority, in the sense of having some degree of power, in itself makes that person or group right or even particularly worth listening to on whatever subject is at issue. The fact that parents, teachers, police, or governments have authority does not mean that they are more likely to be right in their views on any issue than anybody else. The object of stressing rationality as an educational aim is to attempt to do away with the tendency of children to assume that something must be true, or right or good because teacher says so, and of adults to make similar assumptions because the party leader, the newspaper editor, or the local priest says so.

How, then, does one develop rationality in students? And why should one be concerned to do so? The former is largely an empirical question, depending for its answer on the collection of evidence as to what effect various practices actually have. But there are one or two points that follow logically from our understanding of the concept. Since a rational person is, by definition, one who approaches matters with a concern and an ability to assess them by means of relevant reasoning, they need ideally to have, besides this disposition to be concerned, understanding of the type of reasons that *are* relevant in various logically distinct areas, at least a certain amount of information, an ability to conceive of alternative ways of looking at things besides that with which they are familiar, and a questioning attitude. These characteristics may be illustrated by reference to a discussion about the rival merits of comprehensive and some form of selective education.

Imagine that a proposal for comprehensive schools is put to someone who has no experience of comprehensive education and to whom the idea is essentially a novel one. First and foremost, if the individual is rational, he or she will regard the suggestion as up for questioning. She will neither oppose it simply because it is new or unfamiliar nor approve it automatically because it is advocated by people whom she happens to respect. She will want to examine the issue on its own merits. But in order to do that she will need to have or to acquire certain information – information, broadly speaking, about child psychology, sociological factors, and whatever empirical evidence there may be about the actual consequences of schooling on a comprehensive model. One mark of the rational person will be that their judgment on the issue will be more tentative in proportion to the degree in which they lack such information. It is not, of course, part of the meaning of being rational that one should have such information; but it is a mark of the rational individual to recognize the need for it before an informed judgment can be made. But such information alone will not decide the issue, since the question of comprehensive education also involves value judgments: one needs not only to know that a particular system, let us say, is likely to produce greater social cohesion than another, but also to have considered the question of the relative value of social cohesion and various other objectives that might be better served by other educational systems. In order to deal rationally with this dimension of the problem the person in question will need to be able to distinguish between issues that are essentially to be determined empirically and evaluative questions, which are not. If they were to make the mistake of thinking that the fact that most people happen to think that social cohesion is relatively important as an educational objective is a good reason for concluding that it is, then the thinking would in that respect be irrational. Likewise if they were to object to a comprehensive system of education simply on the grounds that they would find it aesthetically displeasing to see a lot of new schools being built and that the system proposed would necessitate such new building, we should say that they did not understand the sorts of reason that were relevant to an educational issue and those that were not. Finally, even when the individual had formed her judgment, it would be a continuing indication of her rationality that she was open to the consideration of alternatives that might be proposed.

It follows from the recognition of these features as characteristics or aspects of a person that are necessary for them to be able to make rational

decisions and to behave rationally that rationality is not likely to be promoted by any educational system that involves an effort by teachers to
instill in children unthinking acceptance of all that is set before them and
all that is demanded of them. If willingness to question and concern for
relevant reasons are to be promoted in children, then presumably they
must to some extent be encouraged to question and to appreciate the reasons for various things, rather than be fobbed off with remarks such as
"Because I say so" or "It just is true, that's why". This point has been well
grasped by a number of educationalists such as Postman and Weingartner,
who in their *Teaching as a Subversive Activity* demand that we throw away
the notion that we (the teachers) know best and know what things are
worth doing, and instead throw everything open to the children's questioning and in this way teach "the most important and intellectual ability
man has yet developed – the art and science of asking questions".[3] What
does not seem to have been grasped by Postman and Weingartner is that
simply to pose questions and give answers is a pretty feeble sort of exercise
if those answers do not have to measure up to any standards of rationality.[4] If we are after the asking of meaningful questions and the search for
rational and significant answers, we shall presumably have to do more
than sit around enthusing over the sound of each other's voices (which at
times one feels would be the characteristic of the Postman and Weingartner ideal teaching situation). If we really wish to promote rationality then
we shall also have to see to it that children acquire information, acquire
knowledge as to what sort of information is appropriate to what sort of
question and how one sets about dealing with different kinds of question,
and, above all, acquire the formal notion that there is a distinction to be
made between relevant and irrelevant, or strong and weak reasons. Thus,
although we cannot say precisely what the best way to achieve these ends
is without a degree of empirical research, we can say that the nature of the
concept of rationality demands that the teacher shall make some positive
effort to discriminate between children's responses and opinions as relatively coherent or incoherent, to provide information, and to initiate children into the various logically distinct types of inquiry and other
fundamental subject matter.

Turning to the question of why we should want to promote rationality we have first to distinguish two possible confusions that may be
involved in the claim that rationality is not an important objective.
First, it is not uncommon to come across people who claim to be
hostile to the aim of rationality, but who are in fact hostile to the
promotion of certain views or opinions which society in general may
happen to regard as rational. However, as we have seen, to object to
the promotion of particular views which are allegedly rational is quite
distinct from objecting to the promotion of rationality itself. Second,
some people claim to be hostile to the aim of rationality when in fact
their objection seems only to be to an exclusive preoccupation with

rationality. It may very well be that an education that was solely concerned with promoting rationality would be inadequate, since there is much more to human experience than reasoning. But to say that rationality is not the only important aim of education is obviously not the same thing as saying that it should not be an aim.

But suppose that neither of these two confusions is being made and that somebody nonetheless asks "Why should I worry about having good reasons for my beliefs, my attitudes, and the way I behave? Why shouldn't I simply act as the spirit moves me? After all, human reason is fallible, why should I not take the view that my intuitive or inspired feeling is as good a guide as reason? What's so good about rationality?" The simple answer to such questions is that it may not be possible to show why the speaker ought to worry about having good reason, but he obviously does, otherwise he would not be asking for a good reason to worry about having good reasons for action and beliefs. More generally, it may be pointed out that it is a presupposition of asking, in a serious frame of mind, such questions as "What ought I to do in such and such a situation?" or "What ought education be concerned to do?" that one is committed to the notion of giving good reasons. What is the point of asking such questions if one is uninterested in whether the reply is well-reasoned or not?

Of course, this only shows that as a matter of fact most of us are committed to the idea of giving good reasons or to rationality as an ideal. It does not show that we ought only, or indeed ever, to act rationally, and it is not inconceivable that someone should claim to be totally uninterested in whether his own or anyone else's behavior is explicable in terms of good reasons. All one can say to such persons, if they exist, is that they are committing themselves to an ideal in which anything goes (for it would not make sense to distinguish between sensible and foolish, acceptable and unacceptable behavior, or defensible and indefensible conduct), and in which there is no room for meaningful communication. A world in which there was no respect for the notion of good reasons would be a world in which a remark such as "I am going indoors because I am cold" would be no more sensible than "I am going indoors because I ate a banana three weeks ago". Furthermore, the man totally uninterested in reason could not make a meaningful objection to anything that happened to him, since there would be no such thing as a good reason for objecting (his objections would merely be subjective grunts of no interest to anyone else), and he could therefore hardly complain if we simply ignored him and his peculiar idea, which is presumably what, in the last resort, we should do. But I think it is clear that although such an individual is conceivable, it is extremely unlikely that anyone should literally believe that the idea of having good reasons is of no importance.

To deny the value of rationality is to do away with the importance of our distinctive capacity for purposive action. To do away with the distinction between good and bad thinking is to deny the purpose of thinking.

Notes

1 Aristotle, *Nicomachean Ethics* (Penguin, 1955) 1.13.
2 'Gender' is a grammatical term used to indicate whether a noun is masculine, feminine, or neuter. Often a noun that refers to a particular sex will be of similar gender (e.g., 'femina' in Latin is a feminine noun and means 'female'. 'Dominus' is a masculine noun meaning 'master'. 'Bellum' is a neuter noun meaning 'war'). But sometimes this is not the case. For example, the word 'nauta', though it means 'sailor' and Roman sailors were male, is feminine. 'Sex' by contrast is a biological term that distinguishes organisms on the basis of their reproductive function.
3 Neil Postman & Charles Weingartner, *Teaching as a Subversive Activity* (op. cit.) p. 34.
4 See Robin Barrow, *Radical Education* (op. cit.) ch. 7.

Further Reading

For a collection of articles relating to the concepts of rationality and reason-ableness the reader is referred to Part 2 of R.F. Dearden, P.H. Hirst, & R.S. Peters (eds.), *Education and the Development of Reason* (Routledge & Kegan Paul, 1972). See also Anthony O'Hear, 'Education and Rationality' in David Cooper (ed.), *Education, Values and Mind: Essays for R.S. Peters* (Routledge, 1986), and Harvey Siegel, *Education's Epistemology* (op. cit.).

Martin Hollis & Steven Lukes (eds.), *Rationality and Relativism* (Blackwell, 1982) contains readings relevant to this chapter and to Chapter 15.

See also Richard Tarnass, *The Passion of the Western Mind* (Ballatine Books, 1991).

Questions

Is it unreasonable or irrational (or neither) to believe in ghosts?

What's the difference between a rational commitment to a political party and an irrational commitment?

13 Critical Thinking and Other Skills

Chapters 4 and 5 considered the view that the best way to approach the question of what should be studied (and to some extent how it should be taught) is to focus on the needs, interests, and readiness of children. I argued that there are serious problems with that approach, and that the curriculum should instead be based on worthwhile subject matter, specifically certain valuable types of understanding or inquiry (Chapter 7). However, there is another school of thought that also rejects the worthwhile knowledge approach, but, rather than advocating a focus on interests and needs, proposes that we should focus on developing particular *skills*, of which one frequently emphasized is the skill of critical thinking.

Critical Thinking

Those who stress the importance of critical thinking have in mind not so much being critical in the sense of pointing out errors and inadequacies in an argument or viewpoint, as assessing things in a dispassionate and rational manner, and thereby coming to correct or at least well-founded conclusions. At first glance, this must seem persuasive. I doubt whether there are any educators, at least in liberal democracies, who do not profess to value critical thinking. After all, we are in favor of rationality, and surely that is tantamount to wanting people to become critical thinkers. It is a normative phrase (it involves *good* thinking), so who is going to say that they want people to think uncritically? The problem, as with the emphasis on needs and interests, is not that the concept is of no value. The problem lies rather in a failure to conceptualize critical thinking adequately and, as a consequence, the provision of an incoherent picture of how to teach or develop it.

In the first place, the very notion that there is an 'it', or that critical thinking is a single monolithic ability like balancing on one leg, is simply mistaken. Critical thinking involves at the very least a *set* of skills (e.g., the ability to spot logical errors, being disposed to examine things critically, having certain information, and being imaginative) and these may each need to be developed in different ways.

DOI: 10.4324/9781003120476-13

In the second place, precisely because these abilities are different in kind, the once common use of the word 'skill' is seriously misleading. Strictly speaking a 'skill' (and here I am simply following the dictionary) is a discrete, physical ability that can be trained and improved by practice. True skills are practical skills, such as the skills of the carpenter or the stonemason, the hairdresser or the plumber. Juggling, swimming, and doing a hand-stand are all instances of skill, whereas exhibiting charm, appreciating poetry and understanding a historical event are not. Or perhaps I should say that they are not skills in the same sense of the word, since in practice what has happened is that some educators have used the word 'skill' as if it were a synonym for 'ability'. But 'ability' is a very broad term and abilities may clearly be of a very different type, as the ability to relate to people is quite different in kind from the ability to play golf, and accordingly has to be developed in a quite different way. To refer to critical thinking as a skill (or set of skills) wrongly implies that it can be developed by practice in any context, just as one can develop one's golf swing by practice on more or less any occasion and in any place. Thinking of it as a skill also suggests that practice necessarily makes for improvement, as by and large practicing physical skills such as the golf swing does. But some abilities such as the ability to philosophize or to feel compassion do not, alas, necessarily improve with time and practice. Today the tendency among educators is in fact to talk of 'competencies', which does avoid the misleading connotations of the word 'skill'. On the other hand, 'competency' is a general term more or less synonymous with 'ability', and thus we are back with the problem that competencies may differ greatly in their nature, and different types of competence need to be developed in quite different ways.

But the most serious problem with standard approaches to the teaching of critical thinking is that they involve what I have termed 'the generic fallacy'. The generic fallacy involves regarding an ability which in fact has specific and limited application as if it were generally applicable. It is the mistake of thinking that any ability can be developed and exhibited in any context, so that if, for example, you have the ability to amuse certain people, you will always be able to amuse people in any situation, which is manifestly not the case. A genuine *skill* may well be generic: if you can stand on your head here and now, the chances are that you will be able to do so tomorrow somewhere else. If the carpenter can produce fine fretwork here, then we should expect him to be able to do so there. But this is not the case with complex intellectual abilities. The fact that a person can think critically (implying among other things thinking *well*) about historical events does not mean that she will be able to think critically and well about scientific issues.

There is a large industry surrounding the promotion of critical thinking, including the publication of books on how to think critically, programs for teaching critical thinking, and various materials for classroom use. But because the authors of this material generally fail to focus on the fact that being able to think critically by definition involves the ability to think well, and that this ability is not generic, most of those who advocate or promote critical thinking exercises, books, and programs are concerned with material that simply ignores the fact that if a person is to be able to think critically about a subject (whether it be an academic subject such as math, chemistry or literature, or a practical matter such as human relations or politics), then they must have a good understanding of the subject matter in question.

It is necessary here to distinguish between the *disposition* to think critically and the ability to do so. The disposition or the ingrained tendency to want to look at matters critically can no doubt be developed by encouragement to engage with any and all manner of material in a critical manner. So, to develop the disposition, the use of much of the marketed critical thinking material may well be adequate. But a focus on a random set of problems or issues ranging from debate about transgender issues to debate about train timetables, from discussion of pandemics to discussion of the removal of statues of discredited figures, while it may obviously help to develop a critical attitude, is not in itself going to achieve the presumed goal of people who can be relied upon to think critically in the sense of rationally, effectively, and to good purpose on matters of importance involving specialist knowledge. For to think critically in the sense of well about, say, pandemics, one needs among other things to understand the medical science and the use of statistics, and to do that involves studying and understanding these subjects themselves.

The question, therefore, that surely needs to be asked first is what do we want people to be able to think critically about, since few of us are equally adept in thinking about everything and anything? The advocates of most critical thinking programs do not have an answer to this, since they do not ask the question. Since most of the material produced is centered on problems and issues that do not rely on specialist knowledge, the most they could claim to be doing is cultivating the tendency or disposition to approach issues in a critical frame of mind, and perhaps the ability to do so where no specialist knowledge is required. But attempting to answer most of the serious questions in life depends to some extent on one or more of the fundamental types of understanding discussed in Chapter 7. It follows that, if we are serious about wanting people to think critically about important issues in life, we do indeed need to cultivate a critical disposition, but we need to do it in the context of the fundamental disciplines and subjects that structure our understanding of the world. To focus instead on such fads and clichés as 'brainstorming', 'lateral thinking', and 'thinking outside the box', without regard to relevant discipline-based understanding and quality in terms of sound-thinking, as distinct from merely welcoming novelty or unexpectedness (which is a marked feature of many critical thinking programs), is to fiddle while the truly educational edifice burns. The goal of cultivating critical thinking will not be effectively served by merely engaging in consideration of a myriad of fictional problems that involve no questions of, say, history, science, or math, and where no particular emphasis is placed on the quality of the reasoning.

In short, developing critical thinking should indeed be one of our educational goals, but it should be developed primarily in the context of those subjects that have been shown to be educationally worthwhile or important. This understanding must of course involve appreciating the rules and limitations of the various forms of inquiry. And there is one further point, the importance of which is becoming increasingly clear: given the reliance nowadays placed on the Internet we need to tackle the various issues to do with manipulation of information. We need to make children aware of the dangers of relying on social media, of trolls, and of other manifestations of misinformation and truly fake news.

There are a number of other intellectual abilities such as creativity and imagination, where the same argument applies. They are not strictly speaking 'skills' and they are not generic. They are normative concepts that necessarily imply judgment of some kind of quality, and they have to be cultivated in particular contexts. To promote imagination is not only to develop in individuals the tendency or disposition to use the imagination, and to think in terms of the unfamiliar, but also to enable them to come up with ideas or products that are good of their kind. An historian who denies the Holocaust is certainly drawing unexpected conclusions, but she is not an imaginative historian so much as a bad historian. While occasionally we hear of individuals such as Leonardo da Vinci, who display imagination in many areas, that is a contingent (and rare) occurrence. It is a necessary truth that one can only display imagination in areas where one has understanding or ability, since an imaginative solution or product is by definition also a good or effective one. (On creativity, see Chapter 16.)

Social Skills

It is common to refer to 'social' and 'emotional' skills as well as to 'intellectual' skills such as critical thinking. But the argument against so doing remains essentially the same. Sometimes, as when empathy, optimism, and patience are referred to as 'skills', this seems absurd. Even to think of them as abilities is surely misplaced and misleading. They are characteristics or aspects of our personality; they may be nurtured, but they cannot be taught or learned in the way that one learns to do hand-stands. Being compassionate, for instance, is a complex matter crucially involving understanding, insight, and feeling, none of which are well characterized as skills. The fact that you are a good friend to your circle of acquaintances does not mean that you will necessarily be able to make good friends in any situation, wherever you go. The fact that you have shown courage in the past does not necessarily mean that you can be relied on to show courage in any and every type of situation.

Another danger of talking in terms of skills, and possibly even in terms of competencies or abilities, is that it tends to suggest that everything from holding a knife and fork to friendship is a matter of behaviors. It is true that to some extent, even in relation to things such as friendship or parenting, we judge a person by reference to how they behave or what they do. Your claim to be a good friend to somebody will not be very convincing if you never contact them, compliment them, or come to their aid when needed. Good parents need to be present, to listen to, and to show affection for their children. But there is more to it than that.

Behaviors and actions are to be distinguished from one another. In talking of a 'behavior' I refer only to a physical movement or procedure such as kneeling down or running. If I talk of an 'action' I refer to both a behavior (or set of behaviors) and the purpose or intent of engaging in the behavior(s). Thus the behavior of running becomes the action of racing if and only if I am deliberately competing with another (or with my own previous timing). Holding up one's hand is in itself simply a behavior. But that behavior may signify a number of different actions, depending on the context, and in particular on the agent's intentions. Thus, the behavior of raising one's arm might be simply an involuntary spasm occasioned by something like Tourette's syndrome, in which case it is nothing more than a behavior; but it might represent the action of wishing to answer a question, a cry for help, a salute, or a greeting, depending partly on such factors as whether it takes place in the classroom, while swimming in the sea, at a parade, or at a gathering of old friends; and crucially it will be dependent on intention. An arm raised while swimming in the sea is a cry for help if I am drowning and intend to attract help, but it is a greeting or an expression of camaraderie if I am quite safe and my intention is simply to signal my good feelings.

Social abilities such as the display of compassion, charm, or consideration cannot be adequately conceptualized in purely behavioral terms. Of course, practice has a part to play. Being polite, being willing to listen, setting out to charm or please, for example, all have elements of trainable and habitual behavior. But it is possible to exhibit these traits without being sincere: one can appear to be polite while simply faking it, one can appear to listen while in fact thinking of other things, and one can successfully charm while inwardly seething with contempt. In attempting to cultivate particular social abilities in the young, we need therefore to encourage certain behavioral habits but also to attempt to encourage the development of appropriate attitudes and feelings.

A typical list of so-called 'social skills' to be developed in young children might refer to sharing, cooperation, listening, following directions, and good manners. Without question these are desirable goals. Nor is there any problem about how to set about doing this: we call for and encourage sharing, cooperation, and good manners; we call for and communicate in such a way as to get children to listen attentively and to follow directions. There is of course the problem of deciding what manners are desirable and what are not, and there will be cases where individual children find it hard to follow instructions, either because they cannot fully understand them or because they are too impatient or inattentive. But dealing with such points is all in a day's work for teachers, and there really doesn't seem to be need for any further discussion on developing characteristics such as these.

By contrast, there are certain putative skills that are of questionable value. Making eye contact, though it appears on almost every list of required skills, seems to me a much over-rated ability; personally, I instinctively distrust people who practice this particular technique in an obvious way, just as the firm handshake seems obviously a learned trick that does not in itself truly tell you anything about the person you are dealing with. Then there are vague admonitions to cultivate one's body language, one's ability to be assertive without being aggressive, to accept criticism without being defensive, and to be positive. Here we surely begin to descend into the more or less meaningless. Certainly, one's physical bearing can convey meaning but we are a long way from any systematic understanding of the matter, and the same physical stance may be interpreted in quite different ways by different people. The difference between aggression and assertiveness is conceptually very fine, yet in practice often so blatant as to need no comment. That is to say, clearly in practice one should stand firmly by one's view that, say, marriage should (or shouldn't) be confined to heterosexual couples, while equally clearly one shouldn't in doing so abuse or insult those who disagree. But when exactly one's assertive defense becomes aggressive is a matter of some philosophical subtlety. Similarly, it is very common in arguments to find one participant claiming that another is being defensive, which the latter (with increasing irritation) denies. As to the injunction to be positive, one can only say that it is about as meaningless and unhelpful as being told to be happy.

Nonetheless, there obviously are a number of social qualities and characteristics that are important and that schools can help to develop. Thus, to develop social qualities such as compassion, kindness, politeness, consideration, generosity, loyalty, and empathy, we need first, at the level of the primary or elementary school, to explain, draw attention to, model, and call for behavior that involves these qualities. We also need to ensure that the community of the school itself, both primary and secondary, is so constituted as to enshrine and exhibit these qualities. But we also need at the secondary level to engage directly in examination of these concepts, giving consideration to questions such as "What does compassion actually involve?", "Are there limits to loyalty?", "Generosity to whom?", "Who determines what is polite?" and "Is it sometimes appropriate to be impolite?". At the same time there should be further indirect contemplation of such concepts in the context of history and most obviously literature.

There is a great deal more to being able to function well in social settings than the mastery of trivial tics such as making eye contact, and the most important thing is to develop understanding of the many things involved in being socially adept, most particularly the concepts themselves.

Leadership

Another concept of educational interest is leadership, both because some schools and faculties of education in colleges and universities profess to teach leadership and because educational institutions along with most other organizations obviously require leaders.

The ability to lead is not generic: the fact that you can successfully captain a ship doesn't mean that you can captain a rugby fifteen, any more than the fact that you can drive a car means that you can drive a tank or the fact that you are good with dogs means you will be good with cats. While we can certainly attempt to list the qualities of a good leader, we cannot reasonably reduce such a list to a list of behaviors or skills. Good leadership is primarily a matter of character; it is more a matter of being a certain kind of person than of engaging in particular behaviors or, as the jargon has it, of having a particular skill-set.

Avoiding the generic fallacy, we must reject the tendency to imagine that the qualities of a good leader for an industrial company will be the same as those required for good leadership in the church, in the armed forces, or in education. There may very well be some characteristics, even some skills, that are common to all, but it should be self-evident that the qualities needed to run a financial business are not entirely coextensive with those needed to run a charitable organization. The entirely distinct objectives and aims of the two necessarily lead to a need for different qualities in their respective leaders. Whether a leader should be effective in getting her way, prepared to be brutal to employees, primarily concerned for the well-being of employees, concerned for customer satisfaction, popular, have moral integrity, be good at making profits, inspiring, unifying, have high standards, be innovative, or whatever, is largely dependent on the nature of the organization in question.

It is depressing to read advertisements for senior positions routinely veer between lists of desirable alleged skills such as 'people skills' and vague notions such as vision or imagination. 'People skills' or the ability to get on with people is not generic; one may find it easy to get along with some people but impossible to get along with others. (This may be because of certain facts about oneself or because what it takes to get on with one set of people will not work with another set.) And getting on with people cannot be reduced to a list of behavioral skills such as a firm handshake, strong eye contact, and seeming to listen. On the contrary, truly getting on with people requires not simply particular mannerisms or observable behaviors, but characteristics that are ingrained and involve both under-standing and holding certain values such as respect for persons, reliability, and integrity.

Sometimes a candidate for a leadership position comes with a track record as a leader. But the fact that a person has, for example, been judged to be adept at getting on with colleagues and to have had a particular and admirable vision while heading a PE department, does not tell us how well they will get on as principal of a large school in a different neighborhood. Plenty of successful department heads fail to make good principals. The question in any case should not be "Does this candidate have vision?" in the abstract, but "What is this candidate's vision?" And, if we are looking for an educational leader as opposed to a political leader or a business leader, it should more specifically be "What is this candidate's *educational* vision?" A track record of imaginative innovations in a history department does not necessarily tell us anything about the capacity to handle a school and its myriad decisions and problems imaginatively. Since leadership is not a generic quality and excellent team coaches may make terrible principals, in looking for educational leaders we need to look for individuals who first and foremost can articulate a convincing and desirable educational vision for the particular institution in question.

In short, there is something rather suspect about the very idea of teaching leadership. We don't need to be taught that ideally the good leader is effective and imaginative. We need to be able to clarify what constitutes effectiveness or imagination in particular contexts and to be able to recognize such qualities in candidates for leadership. As things stand, we seldom face up to the first requirement and we know little or nothing about the second. Though it does not always seem high on the list of requirements for leaders in business, leaders should of course be moral and incorruptible, but again it is hard to know how to make that judgment of candidates since they are hardly likely to proclaim that they are eminently corruptible. The qualities that are most important are, as indicated above, likely to be specific to particular situations: sometimes making a profit is the ability most desired, sometimes creating a happy working environment ranks high, sometimes the ability to clear out dead wood is of paramount importance. When it comes to appointing leaders of educational establishments, I would suggest that our priority should be to look for people who are primarily committed to upholding the highest educational and social standards and who can both articulate what those standards are to our satisfaction and indicate what specifically they would do in respect of such things as curriculum and hiring of staff to maintain or improve those standards. Whether candidates should have pursued a course in leadership remains a moot point.

Conclusion

The argument has been that the misuse of the word 'skill' in an educational context can often lead us to think of various abilities that are in fact complex and involve knowledge and understanding as if they were simple and trainable behaviors. Understanding is a crucial element in so-called social and emotional skills, just as it more obviously is in so-called intellectual skills. But one cannot *train* understanding. To understand is to get inside and come to grips with a body of knowledge. Intellectual abilities in particular, therefore, can only be nurtured in the context of such bodies of knowledge. Given that one needs to have this knowledge and understanding, it seems uneconomic if not downright silly to seek to cultivate the disposition in the context of various problem-solving exercises where no particular knowledge is required. The obvious course of action is to teach the subjects that provide the knowledge and understanding we see as essential to structuring our world, but to teach them in a way that encourages critical appraisal. In other words, we do not want lessons in critical thinking or programs to develop the imagination, but rather teaching in such things as science and history that encourages critical and imaginative engagement. Nor do we need to attempt to develop courses for teachers designed to show them how to teach imaginatively and how to encourage a critical disposition in students. The basic requirement is quite clear: do not simply provide information, but explain what lies behind it or how we have come to these conclusions; encourage students to show both that they understand why historians say such and such, or why scientists have come to this conclusion, and invite them nonetheless to question all of this and if possible to offer alternative analysis and argument. But let us make sure that we also insist that the students' responses make sense.

Further Reading

On skills, see Robin Barrow, *Understanding Skills: Thinking, Feeling and Caring* (Routledge, 2015), Claudia Ruitenberg, 'Plus ca change: The Persistence of "Skill Talk" in Competency Discourse' in *Philosophical Inquiry in Education*, 26 (2), 124–136 (2019), and Gert Biesta & Mark Priestley 'Capacities and the Curriculum' in their edited *Reinventing the Curriculum: New Trends in Curriculum Policy and Practice* (Bloomsbury Academic, 2013).

Of the mass of material relating to critical thinking, I would single out John McPeck's *Critical Thinking and Education* (Martin Robertson, 1981). But see also Harvey Siegel, *Education's Epistemology* (op. cit.), M. Davies & R. Barnet (eds.), *The Palgrave Handbook of Critical Thinking in Higher Education* (Palgrave Macmillan, 2015), and S. Hanscomb, *Critical Thinking* (Routledge, 2017).

On educational leadership, see R.S. Peters (ed.), *The Role of the Head* (Routledge & Kegan Paul, 1976).

William Hare, *What Makes a Good Teacher?* (Althouse Press, 1993) refreshingly argues that the answer lies in specific characteristics (e.g., humility, enthusiasm, and open-mindedness) rather than putative skills.

Related books of considerable interest include: Duff McDonald, *The Golden Passport: Harvard Business School, the Limits of Capitalism and the Moral Failure of the MBA Elite* (HarperCollins, 2017), John Micklethwaite & Adrian Wooldridge, *The Witch Doctors: Making Sense of the Management Gurus* (Random House, 1996), Merve Emre, *The Personality Brokers: The Strange History of Meyers-Briggs and the Birth of Personality Testing* (Random House, 2018), and Franklin Foer, *World Without Mind: The Existentialist Threat of Big Tech* (Penguin, 2017).

Questions

Is the distinction between skills and abilities just a verbal quibble?

What is the generic fallacy?

What would you propose in order to cultivate critical thinking?

14 Freedom and Autonomy

'Autonomy', deriving from the Greek words for 'self' (*autos*) and 'custom' or 'law' ('*nomos*'), means 'self-direction' or 'self-determination'. I have autonomy insofar as I am able to conduct myself according to my own reasoning. This is not a value shared by all cultures. Some, such as ancient Sparta or contemporary China, clearly place the value of homogeneity and adherence to a firm code of social conduct above the value of autonomy. But it is generally valued in the Western world, partly on the grounds that it would be inappropriate for government to dictate all conduct when so much is uncertain, unknown, or unknowable, and partly on the more general belief that freedom is a good.

Of course, most people recognize that there must be some laws and directives that to some extent restrict the freedom of individuals. But we tend to follow the argument famously put forward by John Stuart Mill in *On Liberty* to the effect that we should be free to act in any way that does not harm others, and that freedom of thought and expression should be absolute. Actually, I need to qualify that summary statement of Mill's position if I am to be fair to the argument surrounding exactly what he said and whether he was entirely correct. It is generally agreed, for example, that freedom of expression should not cover instances such as shouting out "fire" in a crowded auditorium, when there is no fire, thus causing panic and possibly a great deal of harm. But if we understand Mill to mean that I should be allowed to hold and express any view, however seemingly repugnant, in a context that is designed for the exchange of views, then I share his view. The argument for this position is basically that the search for truth is best served by such freedom, because it enables good new ideas to emerge and bad or false ideas to be exposed, while established good ideas are strengthened by being unsuccessfully challenged.

The suggestion that the hurt that some might feel on hearing me say things with which they disagree should count as grounds for curbing my freedom does not convince. Feeling upset by what I say is not comparable to people being physically harmed when my words cause a stampede. Of course, words can cause psychological hurt and even, indirectly, physical hurt. For example, some indigenous individuals are believed to have experienced real distress

DOI: 10.4324/9781003120476-14

leading to suicide as a result of repeatedly hearing it said that they tend to be susceptible to alcoholism. But, tragic as this is, the hurt is not a necessary consequence of the claim in the way that anyone who is beaten will feel the blows, and surely we cannot conclude that if there is real evidence that indigenous people are susceptible to alcoholism we should not acknowledge it. To repeat the claim to individuals for no other reason than to taunt and provoke them would certainly be objectionable, because it is wrong to taunt people. But we should surely be free to express this claim in the context of a serious discussion if we believe it to be true (even if in fact it turns out not to be true). I am inclined to accept Robert Manery's suggestion that it would be helpful here to bring in reference to the notion of responsibility.[1] I should be free to hold and express such a view, but I have a responsibility (arising out of respect for persons and concern for their happiness among other things) not to exercise the freedom in circumstances where it will cause unnecessary hurt. But while I take this concern for people being offended seriously, I stand by the view that one must be free to express unpalatable and upsetting views if one is doing so in the interests of a sincere statement of viewpoint. (See further below.)

With regard to freedom of action, there may certainly sometimes be problems in practice in determining whether an action is or is not entirely 'self-regarding' (i.e., has no impact on anyone else), and in deciding what constitutes harm. Nonetheless, the principle that we should be free to engage in any action that does not harm others is both clear in meaning and convincing.

A person's autonomy can be limited either by restrictions on their freedom of action or by restrictions on their capacity to think for themselves. In the latter case, indoctrination is obviously one way in which an individual's autonomy can be curtailed (Chapter 11). But it is not the only way. Exercising autonomy is not the same as simply doing what you want or what you feel like. To act on impulse, driven by emotions such as jealousy or love, under the influence of alcohol, or motivated by a consuming passion for gambling, would all be instances of conduct that was not autonomous. Autonomous behavior is not necessarily rational or sensible behavior, but it does by definition involve one's own reasoning, regardless of the quality of that reasoning.

The question now arises as to whether any of us can truly be self-determining or autonomous. If a person is self-determining then presumably she must have a 'self' that is not itself determined in any way, runs the argument. We must be able to locate in her some independent self that directs her behavior. But can we in fact do this? Common sense alone suggests, even if the studies of psychologists, geneticists, and sociologists did not make it clear, that we are all partly the product of our environment and genetic make-up. The 'selves' that control our behavior are themselves, to some extent at least, formed by external influences including the other people with whom we come into contact as we develop. Such factors as the existence of peer-group pressure, a dominant mother, advertisements, the character of teachers whom we come across, or a broken home influence and help to mold our characters. And our character is part of the 'self' that may determine our behavior. Precisely *how* and *to what extent* various factors influence our development may be a matter for a great deal of argument, but what cannot be doubted is that it is the case that the 'self' referred to in the phrase 'self-determination' is itself originally at least partly determined by something other than itself. In which case, it is concluded, it may well be that the individual who is free to do whatever she chooses may in fact be no more self-determining than a person whose freedom of choice is more obviously and more directly limited.

This argument, although most of what it says about the way in which we develop in response to environmental influences is obviously correct, does not seem to me to be very significant. That is to say, although one must concede that we are all to some extent the product of our environment and genetic make-up, there is still a crucial distinction to be made between people who are free to question the assumptions, habits, attitudes, and beliefs that they may indeed have acquired unconsciously through their environment and those who are not free to question them because they have been successfully indoctrinated. Surely we may quite reasonably regard the former as autonomous (provided that they are not coerced by others or dominated by some passion or craving), in contradistinction to the latter. However, I have introduced this argument because it leads into an important educational debate. Some of those who argue that, as things are, virtually none of us are truly self-determining, go on to conclude that the only way to realize the ideal of autonomous adults is to grant children self-determination from the beginning. In other words, if self-determining adults is our goal, this must be preceded by self-development or self-regulation for children.

Self-regulation for Children

The term 'self-regulation' is used freely by the educator A. S. Neill among others, so it will not be inappropriate to begin by considering what he means by it. He writes that "self-regulation means the right of a baby to live freely without outside authority in things psychic and somatic. It means that the baby feeds when it is hungry; that it becomes clean in its habits only when it wants to; that it is never stormed at or spanked".[2] This means, to take examples from Neill, that when his daughter went through a period of great interest in his glasses, snatching them off his nose to see what they looked like, he "made no protest" and that she was allowed to play with breakable ornaments, that if children go through a period of stealing they should be "free to live out this stage", and of course that they should be free to opt out of school lessons if they choose. "To impose anything by authority is wrong. The child should not do anything until he comes to the opinion – his own opinion – that it should be done."[3] The implication of such passages is clearly that Neill takes 'self-regulation' to mean complete freedom to direct one's own life and that he thinks that the concept can be meaningfully applied even to babies. There are just two things wrong with this: despite the quotations above, Neill does *not* take 'self-regulation' to mean this (alternatively he does, but he does not believe in children being self-regulating), and if this is what 'self-regulation' means it is surely absurd to claim that babies and young children can be self-regulating.

To take the latter point first: what exactly is a self-regulating baby? A self-regulating or self-determining adult, as we have seen, is one who makes her own choices and is not subject to any restrictions on her freedom to do so. But to make a choice in any meaningful sense, even to make a bad or foolish choice, involves by definition a degree of cognitive ability. To determine a course of action for oneself means to reflect upon the options available, to weigh these up and to select one. One is not regulating one's life if one simply drifts along responding automatically to various stimuli. To regulate one's life involves having a grasp of the notion of means to ends, having some knowledge about what will happen if one does this rather than that, consciously making decisions in the light of that knowledge and having some understanding of the idea that one *can* regulate one's own life. To talk in these terms of the baby or young child is just silly. The baby that is not fed until it cries out for food is not 'regulating' its life, it is responding automatically to the stimulus of hunger. Besides, what is this self? The concept of the adult self may be somewhat obscure, but what constitutes the self of the newborn baby? Is not the notion of the individual's self inextricably linked with such concepts as personality and character, and are not these things that develop, come into being, or are acquired as one grows older? Does it make sense to talk of the 'self', 'character', or 'personality' of the newborn baby, or even of its potential 'self' or 'personality'? Isn't the whole point that whether one likes it or not, babies are born without identifiable selves and that the nature of the self and personality they will develop is inescapably bound up with the environment in which they grow up? (This is not to deny considerable significance also to the individual's genetic make-up. See Chapter 3.) While one is regulating the child's life (as of course one will to a greater or lesser extent whatever word one uses to describe the business), by feeding it, putting it to bed, and so on, one is imperceptibly – and no doubt to a great extent unpredictably – influencing the development of a particular kind of self. The mere fact that the mother breast-feeds rather than bottle-feeds, it has been suggested, may materially affect the nature of the self that will develop in the child in some way. Certainly factors such as the degree of security and love and the interests of parents and the other children in the local environment will act as influences towards the development of a particular kind of self. In short, a young child cannot be literally self-regulating from birth, since its self is itself being formed and since it lacks the understanding, cognitive awareness, and knowledge that would be necessary for anything that could reasonably be termed 'regulation' or 'determining'.

But, as already suggested, despite careless remarks such as that "the child should not do anything until he comes to the opinion that it should be done", Neill does not really believe that the child should be entirely self-regulating even if it were possible. Quite apart from the fact that once an adult has made himself responsible for providing and maintaining a particular kind of environment for the growing child – even if that environment is a relatively free or negative one – he has already begun to interfere with the development of the child, and quite apart from the fact that Neill's children are subject in large degree to the regulation of the majority will of other children, there are a number of examples to be found in Neill's writing that indicate that he expects the adults to regulate the child's life to some extent directly. The seven-year-old child, for instance, who has decided to kick Neill's office door, will not find such behavior tolerated. A three year old should not be allowed to paint the front door with red ink. A child should not be free to walk over the dining table, stand on a piano, play on the fire escape, take a wooden mallet to the keys of a piano, or leap onto a sofa with its shoes on. A child cannot be left to regulate for itself the clothes that it chooses to wear, for as Neill admits with reference to his own daughter, if they "had allowed it, she would have run about naked all day in all weathers" and so they felt that they had to "bully her into wearing what we think she ought to wear".

Most of us may feel that the examples that Neill provides of instances in which the adult should interfere are eminently sensible. But the point is that once one has admitted that there are *any* such instances, the simple claim that children should be self-regulating (even if it made sense in reference to babies and young children) is obviously inadequate and it becomes blatantly contradictory to say that "to impose anything by authority is wrong". The term 'self-regulation', pregnant with desirable overtones and emotive force, is serving as a loose slogan to rally support for a particular point of view and obscuring what is really at issue. For what is really at issue is not whether the child should make her own decisions or have them made for her, but *the degree* to which and the *areas* in which she should be left to do what she feels like doing rather than being subject to the deliberate restraints of other children or adults.

It is important to distinguish two distinct questions, which Neill does not always seem to do. They are: (i) what sorts of thing ought children be free to decide for themselves, and (ii) what as a matter of fact is the best way to bring up children in such a way that they will behave in certain ways rather than others? The latter question is of course empirical and a great deal of the time Neill seems to be making the empirical claim that if you leave children free to do what they choose to do (or what they are free to do subject only to the pressure put upon them by other children), they will as a matter of fact in the long run make sound or sensible choices. Clearly his claim that children should never be "stormed at or spanked" is just such an empirical claim, involving the belief that to intimidate the child by storming at him or spanking him is in the long run counter-productive. How true this is is not going to be decided by philosophical inquiry. Intuitively, and in the light of evidence produced by psychologists, one perhaps feels that Neill is right at least to the extent of arguing that storming and spanking are not in general effective means to employ. One's attitude to the wider claim that without adult guidance or control children will make sound choices obviously depends to some extent on one's view of a sound choice. For instance, we are told of the case of Mervyn, who "between the ages of seven to seventeen... never attended a single class. At the age of seventeen he hardly knew how to read".[4] Neill's point is that, though some might feel that here is an example of a less than sensible choice, "when Mervyn left school and decided to become an instrument maker he quickly taught himself how to read and absorbed in a short time through self-study all the technical knowledge he needed". In Neill's view the adult Mervyn was an admirable and successful man. But it would not be unduly cynical to wonder whether Mervyn might conceivably have done better, even in his own judgment and on his own terms, if at an earlier age he had had more possibilities opened to him. And if that seems a groundless suggestion in relation to this particular individual, may one not legitimately wonder whether for every Mervyn there is not another child whose adult life is severely restricted by the choice he made as a child not to attend any lessons?

However, it must be stressed that these are empirical questions. From the philosophical angle the important question is how one decides at what point children's freedom should be limited, on the assumption that at least sometimes children will not make sensible decisions. What criteria does one use to distinguish between what people should be free to do if they choose to and what they should not be free to do whether they choose to or not? What criteria does Neill have in mind for distinguishing between the child who interferes with his work by playing with his glasses and the child who does the same thing by kicking his door?

Perhaps his most well-known answer to this question is his most inadequate. He refers to a distinction between 'freedom' and 'licence.' "The whole freedom movement is marred and despised because so many advocates of freedom have not got their feet on the ground... It is this distinction between freedom and licence that many parents cannot grasp."[5] But what is the distinction? This we are not told. All that we are given are a few examples (many of which have been quoted above) of either. But this simply means that 'freedom' is being used to refer to acceptable or desirable freedom and 'licence' is being used to refer to unacceptable or undesirable freedom. We are no nearer knowing what it is that makes some freedoms desirable (i.e., *bona fide* freedoms) and others undesirable (i.e., licence). What is the distinction between toilet training, which we should not indulge in according to Neill, and regulating the child's sleeping habits, which we may? Why should the child be free to play with her mother's breakable ornaments and not to jump on her sofa?

The distinction between freedom and licence will not get us far, but Neill's other two answers will, at least in principle. They are respectively that children should be free to do whatever does not interfere with the freedom of others and that they should be free to do anything that does not harm themselves. These answers (similar to Mill's) are comprehensible; they explain most of Neill's examples (e.g., the child should not play on the fire escape, wear no clothes, or have unbarred windows, because of the consideration of avoiding harm to himself. The child should not kick down the study door because that interferes with somebody else's freedom), and, in my view, they are in essence acceptable. But before leaving this topic we have to note two points. The first is that, in the light of these criteria for restricting freedom, some of Neill's examples still appear contradictory. Surely the child who plays with my breakable ornaments, thereby breaking some of them, or who plays with my glasses while I am trying to work, interferes with my freedom no less than the child who kicks my door? The second is the point that, though these criteria are comprehensible, they are not easy to make use of in practice. For the real question is what one regards as constituting harm to the child, and what one regards as interference with the freedom of others. It would not be implausible to argue that children who make a lot of noise, who steal, who throw stones through other people's greenhouse windows, or even babies who are fed only and always when they cry for feeding, are interfering with the freedom of others, and that therefore they should be stopped from doing such things. (I am not suggesting that they necessarily should be. I am merely pointing out the complexities involved in the formula 'free to do what does not interfere with the freedom of others'.) Likewise, an individual does not harm himself only by doing things like falling out of windows. Why should one not argue that the child who is given the freedom to opt out of all lessons, and who does so, may also thereby harm himself in the long run? If we conceive of education as initiating people into worthwhile activities then, almost by definition, the child who opts out of education is harming himself.

Precisely what children should be free to decide for themselves cannot finally be settled without reference to one's overall view of what education is and what it is for, and that is why the matter cannot be satisfactorily concluded in a single chapter. If one believed that education was about filling children with information (and hence believed that it was valuable for the child to acquire such information), one would naturally conclude that it would be to the detriment of the child to opt out of this process. If one believed that it was worthwhile for the child to develop rational powers, one would likewise conclude that the child should not miss the opportunity to cultivate such powers. Conversely, to adopt the view that children should be free to opt out of lessons is implicitly to claim that this cannot harm them in any sense, which is evidently a large claim.

All in all, I conclude that the question of how much freedom of action should be granted to children, while obviously partly dependent on various psychological and sociological findings, should in principle be answered by reference to what we regard as educationally important rather than by reference to a list of putative desirable freedoms. After all, notwithstanding the existence of a few schools, such as Summerhill, which allow the child to opt out of formal study, we have a system of compulsory education, presumably on the grounds that we believe it to be advantageous both to the individual and society that people should be educated.

Academic Freedom

Besides the question of what freedom should be granted to students at various ages, there is the question of what teachers should be free to do and say. I do not intend to say any more about freedom of action on the part of either students or teachers, on the grounds that there is little serious dissension on the matter: it is generally agreed for example that students should not cheat, bully, or lie and that teachers should not humiliate, threaten, or frighten. Of course, there is room for debate on various issues such as whether corporal punishment should be permissible or whether it might occasionally be justifiable for either a student or a teacher to tell a lie, but I shall ignore such questions in favor of pursuing the more controversial question of what freedom the teacher should have when it comes to expressing her views. Although this book is primarily concerned with education in the context of schools, and this is an issue most obviously pertaining to higher education, particularly universities, it nonetheless seems important to consider it. First, if autonomy is agreed to be an educational aim, teachers should themselves have autonomy, which involves them having their own opinions. Secondly, secondary schools do also face some questions about what may reasonably be said in the classroom. And thirdly, since most readers of this book are likely to be university students the question may be of some intrinsic interest to them.

I should add at the outset that it is difficult to talk about the question of whether or to what extent teachers should be free to say things that are variously challenging, upsetting, controversial, or offensive without using examples that may upset some readers. For there is not a lot of point in discussing whether we should or shouldn't be free to say things that nobody minds us saying. So if in what follows I defend the right to say something that the reader finds unpalatable or objectionable, I would ask them to remember that we are not primarily discussing the acceptability or otherwise of that particular example, but rather the question of the extent of academic freedom. I should also make it clear that to defend the right of the teacher to hold and express an unpopular view is not to deny that at all times she should have concern for when, how, and to whom she expresses that view. I may be free to express my belief that a certain convention is absurd, but as a teacher I have a duty to consider the appropriateness of revealing this or the manner in which I convey it to particular students.

Today, while academics unsurprisingly cling tenaciously to the principle of academic freedom, they face a number of challenges. For example, during the acrimonious debate which led to Britain leaving the European Union, Michael Gove, a one-time Secretary of State for Education, notoriously asserted that the British people had "had enough of experts". Such a remark of course represents a frontal assault on the ideas of both truth and academic freedom. If we do not trust in expertise, which is effectively to say that there is no such thing as expertise, then there is no distinction between better and worse, knowledgeable and ignorant, or true and false. (No doubt Gove could claim that what he meant was that the British People no longer believed that *academics*, i.e., scholars and researchers in various fields, should be regarded as experts, and that true expertise was to be found among, say, politicians or Twitter users. I'm not sure that that would be any more convincing, but anyway that is not what he said.) This kind of attack from the outside, essentially suggesting that university scholars and researchers have no particular expertise in their fields, is certainly a serious blow to hopes of gaining knowledge. But perhaps more insidious are the attempts to curtail academic freedom coming from inside the academy itself. University lecturers and professors increasingly face restrictions on their freedom to speak the truth as they see it from such things as calls for 'safe spaces' for students, which sometimes seems to mean that the university should be a place where students are protected from feeling worried, challenged, or offended by ideas; from calls to issue 'trigger warnings', sometimes seeming to mean the provision of advance notice that a given class or lecture may upset some students, so that they can choose to stay away; from the issuing of 'dis-invitations' to visiting speakers whose views are unwelcome to some; and from a more general disapproval of whatever is judged to be 'politically incorrect'.

Of course, as always, whether such things as 'safe spaces' and 'trigger warnings' are good or bad depends heavily on what is meant by the terms, and it must be admitted that not everybody understands the terms in the same way; hence my use of the qualification 'sometimes seems to mean'. So, let me be clear: my concern is with these ideas in the senses given above. If, for example, 'a trigger warning' is simply taken to mean alerting students to the fact that something is coming up that they might find shocking, as we may be warned that a film contains violence and bad language (or indeed as I have effectively done in the second paragraph of this section), then I would regard it as an obvious tactic on the part of a good teacher, except when, as can be the case, there is a deliberate intention to shock students for some pedagogical purpose. It is with any suggestion that students should never be shocked or that teachers should apologize for occasionally shocking students that I take issue. Similarly, if by 'safe space' is meant a place where every person and/or idea should be treated with respect, far from objecting, I would say that this is another aspect of good teaching.[6] My concern is with the idea that we should never cause upset or discomfort, for while I have no wish to promote gratuitous pain, it seems to me self-evident that there are a lot of very unpleasant things that students ought to come face to face with. I have placed the phrase 'politically incorrect' in inverted commas because the notion of political correctness is particularly vague and hence dangerously unhelpful. I take it that what the phrase 'politically correct' means descriptively is 'what is judged to be appropriate by our society (polity)' and that it was initially designed to carry positive overtones. However, it appears that it has subsequently been adopted by critics who use it ironically as if it had negative overtones. To add to the confusion there is the problem that there is no reason to suppose that every particular judgment as to what is politically correct or incorrect is truly the judgment of the *polis* or even of the majority. Rather, they are almost invariably the judgments of advocacy groups. To dislike political correctness, as I do, is thus to object to being told that I must adhere to rules with which I do not agree on the grounds that some group has determined that it is offensive not to do so. To say that it is 'politically incorrect' to make jokes about this or that segment of humanity (e.g., cockneys, short people, tall people, fat people, thin people, working class, upper class, New Yorkers) is to say no more than that you, the speaker, and an unspecified number of other people disapprove. So what, if that is the case? More profitable would be to drop the phrase and provide argument for objecting to the jokes in question.

Taking Offense

It will be noted that the notion of offense is common to all these instances. Whatever word we use, be it 'worry', 'upset', make 'anxious', 'challenge', or 'criticize', the fundamental idea is that we must not cause offense to our students. Now, it is certainly a reasonable aim to avoid offending students (or anybody else) in the sense of gratuitously insulting them or demeaning them, but the concept of offense is rather more complex than that. In the first place there is the question of what exactly constitutes offense. Do I have to feel upset? How upset? Is being irritated by a viewpoint the same thing as being offended by it? And so on. I don't intend to pursue the conceptual question further here, however, since whatever its precise meaning there are strong objections to making offense a criterion for suppressing academic freedom.

At any given time and place there may be certain things that are widely agreed to be offensive, but that is a contingent point. We surely cannot accept that certain views or remarks just are intrinsically offensive, whether people recognize it or not. While one can mount arguments designed to establish that people ought to take offense at, for example, a white supremacist speech, the question of whether it is offensive or not is not amenable to straightforward proof and cannot be claimed as a demonstrated truth. There is no agreed and proven list of offensive matter. The alternative is to suggest that what is or is not offensive is a matter of whether people feel offended. But what causes people to feel offense depends primarily if not entirely upon such factors as who they are (including what they believe as well as their psychological make-up) and the nature of the society in which they live. Besides, and more importantly, the fact that some people feel offended plainly does not establish that they are right to do so. The offensiveness of a viewpoint cannot be equated with the fact that people feel offended. Even if the entire population felt that same-sex marriage was offensive, that would not in itself establish that it was. To put it bluntly, it is possible to take offense when one should not do so. Sometimes this is because one has misunderstood what is said or done, sometimes it is because one is taking the matter more seriously than it deserves, but sometimes it is because careful thought and argument suggest that there is nothing objectionable in what is causing you to take offense. The important conclusion to draw from this in the context of a discussion of academic freedom is that restraints on free speech in educational contexts cannot be justified simply by claiming that some people are offended.

Other Aspects of Academic Freedom

Neither the principle of free speech nor the specific principle of academic freedom of course mean that you can say anything you want, in any way you want, in any situation. As noted at the beginning of this chapter, the person who shouts "fire" in a crowded auditorium where there is no fire and thus causes a fatal stampede is not to be condoned. And nothing in the argument above suggests that people, whether academics or not, should be free to insult, abuse, or ridicule people, though of course here again work needs to be done on what constitutes insult or humiliation, and a *feeling* of having been insulted should not be taken as evidence of insult. Something that an individual regards as insulting is not to be confused with what may reasonably be construed as insulting. It must be admitted that in some particular cases it will be difficult, if not impossible, to agree on whether somebody has good reason to feel humiliated, insulted, or offended. But the fact that some cases cannot be effectively determined does not invalidate the point, which is that feeling offended is not the same thing as having good reason to be offended, and in some cases it is possible to determine whether or not there is good reason.

The principle of academic freedom is not designed to protect rudeness, rants, and ravings, nor in itself to express likes and dislikes such as distaste for Romanies or indifference to pedophilia. Nor is it specifically designed to protect the freedom, say, to use the word 'gypsies' to refer to Romanies if one chooses. It is designed to allow one to *argue* – and that word needs to be stressed; while in practice academic freedom also provides freedom to express views or conclusions, in principle it is designed to protect people attempting to provide reasoning for their position – to argue that, say, Israel is wrong to unilaterally annex disputed territory, that the IQ of African Americans is on average lower than that of other Americans, or that polygamy should not be seen as a crime. (Please note: I am neither endorsing nor repudiating these claims here. I am merely citing them as examples of views that one should be free to advance regardless of them being offensive to some. On IQ, see further Chapter 17.) The main argument of those who attempt to defend practices such as the provision of 'safe spaces' (in the sense of places that guarantee no upset or discomfort) or taboos on certain viewpoints seems to be that social justice or the 'cause' (of, say, eliminating racial or sexual prejudice and discrimination) trumps or outweighs concern for truth. Thus, Billy Bragg claims that young people prize "accountability over free speech", while adding that those such as Margaret Atwood and J.K. Rowling, who defend free speech, are privileged and 'safe', which allows them to worry about 'trifles' like free speech.[7] One consequence of this kind of reasoning is that the academy engages in a great deal of self-censorship. As Janice Turner argues, the 'politically correct' or the merely frightened start using the word 'menstruator' in place of 'woman' and 'birth parent' instead of 'mother'. Similarly, motivated presumably by a fear for their jobs, they fail to challenge absurd arguments such as that, because slugs betray a sexual ambiguity, it follows that in a biological sense the male and female distinction is a false binary. At a more serious level, Turner continues, any criticism of Israel, of the Black Lives Matter movement, of conservative Islam, or the seeking of a humane balance between trans activists' demands and women's rights, becomes taboo (*The Times*, Saturday July 11, 2020).

I'm not sure that I can actually make sense of the claim that a cause should outweigh the truth. How are we to establish a just society without regard to truth and knowledge? If the cause is to be sacrosanct, how do we determine whose cause has legitimacy? But in any case, we are concerned with places of learning, places designed to provide education. I too care about social justice, but the place to take action on behalf of that cause is in political and wider social settings. The university (and high schools too) is supposed to give us a place in which people can reason with and against one another without any restraints beyond common politeness. The basis of the argument for a marketplace of ideas is precisely the point that today's heresy is often tomorrow's orthodoxy, and, even when it isn't, its introduction may contribute to strengthening or confirming today's orthodoxy. It may upset some students to hear professors arguing that transgendered individuals identifying as female are not in fact female, and maybe in the future nobody will hold that view.[8] But right now the point of going to university is to advance one's education, and the process of becoming better educated necessarily involves engaging with this and any other argument that is, if not conclusive, at any rate rationally advanced.

Conclusion

The question of the extent to which older children should be self-determining, that is to say the extent to which they should be free to do as they decide to do, is a complex problem that can only be solved in the light of one's other values and educational objectives, for clearly one would not advocate the right of children to determine to do anything that one regarded as in some way unacceptable. Thus, if one believed that people should show respect for others, one would not approve of children being free to determine to show no respect for anyone. A.S. Neill and a number of other self-styled 'progressive' educators argue for a great deal more freedom for children in schools than is traditional. But Neill does not provide any clear and compelling argument for an answer to the question of how much freedom should be granted. One thing that is clear, however, is that any attempt to suggest that only those who have been self-regulating or self-determining from birth can be truly described as self-determining adults must be rejected, since there is no such thing as a self-determining baby. The notion is a logical nonsense and, it is important to add, in practice not even avowed advocates of self-regulation have any intention of literally doing nothing to regulate the life of the growing child.

But the starting point of this chapter was the suggestion that the overall aim of education should be to produce autonomous adults. That is to say, the claim would no longer be that on a number of issues – such as whether they attend lessons – children should make up their own minds, but that the supremely important thing was to bring children up in such a way that as adults they were self-determining. If people are to act autonomously as adults, then education will need to ensure that as they develop children do not succumb to the control of such things as drugs, drink, and distorted passions. It will also be necessary to ensure that education does not become indoctrination and that children acquire the habit of making their own decisions rather than meekly responding to the dictates of others. But these are only necessary conditions of autonomy. They are not sufficient to ensure that an individual is self-determining, for she can only finally be self-determining if she has the freedom to do what she decides to do. And the question of what freedom she will in fact have as an adult is obviously a social or political question that has nothing to do with education. In that regard we have briefly outlined John Stuart Mill's argument for freedom in relation to self-regarding acts and freedom of expression.

There is finally one consideration that has been ignored throughout this chapter and that is the question of the quality of thinking displayed by the autonomous or self-directing individual. The emphasis has been on people making their own decisions rather than acting out the decisions of others. But if these terms are to be regarded as normative, if we are to regard them as necessarily desirable, we surely have to add that what the self determines shall be reasonable. What is the inherent value in people doing what they choose to do, regardless of what it is that they choose to do? Is it a good thing that I bite the heads of whippets, play video games all day, lie in the sun all day, or devote my life to the making of money, simply because I freely decide to do these things? If self-determination is our ideal, what happens when different individuals determine to behave in mutually exclusive ways? Are there not other considerations that must override or modify the claims of self-determination? Is our only concern, for instance, that the individual's allegiance to a particular political party shall be determined by himself? Is that *all* that matters? Are we not concerned about the reasons that he has for his allegiance?

It was pointed out above that the concept of self-determination has a certain amount in common with the concept of rationality: both put the stress on the individual's decision rather than the decision of others. What this and Chapter 12 have really been about is the distinction between the view on the one hand that what matters is that the individual should ideally do what she chooses to do, and on the other hand the view that ideally she should do what there is good reason to do, or that she should do what she chooses to do but that she should choose with rational understanding. In conclusion I wish to suggest that self-determination is an uninspiring ideal unless it is combined with rationality and that the latter should therefore be written into the concept of autonomy. There is nothing particularly compelling about the ideal of a world in which nobody is answerable to anything or anybody except themselves. Whereas there is something very compelling about the ideal of a world in which people are concerned to be answerable only to the demands of rationality. It is the objective of bringing children to question and to think for themselves, provided that their questioning and thinking should be well-informed and ably performed rather than a matter of idle whim, that we should surely embrace. But, as already indicated, it is unlikely that this objective will be met unless a conscious and deliberate attempt is made by teachers to realize it.

Notes

1 Personal communication.
2 A.S. Neill, *Summerhill* (Penguin, 1968) p. 104. Neill founded Summerhill, a co-educational school for children of all ages, in 1921. It is still going strong.
3 Ibid., p. 111. The examples cited occur, in the main, in the section entitled 'The Free Child'.
4 Ibid., p. 107.
5 Ibid., p. 105.
6 B.J. Bartlett, 'Is "Safety" Dangerous: a Critical Examination of the Classroom as Safe Space', *The Canadian Journal for the Scholarship of Teaching and Learning*, 1 (1), 1–12 (2010) discusses the ambiguity of these concepts and convincingly suggests that we should focus on the idea of classroom civility.
7 Billy Bragg (writing in the *Guardian*, July 10, 2020) states that George Orwell's celebrated quotation "If liberty means anything, it means the right to tell people what they don't want to hear" makes him cringe. But he then reverts to A.S. Neill's discredited attempt to solve the problem of freedom by distinguishing between freedom and licence, claiming that Orwell's remark "is not a defence of liberty; it's a demand for licence and has become a foundational slogan of those who wilfully misconstrue one for the other". But, as we saw with Neill, neither he nor Bragg offer any criteria whereby to correctly construe the difference.
8 I realize that my example of the transgendered person may upset some and shock others. But this is a case where I think a shock may be necessary to establish the point I am making, and, while as always I have no wish to upset, I see no good reason for anyone (including the transgendered) to be upset. Granted that a minority of individuals are born intersex (i.e., with ambiguous genitalia) and that there

is room for argument on the precise criteria that should define an individual's biological sex (e.g., chromosomes, genitals or gonads?), the fact remains that about 99% of individuals are born with the genitalia that would conventionally be ascribed to either the male or female anatomy. And it is simply false to assert that there is no difference between those born with female anatomy in this sense and those who, though born with male anatomy, have transitive surgery, those who are born 'intersex', and/or those who see themselves as female while having male genitalia. What is wrong with describing a transgendered person as such or as a 'transgendered female' if preferred? Please note that I am not demanding that transgendered people refer to themselves as such. They can refer to themselves in any way they wish. I am suggesting that there is no good reason to castigate those who choose not to refer to them in this imprecise and slightly confusing way.

Further Reading

For fuller critical attention to Neill, see Richard Bailey, *A.S. Neill* (Continuum, 2013) and Robin Barrow, *Radical Education* (op. cit.).

On autonomy, see Eamon Callan, *Autonomy and Schooling* (McGill-Queen's University Press, 1993), Christopher Winch, *Education, Autonomy and Critical Thinking* (Routledge, 2006), and Stefaan Cuypers, 'Autonomy in R.S. Peters' Educational Theory', *Journal of Philosophy of Education*, 43 (1), 189–207 (2009).

On the role of universities, see Stefan Collini, *What Are Universities For?* (Penguin, 2012).

On free speech and academic freedom, see Timothy Garton Ash, *Free Speech: Ten Principles for an Interconnected World* (Yale University Press, 2016) and Joanna Williams, *Academic Freedom in an Age of Conformity: Confronting the Fear of Knowledge* (Palgrave Macmillan, 2016). See also Diane Ravitch, *The Language Police* (Alfred A. Knopf, 2003).

William Hare, *Controversies in Teaching* (Wheatsheaf, 1985). R.F. Dearden, 'Controversial Issues and the Curriculum' in *Theory and Practice* (Routledge, 1984), pp. 100–110.

Of particular note is Howard Woodhouse, *Selling Out: Academic Freedom and the Corporate Market* (Montreal, McGill-Queen's University Press, 2009).

Questions

What is the problem with the proposed distinction between licence and freedom?

It is argued that the limits on freedom in the context of school should be set by considerations of educational importance rather than by some predetermined list of putative freedoms. What do you understand by this?

Why cannot one legitimately curb speech simply on the grounds that some people are offended? (Or can one?)

15 Relativism: The Challenge to Reason

Previous chapters have emphasized reason and knowledge as key elements in the educational enterprise. Our selfhood is tied up with our minds; our ideal is individuals who can determine what to do for themselves in the light of good understanding and sound reasoning; education is the development of understanding of powerful and distinctive bodies or types of thought.

The time has now come to consider a potential challenge to this emphasis, which I shall refer to as 'relativism'. I choose that term on the grounds that it is a broad enough term to cover various species of an essentially similar thesis. Sometimes a distinction is drawn between *subjectivism*, or the view that there is nothing beyond *individual* perception, and *relativism*, which emphasizes distinct *cultural* perspective, but what they and other similar views have in common is the assumption that there are no truths given in nature, no facts about the world. In Chapter 10 I discussed *moral relativism*, but here I am concerned with a broader thesis to the effect that there are no objective truths of any kind. Everything is a matter of perception. Nothing simply is the case regardless of what anyone thinks. Everything is a viewpoint. Superficially, this thesis may seem straightforward and plausible, as it is certainly true that none of us can avoid interpreting what we see from our own perspective, referring to both how we are physically situated and what complement of beliefs and values we bring with us. But on closer inspection it seems almost absurd.

For some reason, which I confess I find hard to fathom, there have always been some significant thinkers who preached some form of relativism, in some cases even seeming to deny the value of the reasoning in which they are themselves engaged. As early as the fourth century BC, a Sicilian rhetorician by the name of Gorgias was apparently arguing that nothing exists, if it did exist, it couldn't be known, if it could be known, it couldn't be communicated, and if it could be communicated, it couldn't be understood. Unfortunately, though ancient sources make reference to this work, it has not survived, so we cannot evaluate his argument, and it is possible that the work in question was more of an exercise in rhetoric than a serious thesis. Nonetheless, it clearly shows that the idea that knowledge and truth might not be attainable was in the air. Plato introduces us to the historical figure of Protagoras and attributes

DOI: 10.4324/9781003120476-15

to him the remark that "man is the measure of all things, of the existence of the things that are and the non-existence of the things that are not". It is possible that he meant only that, for example, what seems sweet to one may seem sour to another, which is true enough. But it has generally been taken to imply that all statements about the world are the product of human perception, which is variable, rather than indisputable facts about the world. Montaigne wrote "we have no other criterion of truth... than the form of the opinion... of our own country". And Bishop Berkeley maintained that "to be is to be perceived", although he mitigated the implications of this somewhat by adding that since God constantly perceived the world, all its natural phenomena continued to exist.[1]

Postmodernism

Enough has been said to establish that cries of "fake news" and "alternative facts" are nothing new. When the last edition of this book was published a particular form that relativism took was referred to as 'postmodernism'. And, although postmodernism may be thought by some to have been superseded by other post-something or others, it remains a useful source for brief comment.

The term 'postmodern' is in itself not particularly helpful. It means different things to different people and in many cases it is not entirely clear what it does mean. The word seems to have been introduced in an architectural context in the 1930s, in order to differentiate a new contemporary style from the preceding 'modern' style. A similar attempt was then made to define some literature as postmodern in contrast to the fairly well-established notion of modernity in that field. However, it is evident both that the dates that, broadly speaking, separate modern and postmodern architecture and literature respectively are different, and that the criteria that define postmodern architecture and literature are distinct. Even more confusing is the fact that some contemporary postmodernists claim that the very idea of definable periods or distinct epochs is modernist and therefore incompatible with postmodernism. It comes as no great surprise, then, to find Lyotard defining the term obscurely as "an incredulity towards meta-narratives" or that the *International Encyclopedia of Education* should suggest that "it may be better to see postmodernism as a complex intellectual map of late twentieth-century thought and practice rather than any clear-cut philosophic, political, and/or aesthetic movement". It may indeed be better, in the sense of more accurate, to do this, but it is difficult to see it as better in the sense of any clearer.[2]

The truth of the matter is that the word cannot be defined in a clear and consistent manner, given its history, its use in different contexts, and the opaque nature of the language of most self-styled postmodernists. Despite the signs of orthodoxy among many who share an enthusiasm for the likes of Foucault, Lyotard, and Derrida, there are also signs of schism and heresy, not to mention the large number of people who nowadays almost unthinkingly characterize themselves and their thoughts as postmodern and who may mean almost anything by the claim. We therefore cannot talk of the postmodern agenda or even viewpoint. However, there are a number of claims that, rightly or wrongly, are commonly associated with postmodernism, that, however they are labeled or classified, enjoy quite widespread favor today as features of relativism, and that urgently need to be examined and evaluated. Chief among these are claims relating to truth and knowledge, which, if shown to be correct, would substantially undermine the argument for education presented in this book. As mentioned above, they are also, despite their fashionableness, claims that have been familiar, argued about and for the most part rejected repeatedly throughout the recorded history of Western thought since Plato. We should therefore set aside at the outset any idea to the effect that these claims rest on recent advances or insights in thought.

The claims I have in mind are these: there is no truth; we cannot know anything; everything is as you see it; and what is taken to be knowledge is purely a cultural product. The first point to make is a simple, but devastating, logical one: what would it mean to say that such claims as these are true? If there is no truth, how can these claims be true? If we cannot know anything, how can we know this? Simple as the point is, it is sufficient to awake us to the fact that there is something fundamentally ridiculous about such claims: to get away with credit for perceiving correctly that there is no such thing as being correct would certainly be to have one's cake and eat it too. Nonetheless, I shall proceed to give each claim in turn brief consideration. The reason for doing so, the reason for taking this challenge seriously, empty though I hope to show it to be, is that one should not underestimate the damage that such erroneous beliefs have done, are doing, and may in future do to our chances of making tolerable sense and taking appropriate control of our lives both individually and collectively. The malaise, the anomie, the ennui, the frustration, the anger that many people feel today are at least partly related to the insidious effects of these and similar beliefs; the prevalent lack of commitment and the unwillingness to praise or condemn, the assumption that 'realpolitik' rules the world and nothing can be done about it, and the retreat into materialism and instrumentalism can all, I believe, be traced in part to the effects of the common belief that nobody is in a position to say what is true or false, right or wrong. If the world is increasingly riven between indoctrinated and committed believers on the one hand, and cynical relativists, on the other, as there is a case for saying, it is not hard to see who will lose ground. That is fine, if we really have given up on the ideal of reason, truth, and knowledge. But have we? Should we? As Roger Scruton has written, "even those enlightenment thinkers who distrusted reason, like Hume, and those who tried to circumscribe its powers, like Kant, never relinquished their confidence in rational argument... [Yet] reason is now on the retreat, both as an ideal and as a reality".[3] Consequently, as Wheen points out, then Prime Minister Tony Blair, while ceaselessly asserting his commitment to education, astonishingly defended the teaching of creationism rather than evolution as if it was equally valid.[4] (It is true that the theory of evolution is just that, a theory, and as such not an incontrovertible demonstrated truth, but, unlike creationism, it is a rationally defensible theory.)

Truth

Is there, then, truth? This is not the same question as Pilate's "What is truth?", nor is it the same as "What truths are there?" The question is: is it the case that some things are true and some false (regardless of whether we know what they are)? To this question I respond with a few brief points that cumulatively will, I am confident, lead the reader to reply 'yes'. There are various claims that can be formulated in such a way that something must be true: "Either I am writing this at my desk in Vancouver or I am not" – that statement is itself true and one of the two claims within it must also be true. Even if we incline to the solipsistic view that we and the whole world are merely part of some dream, then the claim that that is so must be true (or false). It is true that nothing can be both a circle and a square at the same time. People occasionally try to argue against such an example, perhaps suggesting that magicians can appear to square the circle or that these claims are somehow simply a function of our language, which could have been different. But such responses invariably miss the point: yes, we can be made to think we are seeing a circle turn into a square or an actual metal circle might be turned into a square, but it cannot be square while remaining circular. Nor is this simply the consequence of our language: nothing that is simply what we happen to call a square could at the same time simply be what we happen to call a circle, and no language could be devised to alter that fact though one might be devised that ignored it, glossed over it, or gave some quite different sense to the utterance "This is a square circle". Not only is it clearly the case that there must be some truths, it is also surely evident that to deny this involves a degree of insincerity and bad faith. For who does (who could) live their life on the genuine presumption that there is no such thing as truth? Our daily life is predicated on the assumption that some things are true and others not; that is why we generally catch the bus on time, don't eat rat poison, and take some exercise. No philosopher who claims that he does not believe in truth is telling the truth.

Can We Know Any Truths?

There is truth: some things are the case, some are not. But how do we know what is the case? May the second claim, "that we cannot know anything", perhaps be true? We should distinguish here between knowing something and knowing that we know something. If we define knowledge in a fairly conventional way as believing something that is true in the light of good reason, then surely we shall readily agree that knowledge is possible and, further, that we actually know some things. As in the case of truth, we certainly act as if this were so, and it is barely conceivable that we should do otherwise: it is because

I know that the bus leaves at 3:10 pm that I am leaving the house now; it is because I know that roads can be dangerous that I worry about my young children running into the road. If one really and sincerely believed that no knowledge could be attained, one would inevitably be reduced to a state of existential angst that would be insupportable. Our lives reveal that we believe knowledge is possible and they also reveal a great deal of what we are confident that we know.

Can We Know That We Know?

But can we ever know that we know? This question really boils down to the question of whether and how one can determine that the reasoning that supports one's true belief is good enough. I may be said to know that the sun will rise tomorrow, because the fact that it has done so every day of my life so far represents pretty good reason to believe it. In fact, of course, it may not rise tomorrow, and strictly speaking I therefore shouldn't claim to know that it will. But for practical purposes, it would be absurd to proceed as if it were unknown either in the way that it is unknown whether a vaccine can be found for a new kind of virus or in the way that it is unknown whether God exists. What about my claim to know that the theory of evolution is correct? This can be called knowledge because the reasoning in support of the theory is generally judged adequate, while, by contrast, any reasoning person (as distinct from one whose belief is based on faith) can see that creationism, though it could conceivably be true, is supported by no evidence and rendered implausible by other evidence. But it is of course the case that the theory of evolution (at least as currently understood) could be proved wrong (though only by the acquisition of further knowledge of the truth, it should be noted). It could be, in other words, that what is taken to be 'good reason' to support the belief turns out not to be. Do such examples imply that we cannot ever know that we know? No; they illustrate the fact that many of our claims to knowledge should be recognized as *provisional* – it is not that we necessarily don't know, but that we sometimes are proven to be mistaken. In any case, not all knowledge claims are provisional in this way: some are necessary truths or truths that are logically unassailable. We not only know that all triangles have angles that add up to 180°, but we also know that we know. Similarly, we know that we know that it is true that if all men are mortal and Socrates is a man, then Socrates is mortal.

In practice, once the point is conceded that some knowledge is in principle possible and that there are some things that in sincerity we must acknowledge that we know that we know, the issue becomes one of distinguishing between knowledge claims that we have absolutely no reason to deny and others where we can only be cautious and provisional. In the field of medicine, for example, it is entirely appropriate to say that we know how to set a broken leg or that we know that aspirin, under certain specifiable conditions, reduces the likelihood of strokes, but it would be inappropriate to say that we know that a particular adult's insecurities stem from his toilet training.

Conclusion

In defending the idea that there is both truth and knowledge, there is no need to ignore some of the truth that is embedded in the argument of those who would deny it. It is true that different people perceive things differently. It is true that some of what we regard as true is so only because our culture made it so. It is true that some things are purely matters of individual opinion. It is true that our understanding develops over time (and sometimes regresses). Certainly, there are distinctions such that different degrees of certainty are appropriate to different subject matters, as Aristotle noted long ago.[5] That was part of the reasoning behind the argument concerning forms of knowledge: we can be more certain that we know that $2 + 2 = 4$ or that metals expand when heated than we can that God exists. As was noted in Chapter 7, it is not as clear and uncontentious what the appropriate way to test the latter proposition is, or indeed whether it *can* be tested. But even in the spheres of religion or morality, the difficulty of being sure that we know should not lead us to assume that there is no truth of any kind and therefore nothing to be known – only individual opinion. It is, for example, as obviously true that it is false to say that ugliness is morally wrong as it is to say that $2 + 2 = 5$. Morality is about issues such as honesty and integrity and not about ugliness, and that is a fact.

The important conclusion is that it is not true that everything is as you see it. There are truths and falsehoods, correct and incorrect claims, and it is incumbent on us to use our reason to increase our understanding. The postmodernism of writers such as Lyotard confuses epistemological questions (questions about the nature of knowledge) with sociological questions: there are indeed ways in which what is taken to be knowledge is affected by such things as who has power, the nature of society, and the time and place in which we live, as he maintains. But what may have some influence on some of what we think we know is one thing (and even on a sociological level many relativists exaggerate the degree and extent of such influence). What knowledge is possible and what we do actually know are quite another thing. The essential point of education is to provide individuals with the understanding to make their own rational judgment as to what is known and what is not.

If the extreme relativistic claims considered here were true, it would have serious consequences for education. If everything is how the individual or a given society sees it and anything goes, then how does one begin to construct a coherent curriculum or a persuasive argument for any particular approach to schooling and teaching? How does one make any judgments in a world that denies distinctions of credibility or worth? It may be a bad thing to be too 'judgmental' in the sense of too 'inclined to pass judgments on others', but it is essential to our very way of life to

make some judgments, if only between the edible and the poisonous. Fortunately, the relativist challenge as interpreted here clearly fails.

Notes

1 Gorgias' essay 'On Nature or Non-existence' is referred to by Sextus Empiricus
   in his essay 'Against the Philosophers'. Plato wrote a dialogue involving and
   named after Gorgias. Protagoras' remark is quoted in Plato's dialogue, *Theae-
   tetus*, 152 a. The Montaigne quotation is taken from his essay 'On Cannibals'.
   For Berkeley, see *Principles of Human Knowledge*.
       I cannot resist adding here reference to two limericks that Berkeley's claim gave
   rise to. The first was penned by the theologian and humorist Ronald Knox:

>   There once was a man who said "God
>   Must think it exceedingly odd,
>   If he finds that this tree
>   Continues to be
>   When there's no one about in the Quad."

   To which an unknown author responded:

>   Dear Sir,
>   Your astonishment's odd.
>   I am always about in the Quad.
>   And that's why the tree
>   Will continue to be
>   Since observed by
>   Yours faithfully, God.

2 See Jean-Francois Lyotard, *The Postmodern Condition* (University of Minnesota,
   1994), p. xxiv and *The International Encyclopedia of Education* (Pergamon, 1994).
3 Roger Scruton, 'Whatever Happened to Reason?' *City Journal*, 9 (2).
4 Francis Wheen, *How Mumbo-Jumbo Conquered the World* (Fourth Estate, 2004).
5 Aristotle, *Nicomachean Ethics*, 1.iii (1094 b).

Further Reading

The arguments about truth and knowledge considered in this chapter are as old as philosophy itself; one of the most finely balanced is John Searle, *The Construction of Social
Reality* (Allen Lane, 1995). See also Simon Blackburn, *Truth: A Guide* (Oxford University Press, 2005) and Daniel C. Dennett, *Freedom Evolves* (Viking, 2003).

Christopher Butler, *Postmodernism* (Oxford University Press, 2002) is a clear and
concise introduction. See further, Robin Barrow, 'The Need for Philosophical
Analysis in a Postmodern Era', *Interchange*, 30 (4) (1999), and M. Bonnett, 'After
Postmodernism: Returning to the Real' and K. Kester, 'Postmodernism in Post-
truth Times', both in *Educational Philosophy and Theory: Special Issue: What
Comes after Postmodernism?* 50 (14) (2018).

Those not familiar with their writings might refer to Jean-Francois Lyotard, *The
Postmodern Condition* (University of Minnesota, 1994), and Lyn Fendler, *Michel
Foucault* (Continuum, 2010).

Not to be missed is Alan Sokel & Jean Briermont, *Intellectual Imposters* (Profile, 1998), in which the authors tell the story of how they successfully submitted an article made up of a random selection of incomprehensible quotations from various postmodern articles to a postmodern journal. Mary Lefkowitz, *History Lesson: A Race Odyssey* (Yale University Press, 2008) is a sobering and sad account of the forces of political correctness in general and postmodernism in particular attempting to silence the pursuit of truth.

Questions

In what respects and in what sense is it true to say that truth is relative?

In what sense if any is knowledge possible?

16 Creativity

Over fifty years ago, the Plowden report argued that the primary school should lay special stress "on discovery, on first-hand experience, and on opportunities for creative work".[1] Following that, it was not uncommon to see advertisements for college of education lecturers inviting applicants whose teaching "would offer those taught opportunities for creative activity". Despite the blatant overworking of the term, and consequent attempts by philosophers to elucidate and pin down a variety of distinct species of creativity, it is still frequently encountered and it still, more often than not, has no clear or precise meaning. Richard Florida's *The Rise of the Creative Class*, for instance, is widely and approvingly quoted, despite severe criticism of its failure to adequately define 'creativity' so that Florida appears to regard his house cleaners as being no less creative than Michelangelo. Giftedness, itself one of the most confused concepts to have emerged in educational discourse, is often taken to incorporate creativity. Similarly, research into effective teaching will often refer to students' creativity as an index of success. But in neither of these cases is there a serious attempt to analyze the concept. Instead, uncritical reliance is placed on some standard creativity test.

Creativity tests, of which examples are the invitation to think of uses for a brick or to fill in circles in such a way as to produce pictures of some kind, are among the more embarrassing of educational absurdities. If all that is required is that the student lists some uses (e.g., to build a wall) or fill in a circle (e.g., draw a smiling face), then 'create' means no more than 'produce'. If it is assumed that the more creative students are those who think of more uses or fill in more circles, then we are simply equating creativity with the number of responses a person comes up with, and if we factor in speed of response we are simply saying that creative people are those who come up with a lot of ideas very quickly. The trouble is that this is not what we mean when we refer to creative giants such as Einstein, Beethoven, Rembrandt, or Shakespeare, or any of today's leading creative figures in technology, art, science, skating, film, or anything else. Creative people do not necessarily proceed with great speed and they are not always particularly productive in terms of quantity. More to the point from an educational perspective, why should we think it important or valuable to

DOI: 10.4324/9781003120476-16

rapidly produce a lot of responses in relation to trivial exercises such as thinking of uses for a brick? If performing well on tests such as these is what is meant by 'being creative' then creativity does not appear to be a matter of any great concern. Similarly, in what sense of 'creative' would it be true to say, as Lytton does, that "we cannot... deny the epithet 'creative' to the five-year-old child who produces a picture of square cows and peopled with round-bellied neckless mums and dads"?[2] Surely the sense of 'creative' here bears little relation to its meaning in the suggestion that Harold Pinter was a creative playwright or James Watson and Francis Crick creative scientists.

One's Own Work

Our concern must be with the normative use of the term, which is to say with a sense of 'creativity' that is taken to be desirable by definition. No one would champion creativity unless they assumed that creativity was valuable in some respect. Clearly the mere business of making something, without any reference to what is made or produced, how it is made or why it is made, is not necessarily valuable. The normative sense of 'creative' must therefore have certain other conditions written into it besides the mere condition of producing. What are these further conditions?

One fairly obvious condition is that what the creative person produces should be her own. In one sense, of course, anything that anybody produces is their own. If I offer an opinion it is my opinion. If I write a book it is my book. But what is meant here is that whatever is produced must be the agent's own in the sense that it is the outcome of her reasoning, planning, or working out: it must represent her way of looking at whatever it is she produces. What a creative person produces cannot simply be a copy, an imitation, or a representation of somebody else's work. To be a creative thinker I must do my own thinking and not simply parrot the thinking of others. It follows from this, incidentally, that a skilled craftsman, whose sole concern is to make reproductions of antique furniture, cannot be called creative. Such a person may be highly skilled and deserving of great admiration. One may feel that those forgers who have reproduced the paintings of great masters, sometimes even reproducing their techniques as well as their products, deserve greater credit as painters than they have usually received. But they are not *creative* artists.

But these two conditions alone (that one should produce and that it should be one's own) are still not sufficient to characterize a creative person. If they were, then all novelists, all architects, all hairdressers, all scientists, and all painters, provided that they worked with some understanding of what they were doing so that their products were the outcome of their way of looking at things, would be creative. But if virtually everybody is by definition creative the term ceases to pick out anything of significance.

Originality

A third necessary condition, I suggest, is that what one produces should be original in the sense that it breaks new ground. Thus, Einstein would not be regarded as a creative scientist if, besides the theories that he produced being his own, they were not also theories that broke new ground. Originality sometimes involves a break with traditional ways of proceeding in a given sphere. Thus, the Impressionist school may be said to have evolved a new approach to painting as well as producing original paintings, Wagner may be said to have conceived a new kind of opera or music-drama, and non-Euclidean geometry may be said to have involved a new kind of mathematics. But originality of form or technique in this sense is not a necessary condition of creativity. If it were, composers such as Mozart and Haydn, novelists such as Dickens, and painters such as Constable could not be called creative. The originality of a creative individual, though it may include pioneering techniques, may reside simply in the product.

The distinctive element that makes a work original may be very slight in terms of the measure of difference between it and other works. For instance, a creative photographer may concentrate on often photographed and familiar scenes, and the originality of her work may depend entirely on the angle from which she takes her shots. Or a composer may produce a piece of music that substantially consists of quotations from other composers: the originality in this case may lie entirely in the selection, arrangement, or juxtaposition of the quotations. But however slight the difference, originality is one crucial factor in a creative work.

Intention

Could a person be creative by accident, or should we add intention as a fourth criterion of creative activity? (The intention referred to is the 'intention to produce a particular work', and not the 'intention to produce creative work'; one cannot legitimately include the term that one wishes to define – in this case creativity – in the definition.) This question has become of particular interest now that some believe that computers might be programmed to produce works such as Virgil's *Aeneid*, or that given enough time monkeys provided with keyboards might bash out works that *prima facie* stand as works of art, and with the knowledge that many works of art exhibited in recent years, particularly in the sphere of painting, are produced at least partially by random means (e.g., simply upsetting various tins of paint on a canvas).

We have to distinguish here between a creative person and creative work. We perhaps tend to think that the two are inseparable: creative work is the work of creative people and creative people produce creative work. But the existence of computers and keyboards, which provide the means for monkeys to write, raises the possibility of creative work that is not the product of creative beings. If, then, a computer or a monkey could produce a work that was comparable with a

Shakespeare play there seems no reason why we should not call it a creative work. But it would nonetheless seem very odd to describe the monkey or the computer as creative, except in the purely descriptive sense of productive. The condition that a creative person should produce work that is his own already implies that a creative person must be conscious of what he is doing. For if an argument, a theory, a play, or a painting is really my own, this is to say that it is a genuine product of my way of looking at things, and my way of looking at things presupposes consciousness. Monkeys and computers do not have their ways of looking at things, they do not produce their work in response to a conscious process, their work cannot be their own in the sense intended, and therefore they cannot be creative.

To say that a creative person must be conscious of what she is doing is not to say that if Shakespeare was creative then he must have intended to write *Hamlet* in the way that *Hamlet* turned out. It is to say that *Hamlet* must have arisen as the result of a deliberate intention to produce a play on a certain broad theme. As far as this condition goes, therefore, there is no reason to deny that the painter who deliberately drops tins of paint at random onto a canvas is creative. The painting that results is not a painting designed and planned in the manner that the *Mona Lisa* was planned. But it is a painting that is the outcome of a deliberate plan nonetheless. Had the painter accidentally spilt his paint then the case would be different – the product might be regarded as a creative work, but the artist could not claim to be a creative artist on the strength of this accidental product.

There is another reason why we should hesitate to call monkeys creative. To call somebody creative is to attribute a tendency. One can imagine a situation in which one would describe somebody as creative on the strength of one work – 'Did James really write this? I had no idea he was creative' – but nonetheless the implication of calling someone creative is that he is more than a one-shot artist. Shakespeare differs from the monkey not only in that he had some idea of what he was doing, but also in that whereas with the monkey we await the possibility that given time random tapping of the keyboard will produce a coherent work, with Shakespeare, precisely because he did know what he was doing, we may expect all of his attempts at play-writing to result in plays. I have already suggested that we should not tie creativity directly to output. We cannot say that the more one produces the more creative one is. Haydn composed more than Brahms, but that does not in itself make him more creative. Some creative people have in fact produced very little. Nonetheless we should generally expect a creative person to give evidence of her creativity consistently. The fact that on one occasion I produce an original thought that is my own does not make me a creative thinker if every other thought that I produce is unoriginal.

Quality

We thus arrive at the view that a creative person in any sphere is one who tends to produce original work that represents their own way of looking at things in that sphere. The obvious and crucial question now arises of whether we have to add some reference to the *quality* of the work produced. If we do not add reference to quality as another condition of creativity, certain consequences have to be accepted. First, virtually anybody who had a spark of independence could be said to be creative. The very fact that I know very little about painting, with the result that any daub I produce on a canvas is very much my own, would paradoxically make me a creative painter. The mere fact of my sitting down to write a novel would turn me into a creative novelist. For what I wrote would be a product that was my own and was original in some degree; it would be consciously produced and there need be no problem about tendency, since presumably I could then write another novel. This consequence, I suggest, is quite unacceptable. I do not know how to paint, my novels have no merit whatsoever: I am neither a creative painter nor a creative novelist.

Secondly, though obviously related to the first point, if any distinctive product consciously produced is evidence of creativity then the assumption from which we started – that it is desirable that people should be creative – is thrown open to question. It is one thing to say that it is desirable to produce creative writers and scientists if we have in mind examples such as Shakespeare and Einstein (examples which carry the implication of quality), quite another if we have in mind virtually anybody who puts pen to paper or has an idea. The only way in which one could defend the thesis that creativity without reference to standards or quality was a normative concept or a desirable quality would be to argue that the mere fact that somebody produces something original is a praiseworthy feature of that individual. The reader must decide whether a scientist who produces a theory that is absurd but original (because nobody else would countenance such absurdity) is to be praised on that account, whether an artist who produces a smashed pane of glass, smashed in a subtly distinctive way, is therefore to be admired, or whether a photographer who takes a series of photographs without removing the cover from the camera lens is on that account alone to be revered. I suggest that none of these people are necessarily to be admired, and that therefore either we cannot necessarily attribute creativity to them, or else 'creative' must be understood as a purely descriptive value-free term, and it is a separate question as to whether we wish to promote such creativity.

Thirdly, if we do not write into the concept of creativity some reference to quality, then the word is in fact redundant. All novelists would be creative, since no two novelists have ever written the same book and no novelists have ever written books that are not their own work. All people who thought at all would have a claim to be creative thinkers, since no two people think exactly alike; every individual, by the mere fact of being a unique personality, is in some respect a distinctive or original thinker. If the word 'creative' were redundant, it would make no sense to talk of promoting creativity. The demand for creative persons would simply be a demand for novelists, scientists, mathematicians, and so on.

We therefore have to add as another necessary condition of being creative that the individual should produce good work. But this raises the question of what the criteria are for good work. In the sphere of science and mathematics this is not a great problem: a creative scientist is one who makes genuine advances in knowledge. One can judge that the Russian scientists who produced the first rocket to orbit space (the sputnik) were creative because, to put it crudely, the rocket worked. But in the sphere of art, for example, assessing creativity will involve reference to aesthetic criteria, which are notoriously difficult to assess. This is why in the example of the photographer who does not remove her lens cover I had to write that she was not 'necessarily' creative. My point there was that the fact that she was being original would not alone make her creative. But some people might accept that, and go on to argue that she was nonetheless creative because her blank photographs were works of art. If that seems preposterous to some readers one has only to think of John Cage's *4'33"*, heralded by many as an artistic work of quality, which consists of a pianist sitting at a piano with the lid down over the keys and playing not a note. The point to be stressed is that given that there are some standards, that there is a distinction between good art and bad art, then the mere fact that I produce a color pattern that nobody else has done does not make me creative: the pattern must have some quality; it must come up to certain standards. (On aesthetic standards, see Chapter 18.)

Creativity and Education

If the analysis of creativity given above is acceptable, then certain things follow. The first point is that one part of what it means to be a creative artist, scientist, or whatever, is that one is a good artist, a good scientist, or whatever. The converse of course is not true: I may be a good mathematician without being a creative one, because I may not produce any original work in mathematics. But if I am a creative mathematician then I shall both produce original work and work that is good work according to the standards of mathematics. It follows from this that in order to assess whether a person is a creative scientist we shall need to refer to different criteria than those that we shall need to refer to assess whether she is a creative photographer. Math, science, novel writing, photography, and so on are distinct activities and to be good at any one of them requires distinct talents and reference to distinct standards and ways of proceeding. And it follows from this that there is no necessary reason why an individual who is creative in one respect or sphere should be creative in any other. It therefore does not make much sense to refer to one individual simply as creative or more creative than another. When we do pick out an individual such as Leonardo da Vinci as especially creative, we mean that he showed himself to be creative in many spheres. Da Vinci was not more creative than Beethoven as one might say he was more good-tempered. He was creative in more spheres.

How do these points affect the stress on creativity in education? Before going any further we may as well face the fact that despite the impression one may get from some educational writings, virtually nothing is known about what as a matter of empirical fact produces creative people in various spheres. That is to say, virtually nothing is known about how one may best hope to produce a Shakespeare or a Stephen Poliakoff, a Mozart or a Poulenc, a Darwin or an Einstein. It well may be that such people are born and not made at all. There is a certain amount of plausibility in the idea that where children are given a certain amount of scope for free expression in any sphere, they may grow up less restricted in their work in that sphere than those who are not given such freedom. But it should now be clear that that is not really to say anything about creativity. One is hardly surprised at the suggestion that those who are brought up to express themselves freely in paint or to take a delight in problem-solving should tend, as adults, to feel free to express themselves in paint and enjoy problem-solving. But the questions still remain as to how important these things are, as to whether there are not other things equally important even in the sphere of painting, and as to whether such children can be called creative. To express oneself is not to be creative, despite the fact that to be creative involves among other things expressing oneself. To solve problems seems an admirable thing to do, but practice in solving problems in school does not automatically mean that one will be skilled at solving problems as an adult (see Chapter 13 on the generic fallacy).

If our intention is to promote creativity then clearly we have to meet the following requirements: (i) We have to avoid instilling in children the idea that everything is known and determined, and that they cannot follow their own distinctive way of looking at things; (ii) We have to promote a disposition towards ingenuity and imagination so that individuals are eager to make the imaginative leaps necessary for breaking new ground; (iii) We have to produce ability and understanding in any given sphere, for without these how, except by chance, is the individual going to be a good scientist, artist, or whatever; how is she going to display the excellence that is a part of creativity?

Creativity and the Arts

Once these considerations are spelt out one immediately has grave doubts about a lot of so-called creative activity in schools, for it neither is creative nor is there any reason to suppose that in isolation it will promote creativity. There is absolutely no evidence, for instance, to support the suggestion that young children who come up with unexpected uses for a brick (e. g., use it as a bed warmer) or fill in a lot of circles in intriguing ways will be more likely than others to end up as creative in any field, be it business, science, technology, art, or parenting. And what could be meant by a 'creativity hour' or a lesson simply entitled 'creative activity'? As we have seen, it does not make sense to talk of creativity in a vacuum: individuals can only display creativity in particular spheres of activity. The idea of children being creative, as opposed to having a creative math lesson or a creative writing lesson and so on, is a simple nonsense. It is also worth raising the question of why there is so much emphasis on producing creative artists. Creative scientists have an obvious utilitarian value, but why do we need to be so concerned about producing creative artists? Surely, by definition they should be few and far between, and one might almost say that they must arise of their own volition and impetus rather than be produced by the educational system.

What are we to say in respect of artistic creativity when, for example, Anderson remarks that "the creative environment must provide freedom for each person to respond truthfully with his whole person as he sees and understands the truth"?[3] Clearly the reply must be that this is indeed one thing that the creative environment must provide, but it is not all that it must provide. If children are simply given access to the materials for painting and left to respond truthfully with their whole person (the very idea of which, incidentally, I find perplexing in reference to young children: does not a truthful response involve the idea of considerable self-awareness?), they are not necessarily being creative. What is happening in such a situation is that the first of the three requirements outlined above is being met: the children are being encouraged to paint as they feel inclined and not in response to the instructions of others. It is possible that they are being imaginative and that therefore the second requirement is being met, although it is not at all clear how one best promotes ingenuity and imagination. But it is the requirement of ability and understanding that is all-important and that requirement is not being met at all. How are children expected to become creative artists if they are brought up under the impression that anything they do with their heart in it is creative? How does one expect to produce a creative composer or painter if one does not teach the child how to compose and how to paint and if one does not familiarize her with what has already been done in those fields and with what at the present time counts as music or painting?

Creative Writing

Much the same may be said of 'creative writing'. In so far as an emphasis on creative writing means that there is a case for suggesting that repeated corrections of stories on the grounds that they are mispunctuated or misspelt may stunt the child's enthusiasm and spontaneity, the claim has some plausibility. But it is not true that any spontaneous writing is creative writing, and it therefore does not follow that a systematic acceptance of anything the child writes promotes creativity. It is no doubt true that spelling and the accepted rules of grammar do not generally have much to do with being creative. It is probably also true that some creative artists have not been particularly gifted as spellers and grammarians. It is certainly true that some creative writers, such as James Joyce, have deliberately abandoned conventional rules of grammar and spelling to a large extent. But Joyce proceeds as he does in order to make a point and he could not do this without full awareness of the rules that he chooses to flout. And it is equally true that many creative artists have emerged from a schooling that taught them to spell and punctuate, that much creative work has been written according to such rules, and that there is a limit beyond which not even a Joyce can go if his work is to be read by others. Certainly if one wants to produce creative writers one does not want to curb their spontaneity. All that is being said here is that it is not in fact clear that concern with such things as spelling and grammar need curb spontaneity, that, more importantly, spontaneity alone does not produce creative writing, and that treating a child's writing uncritically and undiscriminatingly as creative cannot help to promote creativity in that child. To become a creative writer she needs to acquire skills, understanding of other creative works, and familiarity with what has been written. She needs knowledge and critical standards, neither of which are promoted by creative writing lessons understood as spontaneous writing lessons. The only way out of this impasse is to argue, as Britton has done, that the definition of literature is a piece of writing that is written for its own sake and involves the writer in reflecting on his own past experience.[4] If that is what literature is, then children may be said to be writing literature. The reply to this is that this is not what most of us mean by literature, but that if we accept the definition it becomes, as White has pointed out, an open question as to whether there is necessarily any value in people writing literature.[5]

Math and Science

Even more obviously, if we wish to produce creative mathematicians or scientists, it is insufficient simply to leave children to proceed as they see fit. What usually seems to be meant by creative math lessons are lessons in which the child is encouraged to discover solutions for himself from certain data rather than being simply given the answers. There may be good grounds for advocating this discovery method (see Chapter 4), but the fact remains that such a procedure does not mean that the child is being a creative mathematician, that such a procedure alone cannot produce creative mathematicians, and that, for what it is worth, creative mathematicians can, as they have done throughout history, arise without having had the benefit of such teaching methods. The situation is quite simple: to be a creative mathematician is to be a good mathematician and to have the ability and the originality to go beyond the current bounds of mathematical knowledge. If all we wanted from math lessons was a host of creative mathematicians, it would still be an open empirical question as to how much one needed to instill mathematical knowledge and to what extent one could do this without stunting the originality and questing frame of mind that are also necessary for creativity.

To be creative in any specific sphere demands knowledge and under-standing of that sphere. Any education that ignores this point is not making a realistic effort to promote creativity. Originality is also a necessity and it may be that discovery techniques and problem-solving activity will sharpen the tendency towards originality, or at least avoid the stultifying effect that traditional inculcation of information may have. All that can be said here is that these are empirical points and there is not as yet any convincing evidence that such teaching techniques make a material difference in terms of producing creative scientists. Such techniques may of course be advocated for reasons that have nothing to do with creativity (e.g., that the child understands better what she sees for herself, that her interest is sustained, that she thinks for herself) but that is a separate question.

Self-expression

Self-expression is a necessary condition of creativity and therefore if creativity is our goal self-expression must play a part. But, since it is not a sufficient condition, it cannot be our sole consideration and since it is unrealistic to pretend that we even want all our children to be creative writers, let alone that they will be, we have to ask whether the emphasis on self-expression can be justified without reference to creativity. Presumably it may be defended to some extent on therapeutic or psychological grounds. That is to say it would not be implausible to suggest that some opportunity for self-expression without reference to critical standards may be valuable in that it provides relaxation and promotes self-confidence in children. Further than this, it may lead children to reveal more of their inner-self, which may have psychological value. For example, a child with a troubled home background might derive some benefit from writing freely about this. But clearly not all children are in need of such therapy and even for those who are, there are other things to be done in schools besides provide it. If all writing lessons become exercises in self-expression they cease to provide relaxation, and if all writing is self-expression only it ceases to promote self-confidence. For why should being able to do what anybody can do promote self-confidence?

The conclusion that seems inescapable is that self-expression in the artistic sphere has a part to play both because it can be educationally valuable and because it is one necessary part of artistic creativity. But self-expression alone is not sufficient to warrant talk of creativity. Finally, then, what can be said of the five-year-old child who produces "an image of the world as he sees it, littered with square cows and peopled with round-bel-lied, neckless mums and dads".[6] Lytton, it will be remembered, claims that we cannot deny the epithet 'creative' to such a child. Now certainly Lytton may use the term in such a way that it makes sense to regard the child as 'creative', which is precisely what he does. For him, the term can be understood to indicate that someone has had a subjective feeling of 'effective surprise' in producing a work, and therefore the child may have been creative. As against this proposed definition it may be pointed out that (i) it is a strange use of the term: when people call Shakespeare a creative writer they simply do *not mean* that he had a feeling of effective surprise when he wrote *King Lear*; (ii) it is not really a definition that serves any useful purpose, since the notion of effective surprise is at least as obscure as creativity itself (What *counts* as effective surprise?); (iii) little use could be made of such a definition, since it is entirely unclear how the teacher is supposed to know whether the child has indeed experienced effective surprise; (iv) and, above all, if this is what creativity is taken to involve, it is difficult to see why one should regard it as valuable.

It is difficult to avoid the conclusion that Lytton has offered us a *persuasive definition* of the term. That is to say, conscious of the fact that creativity has overtones of desirability for most of us, he has defined it in terms of what he thinks desirable. But there seems no obvious reason to agree with his judgment that this sense of 'creativity' is in itself desirable, and there are many reasons such as those outlined in this chapter for claiming that to feel effective surprise is not in itself to be creative.

Notes

1 Lady Plowden, 1967, vol. 1, p. 187.
2 Hugh Lytton, *Creativity and Education* (Routledge & Kegan Paul, 1971) p. 3.
3 H.H. Anderson, 'Creativity in Perspective' in H.H. Anderson (ed.), *Creativity and its Cultivation* (Harper, 1959) p. 253.
4 James Britton, 'Literature' in *The Arts and Current Tendencies in Education* (University of London Institute of Education, 1963) p. 42.
5 J.P. White, 'Creativity and Education' in R.F. Dearden, P.H. Hirst, & R.S. Peters (eds.), *Education and the Development of Reason* (Routledge & Kegan Paul, 1972).
6 See note 2 above.

Further Reading

Richard Florida, *The Rise of the Creative Class* (Basic Books, 2014).

For a general survey of creativity tests from the psychologist's point of view see Hugh Lytton, *Creativity and Education* (Routledge & Kegan Paul, 1971).

For philosophical approaches to the concept see R.K. Elliot, 'Versions of Creativity' in *Philosophy of Education Society of Great Britain, Annual Proceedings*, July 1971 Vol. V.2, and Sharon Bailin's lucid *Achieving Extraordinary Ends* (Kluwer, 1988).

See further, Michael Beaney, *Imagination and Creativity* (Open University Press. 2005), and Berys Gaut & Matthew Kieran (eds.), *Routledge Handbook on Creativity and Philosophy* (Routledge, 2018).

Questions

What are the criteria that define creativity according to the text? Do you agree that they are both necessary and sufficient?

Why might one argue that creative artists should arise of their own accord and that schools should not attempt to produce them?

Would you regard a prominent pop star or popular novelist as creative in the same sense as a famous classical composer or 'literary' novelist?

17 Multiculturalism and Racism

Two Senses of Culture

There are two distinct uses of the word 'culture', failure to distinguish which leads to considerable confusion. Generally when one refers to various cultures within a society, and often even when one refers to the culture of a society, one is using the word as an anthropologist or sociologist would. This is quite distinct from use of the word to refer to works of art or works of a high aesthetic standard. This latter sense is what the poet T.S. Eliot referred to more specifically as 'high culture', and in what follows I will refer to it as Culture with a capital 'C' in order to keep the distinction clear.

When the anthropologist refers to the culture of a society or the sub-culture of a group within society, she means to pick out or identify a way of life or a code of living that is distinctive of that society or group. Thus, she can talk of the Inuit culture, meaning simply to refer to the behavioral customs, the manners, the interests, and so on, of the Inuit. Likewise, she can contrast an aboriginal culture with that of a 'settler' society, or pick out the distinctive features of the way of life of a commune and refer to it as the commune culture.

In theory this use of 'culture' is purely descriptive; it contains no implications about the value or otherwise of any culture referred to. Furthermore, there is no particular stress on the sphere of art. In the anthropological sense of the term we may say that it is a feature of our culture that men generally wear trousers, that there is a monogamous institution of marriage, that pubs usually have dart boards, and so on.

When we talk of Culture (i.e., in the aesthetic sense) we are not simply using the word in a neutral descriptive way. Culture (with a capital C) is a normative notion. Culture in this sense, though we may disagree as to what constitutes it, is by definition presumed to be desirable.

The adjective 'cultured' is almost always used in the aesthetic sense. An individual is not regarded as cultured simply because she belongs to a group with an identifiable culture in the anthropological sense. The sociologist may inquire into the culture of the Hell's Angels, and he may tell us what it involves, but we do not therefore conclude that members of the group are necessarily cultured people. A cultured person is not simply a person who

DOI: 10.4324/9781003120476-17

abides by some identifiable code of living. Only a particular kind of code of living, a particular kind of way of life, will count as a cultured way of life in the non-sociological sense. And one aspect of the cultured individual's way of life, at least, must have some reference to the sphere of art. A woman who has absolutely no interest in and no knowledge of any kind of artistic endeavor may be a number of admirable things, but she is not a serious contender for the title of 'cultured'. In the same way, whereas initiation into the culture of a society in the anthropological sense means initiation into the way of life of that community, initiation into its Culture must involve introduction to what are regarded as works or practices of some artistic value.

In the remainder of this chapter, I shall be concerned with the socio-logical or anthropological sense of culture, while questions relating to the aesthetic sense will be examined in the following chapter.

Multiculturalism

With regard to the anthropological sense of culture one contemporary issue is of particular interest, and that is *multiculturalism*. Most Western societies nowadays are distinctly multicultural in that, thanks to widespread colonisa-tion and immigration, the population consists of many different ethnic groups, each bringing with it its own culture and very often a number of fur-ther sub-cultures within it. Generally speaking (although there are dissenting voices) this multiculturalism is welcomed and celebrated. The idea is that we should not simply tolerate or accept difference, but that we should embrace it. It is regarded as self-evident that cultural diversity is in itself a good.

I should make it clear at the outset that I do not in any way wish to object to or denigrate the idea or the actuality of a multicultural society. But I do wish to suggest that the idea that multiculturalism is inherently valuable is questionable, and that there are problems with the simplistic view that diversity is to be celebrated for its own sake.

Different cultures may indeed often be equally valuable in their own way, but it is not the case that all cultures are *necessarily equally* admir-able, and indeed some cultures, such as perhaps the culture of Nero's Rome, Pol Pot's Cambodia, or Kim Jong Un's North Korea, and some cultural beliefs and practices, such as slavery, honor-killings, female cir-cumcision, and the activities of the Ku Klux Klan, may quite coherently be condemned as bad. Whether these judgments can be said to have *objective* validity depends on one's view of whether and to what extent moral *knowledge* as distinct from *belief* is possible (see Chapter 10). But even if we take the view that moral values are relative to different societies, it is evident that certain practices and beliefs may be morally unacceptable (and/or illegal) in a given society. For, if moral values are purely culturally specific, then the arbiter of right and wrong is the host culture. The broad assumption that multiculturalism is a good thing therefore cannot lead us to the conclusion that any imported value has to be recognized and respected. A given society may quite justifiably condemn and reject particular values held by a minority culture within it, if they are incompatible with its own core values.

So, why do we tend to value multiculturalism? In the first place, in many countries it is now a fact of life that there are citizens who come originally from a variety of different cultures, and the principle of *respect for persons*, which we have argued for in Chapter 10, requires that we acknowledge and accept the different cultural values they bring with them, provided that they are not actually incompatible with or detrimental to our current established values. Secondly, it may well be the case that some aspects of a culture that is newly arrived in a given society represent a positive addition to the host culture, while even ideas and values that are not regarded positively may have value in challenging us to think more carefully and deeply about an issue. If, for example, a new wave of immigrants brings what the host nation sees as a welcome ethic of hard work or an enlightened attitude to marriage, that is self-evidently to be welcomed. But even if what is at issue is a cultural practice that is at best contentious (such as the requirement that females should be veiled), having to engage seriously with this issue has its own value. For many, there is, thirdly, the claim that the fact of diversity is good in itself. On this view, a monolithic society in which broadly speaking all think alike and act in similar ways is inherently less admirable than one in which there are many different values, customs, and beliefs.

The point that the principle of respect demands that we do not dismiss cultural differences just because they are new or different is surely correct as far as it goes, and should be sufficient to establish that cultural differences should be welcomed, other things being equal. 'Welcomed' in this context, however, does not mean that they have to be enthusiastically embraced, although sometimes they may be; it means minimally that the new values should not be treated with contempt or dismissively, but at the very least neutrally. 'Other things being equal' refers to the point that the values in question should not be incompatible with the accepted social norms of the society in question. Of course, if a society is not to stagnate and become ossified in its ways, it must allow people to champion even values that may initially be regarded as antithetical to its beliefs and customs. But that leads to the conclusion that people who hold beliefs that differ from mainstream thought, whether they are newcomers or citizens of longstanding, should be allowed to articulate those beliefs and argue for them – a conclusion argued for in Chapter 14, on the grounds that increasing our understanding and grasp of the truth is dependent on the free interchange of ideas. It does not, however, lead to the conclusion that, while being free to argue in favor of, say, female circumcision, I should be free to practice it.

The importance of the second point, that newly imported ideas may be valuable regardless of their *intrinsic* value, in that *extrinsically* they provoke us into some serious thinking, is implicit in the standard argument for freedom of thought: the existence of competing ideas, even when they are bad ideas, may serve to strengthen our understanding of and commitment to current beliefs.

The third suggestion, that diversity is good in itself, is less obviously convincing than the previous two claims. One might hold a stereotypical view of the Soviet Union in the past or the Republic of China today as places of drab uniformity, lacking in many freedoms we value, including most notably freedom of thought. And one might therefore conclude that they are inferior to more variegated societies. But there is a danger here of confusion between moral or ethical value and non-ethical value such as aesthetic value, or simply the value of preference or taste. Certainly, I would prefer to live in a country such as Canada that welcomes multiculturalism rather than in China, which, while being in some ways extremely diverse, aims to iron out difference as far as it can. But the fact that I might prefer to live in Canada clearly does not in itself show that Canada is a superior country in a moral sense, or indeed in any other sense.[1] I am inclined to conclude that multiculturalism, though attractive to many, is to be welcomed morally only on the grounds of respect and the assumption that in the long run diversity of values and beliefs leads to the winnowing out of poor ideas and the survival of better ideas.

Melting Pot versus Mosaic

Another question to be raised in this context is whether there is reason to prefer the so-called '*melting pot*' approach to cultural integration or the '*mosaic*' view. The former, traditionally associated with the United States, has it that, while people from diverse backgrounds are welcome, the presumption and wish is that in time they will assimilate to the host culture, perhaps while at the same time unobtrusively modifying that culture in certain ways. The mosaic metaphor, often applied to Canada, suggests that the ideal is for different cultures to survive in their pristine form, thus making society as a whole appear as a colorful picture of distinct subcultures, akin to a mosaic which, though made up of individual distinct pieces of glass, ends up presenting a coherent and harmonious picture.

Whether these two approaches are in fact represented by the United States and Canada may, to say the least, be doubted. I doubt whether many African Americans, Mexicans, or Puerto Ricans would assent to the view that they have either been able or in any real sense invited to assimilate or mix in with the dominant culture. Similarly, though some may feel primarily locked into their ethnic culture rather than assimilated into a wider Canadian culture, the suggestion that Canada is a harmonious collection of distinct sub-cultures is not very realistic.

But the more important question is whether we should aspire to either of these models. I have already suggested that no society can be expected to allow a sub-culture to engage in practices that are abhorrent to the dominant culture; nor will it in fact allow such to happen whether the dominant culture is imposed by a dictator or a democracy. In the latter case, of course, one is implicitly saying that sub-cultures must concur with the fundamental moral values of the majority. It is worth stressing that it is *moral* values we are talking about. There are surely no grounds for concluding that diverse artistic values or preferred social customs that have no moral significance should always be subordinated to the majority viewpoint. But, while the moral values of the host culture may be challenged in argument, they must be accepted and abided by until such time as the argument is won.

Secondly, and more contentiously, I would argue that minority cultures, while under no obligation to do so if there is no moral issue concerned, should nonetheless try to assimilate to those customs and procedures of the majority culture that have to do with social interaction of one kind or another. The concern here is for unity and harmony. Common sense suggests that any society, if it is to function well and provide security and comfort for its citizens, needs to be based upon some commonalities. To this extent assimilation is to be preferred to the mosaic. Thus, there is no reason why different groups should not continue to follow their own religious practices, wear their own preferred style of clothing, stick with their own culinary practices, celebrate their own festivals in their own ways, and speak their own languages with those who can also speak them. But there is good reason to insist on them mastering the official language(s), recognizing if not observing the majority festivals, providing a schooling for their children that is not exclusively based on their own culture, as well as abiding by the moral values that govern the wider society.

One of the concerns of many of those who have argued for deschooling society has been that the school system promotes an uncritical acceptance of our culture (Chapter 4). To this general concern may be added the more particular objection that the culture promoted is not representative of our multicultural society and is still overlaid with a colonial outlook. We can readily agree that schools should not promote an uncritical acceptance of our culture (or anything else) and also that there should be recognition and respect for the principle of cultural diversity and for different cultural practices that do not undermine the dominant culture. It is surely also reasonable to suggest that the teaching of subjects such as history should eschew out of date imperialistic and colonial overtones.

However, these important admissions should not lead us to conclude that history should be primarily a tale of acknowledgment of guilt and redress, or that any cultural practice is sacrosanct.[2] Above all it should not incline us to cease promoting a common culture. Far from being a defect of schooling, promoting a common culture and thereby helping to foster a sense of common identity is surely one of the valuable functions of the school system.

Systemic Racism

When thinking about our culture, it is hard to avoid the topic of racism. It is an evident social problem to some degree, and schools both have to deal with racist incidents and attempt to combat it through education.

In recent weeks, as I write, an unexpected difference of opinion between the Chief of the Vancouver Police Department and the Mayor of Vancouver has been publicly aired.[3] The former asserts that the police department does not suffer from '*systemic racism*', while the latter asserts that it does. It would be hard to find a better example of the way in which philosophy, while not being able to prove or establish beyond cavil that one of them is right and the other wrong, can at least point out that the disagreement is meaningless as it stands, since it is quite unclear what 'systemic racism' means. It well may be that both men are in fact correct in their opinions because they mean quite different things.

Racism is obviously a debated concept, to which we will come in a moment, but the much in vogue word 'systemic' is also problematic. It is primarily a physiological term used of a poison or disease that affects the entire body, and it is usually unwise and confusing to take a word that has a specialist meaning and apply it in another context. But assuming that 'systemic' racism in this case means racism that affects the entire police department, and assuming that we can make sense of that (the *entire* department? The cleaners, the computers, every single policeman and woman?), there remains the serious and difficult question of what we are suggesting when we say that the whole system is inherently racist. Presumably we don't mean that every officer is racist, because that is palpable nonsense.

I take it that 'systemic' is meant to have overtones of, perhaps is actually synonymous with, 'systematic', so that what is being claimed has less to do with the amount or degree of racism than with the way in which the department is organized, set up, or administered. Systemic racism is racism that is inherent in the system. Thus, the claim would be that when it comes to procedures for hiring and promoting officers, and for detaining, questioning, or arresting people, the standard or approved procedures are racist; similarly, when it comes to policy on such matters as where to put resources, the criteria are racist. Now, I am in no position to judge whether what the Chief of police claims is true or false of the Vancouver Police Department, but I am fairly sure that, in denying that the racism was systemic, he was saying that department *policy* does not involve targeting people, hiring and promoting officers, and decision-making generally, on the grounds of race. I presume he meant that the problem is with individual officers being racist; there may of course be a tendency for racist officers to associate with each other, and thus there may be groups that can be said to share a racist culture. But that does not make the organization as a whole in itself racist.[4]

As to the mayor, while it is possible that he has evidence that the Department is indeed racist in its policy, structure, and administration, since he has not provided any such evidence, it seems more charitable to assume that he means by 'systemic' racism little more than *widespread* racism. In other words, if I am right, what appears to be a major and potentially damaging difference of opinion is in fact just a misunderstanding based on conceptual confusion. Both men may be right: the Department may not be systemically racist in the sense of organized on racist principles, but there may be rather a large number of racist cops. (There are of course other possible senses of 'systemic' racism besides those mentioned, and the VPD may for all I know be systemically racist in some sense. My point is that argument about this is pointless until we clear up the conceptual uncertainty.)

Racism

And what precisely is a 'racist' cop? Racism is usually defined as a belief in the innate superiority and inferiority of particular races. Racists are those who dislike or look down upon certain people purely because of their race; it involves judging individuals on the grounds of their race, either failing to take into account any particular characteristics of the individual or assuming that they are irrelevant to the question of that person's worth. That is clearly wrong: being Welsh, Scottish, Irish, or English is not a valid criterion for a judgment on the merits or demerits of an individual.

At this point, some would add further criteria, suggesting for example that racism necessarily involves abusive or aggressive attitudes and behavior towards those thought to be of inferior race, or that any stereotyping of 'the English are self-deprecating' kind is racist. But this is to be resisted. Superficially it may seem that the more criteria we add for depicting racism, the more widespread we will find racism to be. But the conclusion is incorrect. There is a difference between determining the *criteria that define* a concept and merely producing *examples*. If one simply lists examples that one regards as racist (e.g., refusing to employ a person of a different race, insulting them, demeaning their beliefs or behavior, physically attacking them, displaying contempt) then it may look as if one is expanding the concept so that many more people can be considered racist. But, if the examples are indeed examples of racism, that must be because they all share some common defining characteristics that are necessary and/or sufficient. But they don't. Not all insults to those of another race are racist insults and not all racists engage in insulting people. If these examples are all to be taken as instances of racism it must be because racism is being defined as more or less any kind of objectionable behavior. But racism must involve objectionable behavior based on race. It is not being insulting that is racist; it is being insulting (or doing anything else) purely on grounds of race.

The more criteria we add to the concept of racism, the fewer people can be found who are truly racist. Many more people are likely to regard some other race as inferior than are likely also to engage in hostile behavior towards them. Hostile behavior towards a member of another race may certainly be the result of racist feelings, but it should not be made part of the definition of racism. It is neither a necessary condition (one can be racist without being overtly hostile) nor a sufficient condition (one can be hostile to a person of another race without it being because one is racist). This last point is of particular importance because there is a marked tendency for people to assume that all hostility towards a member of a different race must be racist; but that is clearly not so.

Stereotyping is often classified as being in itself objectionable, but this too must be resisted. It is true that some people use the term pejoratively to mean an 'oversimplified' or even 'unwarranted' standardized description, but such connotations are the consequence of the speaker happening to dislike or object to the practice; such objection may sometimes be reasonable in respect of particular instances, but in itself stereotyping is not a value-loaded term. Most of the so-called 'social sciences' are referred to as 'so-called' precisely because they are not true sciences uncovering laws but fields of inquiry that for the most part draw generalizable conclusions. They may be well-founded, reasonable, and important, but they remain generalizations. A stereotype is merely a form of generalization. One can certainly misuse either, as one does when one judges an individual to necessarily conform to the stereotype, but there is nothing inherently wrong with a stereotype such as that the English are self-deprecating (though of course it may be untrue).

I would define racism as the harboring of feelings of superiority towards others on the grounds of race. There is no need to extend it. Racist acts are those motivated by racism. To hold the view that overall, historically speaking, a particular race has been superior in the sense of achieved more of value than another, for example, though fraught with danger (especially in that race may here become confused with society, culture, or ethnicity) and generally hard to sustain, is nonetheless not in itself racist, provided that one does not go on to assess individuals of that race in terms of that overall view. (Note that by this definition it is possible to have a condescending, patronizing, but entirely *benign* attitude towards an individual of what one regards as an inferior race, but that that is equally racist, and hence reprehensible.)

The truth is that we are failing to distinguish, (i) *treating* people differentially solely on the grounds of their race, which is surely racist and hence unacceptable; (ii) *looking down* on individuals solely on grounds of their race, which is equally racist and hence reprehensible; (iii) *looking up* to them on the same grounds, which, though it seems slightly odd to object to it, is also racist; (iv) looking down on *particular characteristics* of an individual, such as arrogance or self-deprecation, which happen to be *thought of as stereotypical of a particular race by some (possibly but not necessarily including oneself)*, which is surely not in itself racist; and (v) looking down on particular characteristics of an individual *which are not associated with a stereotype*, which is clearly not racist.

In *The Bell Curve*, Richard J. Herrnstein and Charles Murray re-ignited the longstanding debate on nature and nurture, IQ testing, and race, when they concluded that, on average, African Americans have lower IQs than white Americans.[5] Let us set aside the following points: the fact that IQ is nothing more nor less than what IQ tests test and has no conceptual connection with what people ordinarily mean when they judge individuals to be more or less intelligent; the fact that there is no significant empirical evidence of a connection between high IQ and intellectual or other social achievement; the fact that IQ tests are inescapably partly tests of learning (and may therefore favor people from one kind of background or environment over those from another); and finally the fact that the variation between the IQ of individuals of the same race may be greater than the average difference between races. These are all grave defects, which should be sufficient, but evidently are not, to bring an end to the business of IQ testing; but let us ignore them. The question that is relevant to us here is whether it is fair to accuse Herrnstein and Murray of being racist, as some have done.

It is true that they conclude that African Americans are different in respect of IQ and it is true that they regard this difference as innate or due to race rather than environment. But they say nothing about the superiority or inferiority of any group or race, and for that reason alone, while thinking that the concern with IQ is a complete and in many ways deplorable waste of time, I conclude that they cannot be called racist. Merely observing or believing that there are inherent differences between races, whether true or false in particular cases, and whether the differences are regarded as more or less valuable, cannot count as racism. For it is true that there are differences, and some differences arguably may be preferable to others. (Once again, I need to make it quite clear that I do not endorse the view that African Americans have been shown to have a lower intelligence than other Americans. The most that could be claimed by this research is that on aggregate African Americans score less well on IQ tests than some other groups, but, as noted in the previous paragraph, IQ tests for a number of reasons are of little or no consequence. My argument has been simply that drawing an unpalatable conclusion about a racial group from research that, whatever its shortcomings, has been conducted honestly and sincerely does not in itself make one racist.)

There are other kinds of mistake and bad things besides racism, but it does not help to define racism in wider terms. It is not *necessarily* racist to happen to dislike every Slav you meet, to make Polish jokes, to criticize Israel's government, or to generalize about the Irish. It has recently been argued that the television show *Spitting Image*, which satirizes well-known individuals who are represented by caricature puppets, is racist, because it presents black celebrities as 'grotesque puppets'. But since it presents white (and Asian, etc., etc.) celebrities as equally grotesque puppets it is hard to see what is racist about it. Nor can one take seriously (although the television program *The Simpsons* did) the further suggestion that it is racist to have individuals of a different race provide the voices for these various animated figures. When it comes to the suggestion that it is racist to allow writers of one race (in this case white) to write for the puppets (black) of another, one begins to wonder whether we are not going insane. There may be reasons of some sort to uphold objection to some or all of these examples, but none of them can reasonably be said to involve racism.

There are real racial problems, but they boil down to the fact that some people think that being a member of a certain race in itself means you are not worthy of respect.

Unconscious Racism

In July 2020, Keir Starmer, the Leader of the British Labour Party, referred to Black Lives Matter as a 'moment' rather than a 'movement'. I am not sure exactly what point he was trying to make, but it hardly seems an objectionable remark, and it is clear that Starmer himself did not intend it to be derogatory. However, he was immediately criticized for being racist and, in response, announced that he would undergo 'anti-racism' training. Of course, he had not thought of himself as racist when making the remark, so now we are in the territory of 'unconscious racism'. There is always something a little suspect about 'unconscious' anything, and something equally suspect about the programs designed to expose and vanquish it. (It is also extremely irritating to be told by other people that they know more about your motivation than you do yourself. They, after all, are only able to infer your motives from their interpretation of your behavior.)

It is argued that the unconscious makes rapid judgments rather than draws slowly reasoned conclusions.[6] To make this point, subjects may be told that a bat and a ball cost $1.10 and that the bat costs a dollar more than the ball. They are then asked, how much does the ball cost? Apparently most people answer 10 cents, whereas the correct answer is 5 cents. (Think about it!). The idea that such a mental test establishes anything of significance about the unconscious borders on the ridiculous. What of those who give the correct answer? Is their unconscious not guilty of making rapid judgments? Do we really need tests to establish that sometimes our 'immediate' (which is what we are actually talking about rather than 'unconscious') responses are wrong?

Having supposedly thus established that the unconscious makes bad judgments, we proceed to establish that the individual is making bad racist judgments. How do we do that? In one example you are asked to consider your seven most trusted friends and then to answer certain questions relating to this group. Examples of the questions are: are they of the same age as you? Are they of the same race? Do they have the same educational background? Are they the same sex? In many cases the answers will more or less all be in the affirmative. This doesn't seem particularly surprising since like tends to appeal to like and we tend to make friends among those with whom we associate (e.g., go to school, play sport, work with). But in this case the conclusion is illegitimately drawn that unconsciously we reveal our preference for people of our own sex, age, race, and educational attainment. And that is supposed to establish that we are unconsciously racist, though to most people it would surely only establish that for unknown reasons, of which there could be hundreds, our closest friends happen to be of the same race. Basically, as often in social science research, the conclusion is established by defining what is being examined (in this case 'unconscious racism') in terms of the tests involved: 'unconscious racism' *is* 'answering such questions in the affirmative' (see Chapter 19).

Not only is it not necessarily racist, it is also not necessarily wrong to want to be with people of one's own educational attainment and age (which may imply of the same experience). The race of one's friends is unlikely to be, and is certainly not *necessarily*, a consequence of bias or desire, whether conscious or unconscious, so much as of circumstance. Granted it tells us something about our society that I did not go to school with, grow up in a neighborhood with, or, until late in life, work with many people of a different race, but this, while it at least partially and perhaps wholly explains the lack of other races among my closest friends, does not tell you anything about my attitude to them.

If there is such a thing as 'unconscious bias', this kind of approach would not appear to be a convincing way of getting at it. But it is hard to avoid the conclusion that the very notion of 'unconscious bias' is dubious. Most of us accept the idea that we may have motives of which we are unaware, but it is hard to see how a concept such as bias can be unconscious.

A bias is simply a preference or an inclination though it is often given a negative tone by implying that the tendency in question is irrational. In this sense I am biased against an individual if I target them for no good reason. So one can certainly be racially biased, i.e., target someone on grounds of their race. But strictly speaking I can't be unconsciously biased, because bias implies some form of deliberate attitude or action. The only sense I can give to the notion of unconscious racism is if the evidence shows that I am inclined to disfavor members of some race and that I am not even aware of the fact; that is to say, for example, that it genuinely takes me by surprise to discover that over a period of years I have only ever promoted white people. But even then something further is required to establish that this was *because* they were white. It might have been that I genuinely thought they were best (rightly or wrongly), because I wasn't really paying attention, because I thought they were good looking or for any number of other good or bad reasons. E.P. Thompson recounts the case of an eminent scholar who marked all those passages in a book on France that referred to the French in some manner as wretched; on reading the book again several years later he discovered to his surprise that he had made no note of all the passages that referred to happy, prosperous French people.[7] But the implication that he had been *unconsciously* hostile to the French when he first read the book seems quite unsustainable. Certainly, one can believe that he might be surprised to discover how hostile he was to the French all those years ago, but it is beyond belief that at the time he was unconscious of the fact that he was noting only hostile comments.

Imagine a situation in which a critic of the state of Israel (A) is accused by another (B) of being anti-Semitic. Imagine further that A denies being anti-Semitic and claims that she is simply opposed to some action(s) of the

Israeli government. To this B responds: "you may think that is all you are doing, but subconsciously you are against these actions because they are carried out by the Jewish state, which is to say Jews". But on what grounds can one possibly claim that in general this is the case? A, one may imagine, will say something like, "I don't feel any animosity. I am not aware of hostile feelings. I have many Jewish friends" and so forth. "Well", says B, "your animosity is subconscious". But what does this mean when the alleged animosity does not stop A liking Jews or indeed supporting the existence of Israel? In particular cases it could possibly be true that A is anti-Semitic, but even then it is hard to believe that the individual would truly be unaware of their prejudice, as opposed to dissembling.[8]

I suppose I must allow, despite my argument, that it is possible for a teacher to be particularly hard on a student and to think they are so because he is lazy, insolent, or some such, whereas in fact it is because the teacher simply doesn't like him. But is it conceivable that the teacher dislikes him because of his race without realizing it? If it is possible (and this seems to be the standard assumption of those who detect widespread unconscious racism), I have to say that it seems to me a fairly rare scenario. Racists may often choose to hide their racism for practical reasons, but by and large I should have thought that most people who genuinely dislike a particular race are well aware of the fact.

Crash

Paul Haggis' film *Crash* is an exploration of the topic of racism.[9] In my view it is a particularly good and useful contribution to thinking about the subject. That was also the critical consensus when the film first appeared. Roger Ebert called it "the best film of 2005", while ten other leading film reviewers listed it among their top ten films of the year. But then comment turned against it, with cultural critic Ta-Nehesi Coates going so far as to describe it as "the worst film of the decade".[10] This is surely partly a sign of changing times: today there is a greater concern for and therefore an increased tendency to see racism in any remotely negative comment about anybody, if they happen to be of another race. The reason that I think *Crash* a good exploration of the topic is that it introduces a number of individuals of different race each of whose character is complex, as of course most individuals are, and who together represent a wide variety of attitudes to race. There is the well-to-do white woman who instinctively swerves away from two black people walking by her in a largely white neighborhood and who distrusts the man fixing the locks in her house because, she says, of his prison-style tattoos and style of dress. She does not add "and because of his color". But perhaps that is what is really of concern to her. She is certainly presented as an unsympathetic character. On the other hand, is it not rather presumptuous of us to assume that this is racial prejudice in the sense of hostility to a person of color, when she has provided a perfectly coherent reason for her concern about the locksmith? And while moving away from people of a different color is regrettable in various ways, is it altogether objectionable given the racial tensions in Los Angeles, and is it necessarily evidence of racism? One of the good guys is a black cop, but even he gets into trouble with his girlfriend when it turns out that he unthinkingly assumes she is Mexican, being unaware that she is of mixed Latin–American parentage. Ungallant, insensitive, no doubt, but racist? The good guy's brother is one of the bad guys, primarily an auto-thief, reminding us that indeed good and bad are not tied to race. Meanwhile, another of the good guys, also a cop, ends up killing another of the bad guys who happens to be of another race. But he kills him by accident because he thinks that a gun is being drawn on him, which is unfortunate since, on the face of it, he is the least racist character of all. The nastiest character of all (though even he has redeeming features such as devoted caring for a dying father) who is racist on almost any view, nonetheless risks his life doing his job as a policeman to release a woman of another race (whom he has previously humiliated) from a burning car as it is about to blow up. Those who dislike the film presumably think all of this is sentimental and designed to reassure us all that racism is not a real problem. For instance, another criticism has been that one of the characters, a Persian immigrant with limited English, who fails to understand what he is being told about security and whose shop is consequently subsequently trashed, is depicted as deranged and delusional. But some people are deranged and delusional. It is almost as if for some people the imputation of any negative characteristic to any individual of a different race must be evidence of racism. But that is absurd.

I see the film very differently. Because it is extremely well directed and acted, we believe in all of these characters and we see that no simple explanation of their actions, such as that they are or are not racist, is adequate. Each one exhibits racism, if at all, in a different way, to a different degree and for different reasons. And – and this is the important point – in real life, without the benefit of seeing how the story ends, so to speak, and without all the information about them that the film can provide, we would not be in a position to make any kind of *informed judgment* about whether and in what sense any of these individuals was racist. The moral, in other words, is that we should be careful about judging people to be racist when we do not know either their motives or intentions in saying or doing what they do.

David Hume

I feel I must comment briefly on the University of Edinburgh's 2020 decision to remove the name of that great figure of the Enlightenment, David Hume, from the David Hume Tower.

The two main charges against him are first that, despite being opposed to slavery, he advised and abetted his patron in buying a slave plantation, and secondly that he wrote, in a footnote added five years after first publication of his *Of National Characters*, "I am apt to believe the Negroes and in general all other species of men... to be naturally inferior to the

Whites". Edinburgh University, in removing his name from the David Hume Tower, explains that this remark 'rightly' causes distress to students working there and that it has acted to 'protect student sensitivities'. Students today must be very sensitive indeed to be distressed by such things; indeed, one might prefer to call them pathologically 'tender', 'delicate', 'thin-skinned', 'impressionable', or 'easily upset'. In fact (though an online petition received 1700 signatures in favor of removing his name), no evidence has been provided that anybody is genuinely distressed by working in the Tower. But why does the university unhesitatingly pronounce that these putative students are 'rightly' distressed? Should we be distressed by any mention of or memorial to anybody who holds views we think mistaken? And what exactly is the view in this case? What precisely did Hume mean by 'naturally inferior'?

By 'naturally' one presumes that he held the view that there were *inherent* differences between the races in respect of whatever the characteristics pertaining to quality of persons might be. In this most of us believe Hume was simply wrong as a matter of empirical fact. But it can hardly be held against a person living several centuries ago that we now think that they were mistaken on certain matters of fact. So the burden of the argument falls on what Hume meant by 'inferior'. If he meant they were not deserving of any respect in Kant's sense or that they could rightly be used as means to our ends, then we would have grounds for judging his position to be morally objectionable. But he did not mean that. He clearly meant something along the lines of 'non-whites are [inherently] less capable than whites in various respects that go to advance the sort of achievements that we value'.[11] This, most of us now think, is plainly not true; but it does not make Hume a racist. To be a racist he would also have to believe that non-whites did not deserve respect as persons and as such could be treated badly and as means. Following the definition provided above he would have to "dislike or look down on" non-whites but his remark does not provide evidence of this.

And so we come to the fact of his advising his patron to buy a slave plantation. That certainly seems hypocritical in one who rejects slavery and must seem objectionable to those of us who today regard slavery as morally repugnant, but it seems logically very little different from the hypocrisy that many of us who use a bank that engages in corrupt practices such as selling sub-prime mortgages (and worse) are guilty of. The fact that we are equally guilty of hypocrisy doesn't of course mean that Hume is off the hook. But it suggests that we are being rather precipitate in taking the moral high ground. We might be better advised to worry about the serious forms of slavery that persist today than worrying about hearing the name of David Hume.[12] My point here is not to defend Hume's stated position, but to argue that it is not strictly speaking racist, and that concern about memorializing individuals of towering historical intellectual and other importance is trivial compared to concern for manifest contemporary injustices.

Education

Two conclusions with regard to schooling are obvious: it is desirable that schools should have a multicultural intake in order to develop familiarity and ease between children from different cultures, and it is vital to promote knowledge of other cultures, for clearly ignorance may be as much the cause of inter-racial tension as actual racism, and genuine racism is generally the product of ignorance.

There are of course other questions to contemplate. Should there be more teachers from minority groups? Should the curriculum be de-colonialized? Should schools be doing more to promote understanding of minority cultures? These are legitimate questions, but they will not receive extended discussion here, not because they are unimportant but because they are largely issues beyond the purview of philosophy.

Given the multicultural nature of our society it would surely be advantageous to have more teachers from more varied backgrounds both to represent our diversity and perhaps to better teach some aspects of it. But this is one issue on which there is little or no evidence to suggest that it is the education system itself that is at fault. The problem, for whatever reason, appears to be that while the system positively encourages such representation, many minority cultures are not drawn to the profession of teaching. That in itself might be because individuals from certain groups such as, say, indigenous groups have been denied adequate educational opportunity themselves. So this is sometimes an educational issue, but it is also often a social issue, as for example when immigrant groups lack the economic means to pursue education and teacher training or when there are cultural norms to the effect that teaching is not a prestigious calling.

The call for de-colonialization is more problematic because it can mean so many things. If it means that we should be alert to the faults and the crimes in our history and to literary talent regardless of where it originates there will be little dissent. I have already acknowledged above that history, for example, should not be taught from an uncritical imperial perspective, and that the literature studied should not be exclusively that of dead white males. As we shall see in the next chapter, advocates of something like a literary canon such as Matthew Arnold were always very clear that they wanted the best, regardless of when, where, or by whom it was written. It is certainly true that Arnold's own view of the best of what had been written would have been less varied than we would expect today. But it is also the case that in most jurisdictions today the English curriculum is expected to include a variety of work from authors of any sex and of many different racial and cultural backgrounds.

But if, to pose an extreme view, de-colonialization were a call to routinely condemn all past actions by colonizing powers, for example, or to refrain from all mention of colonial figures such as Cecil Rhodes on the ground of their faults as we now judge them, it should be roundly rejected.

History is the attempt to understand what happened, not to write an essay in wish fulfillment or to engage in moral hectoring of the past. Similarly, if the intention is to exclude some or all of the great writers of the past from colonizing nations and to replace them with writers from a colonized background as matter of principle or on some kind of quota system, it is to be resisted: we want students to read the best, whatever its provenance.

When it comes to promoting minority culture there is again a certain ambiguity. If we are taking care to recognize the achievements, including literary achievements, of those from minority cultures in our teaching of history and literature, as we have said above we should be, then we are promoting minority cultures in an appropriate way. It would be another matter however to suggest that it is the job of the school to focus on the study of other cultures as such, as distinct from studying them in the context of a broader historical and literary perspective. The primary function of schools in respect of culture should be to foster a common culture in the interests of helping to cultivate a society of people who, whatever their differences, feel a common bond.

Conclusion

Cultural differences exist and there is nothing inherently wrong with the idea that some cultures may be superior to others in particular respects. Some may be argued to be morally superior; some produce superior art; some are more friendly, and so forth. There is no reason that we should necessarily admire all cultures equally and there is no reason that we should respect all aspects of a minority culture within a given society. There is however much to be admired in many widely differing cultures and it is both morally right and culturally beneficial to welcome and respect cultural differences that do not run counter to the dominant culture, while at the same time demanding a similar welcome and respect for the dominant culture. The notion of some form of partial assimilation to the host culture on the part of newcomers seems a considerably more coherent approach than the so-called mosaic pattern.

There are a number of claims that, especially when taken together, may be thought likely to prove contingently counter-productive to the ideal of ending racism: for example, expanding the list of supposedly racist (or otherwise offensive) behaviors so that it becomes racist for an actor to take on the part of a character of a different race or, taken to its logical conclusion, a matter of 'cultural appropriation' for a British band to play country music; the increasing frequency with which governments and other institutions issue apologies and recompense for historical sins; and the continued acceptance of the self-contradictory notion of 'positive discrimination'.[13] In calling such things potentially counter-productive, I am suggesting that many of those who, for instance, entirely accept that past discrimination against gay men was morally wrong and who now also approve, whether enthusiastically or reluctantly, same-sex marriage, are going to think it a push too far when told that only gay actors can legitimately play gay characters.[14]

Racism involves judging an individual simply as a member of a given race. Our concern is generally with negative judgment, as when a person looks down on another and/or treats them with some form of contempt because they are a member of a certain race. Attempts to widen the net to catch more racists by adding other criteria to the definition do the opposite: the more necessary conditions we add to the meaning of racist the fewer people will be found to be racist. We do not need to extend the definition. There are plenty of other critical terms to pick out bad behavior. It is not morally wrong or unacceptable to generalize about a race. It is not morally wrong to argue that something is both commonly true of members of a group and objectionable, though any such argument needs to be very carefully phrased and presented to avoid misunderstanding. It is not necessarily morally wrong to discriminate between people of different race on particular issues (in the basic sense of discriminate, i.e., recognize actual differences). But it is wrong (it is racist in fact) to favor or disfavor an individual in thought or deed simply on the grounds of their race.

The notion of unconscious racism seems particularly unhelpful. To combat racism all we can do is argue for the value of respect for persons, exhibit and preach tolerance and open-mindedness, and reinforce positive attitudes through a proper understanding of philosophical issues, historical fact, literary explorations, and our differing cultural beliefs and practices.

Notes

1   While one can obviously attempt to compare cultures in respect of particular issues, to attempt to rank them overall raises the difficult question of how one determines the criteria and what they should be. See note 11 below.
2   While it is evidently right for a society to recognize and show contrition for certain recent sins of the past, the questions of how far back one should go, whether or how much material recompense is due to descendants of past injustice, and whether we are responsible for the sins of our forebears are all very problematic.
3   The story was reported by Dan Fumano in the *Vancouver Sun*, June 29, 2020.
4   It is clearly reprehensible, however, for the department to turn a blind eye to or fail to root out racist activity on the part of any of its members, whether we call it 'systemic racism', 'racism', or simply morally wrong. The issue that lay behind this disagreement, incidentally, was 'carding'. Police stop and question indigenous and black people disproportionately more than whites. There might be reasons to justify this practice or it might be unjustified, but even if unjustified, though it *might* be racist, it is not *necessarily* racist.
5   Richard J Herrnstein & Charles Murray, *The Bell Curve: Intelligence and Class Structure in American Life* (Free Press, 1994).
6   I owe most of this account to Rhys Blakely who wrote of his experience in *The Times*, July 11, 2020: 'I've confronted my unconscious bias but will it change a thing?'
7   E.P. Thompson, *The Making of the Working Class* (Pelican, 1980).
8   H. Blanton & J. Jaccard, 'Unconscious Racism: A Concept in Pursuit of a Measure', *Annual Review of Sociology*, 34, 277–297 (2008), distinguishes between unconscious racism in the sense of being unaware of the racist effects of one's actions and in the

sense of being unaware that one has a racist attitude. The former is of course possible and has wider application than to racism alone. Ignorance concerning possible consequences of one's actions can often be harmful and is one very good reason why, through education, we try to both make people aware of the dangers of ignorance and to combat it as far as we can. But the latter, the idea that one might be racist without being aware of it, they conclude, is not supported by the empirical evidence. They also propose a third sense of unconscious racism as an inability "to gain subjective access to the determinants of [one's own] actions", which I take to mean that one doesn't know why one acts as one does. But I find it hard to understand how being racist without being aware of it, which we have just learned is not a possibility supported by the evidence, is not an instance of this third sense. Certainly, as noted above, one can in some cases be unaware of one's real motivation, as, for example, I may not realize that my attitude to someone is actually caused by my envy of that person. But racism necessarily involves an attitude (usually negative) towards some person on grounds of race, and I cannot see how a person can be unaware of that negative attitude or unaware that that attitude is related to race, if it is. Whether or not I have correctly understood this alleged third sense of unconscious racism, it is to be stressed that the study concludes that empirical evidence does not support the idea that people can be unaware that they have a racist attitude.

9 Do not confuse Paul Haggis' 2004 film with David Cronenberg's 1996 film, also titled *Crash*.

10 *The Atlantic*, December 30, 2009.

11 Martha Nussbaum, *Creating Capabilities: the Human Development Approach* (Harvard University Press, 2011), suggests a set of capabilities that are necessary to human flourishing and argues that the extent to which individuals can exercise these capabilities in a given society is a measure of the justness of that society. Though the argument is entirely benign, this and similar attempts to assess the relative 'justness' of societies would seem in principle to be little different from Hume's attempt to assess their relative 'superiority', since a more just society is presumably to be accounted superior to a less just one. Of course, Nussbaum offers certain criteria and thereby some evidence for her judgments, which Hume does not. And it has been conceded that Hume (who ignores for instance the historic Arab contribution to learning) is in our view simply mistaken as to matters of fact. But my point is that the making of judgments about the varying achievements of a race, culture, or civilization is not in itself reprehensible.

12 Ian Urbina, *The Outlaw Ocean: Journeys across the Last Untamed Frontier* (Knopf, 2019) is an eye-opening and frightening account of modern-day human trafficking, press-ganging, and other types of slavery.

13 'Racial discrimination' involves inappropriately treating people differently (usually worse) on grounds of race. 'Positive discrimination' equally involves treating people differently (in this case always worse) on grounds of race. Two wrongs don't make a right. Our moral duty is to treat all people fairly now regardless of what we or our forebears did in the past.

14 See Douglas Murray, *The Madness of Crowds: Gender, Race and Identity* (Bloomsbury Continuum, 2019).

Further Reading

Anne Phillips, *Multiculturalism Without Culture* (Princeton University Press, 2007); P. Eslin & N. Hedge, 'Inclusion and Diversity' in *The Sage Handbook of Philosophy of Education* (op. cit.); J. Suissa, 'Multiculturalism and Diversity' in P. Smeyers (ed.), *International Handbook of Philosophy of Education* (Springer, 2018).

On systemic racism and related terms such as 'systemic oppression', 'institutional racism', and 'institutional bias', see C.D. McIlwain & S.M. Caliendo, 'Race, Politics and Public Policy' and other papers in their edited volume, *The Routledge Companion to Race and Ethnicity* (2010), pp. 38–46, and D. Chandler & R. Munday on institutional bias in *A Dictionary of Media and Communication* (Oxford University Press, 2020).

Antony Flew, 'Three Concepts of Racism', *Encounter*, July 1990, pp. 63–66, offers an argument similar to that outlined in the text.

Questions

There are so many questions that arise both in relation to the arguments in this chapter and the topics of multiculturalism and racism generally that I feel it hardly necessary for me to suggest some. But I will ask:

What arguments are there for and against pulling down or otherwise blocking out what kind of memorials?

In some cultures, spitting in public is rife and regarded as a good thing to do, in others it is regarded as revolting and undesirable. What stance should a host nation that deplores the habit take in respect of an immigrant population habituated to it (or vice versa)?

What should the aim(s) of multicultural education be?

18 Culture

The Cultural Elitists

There are a number of educationalists, sometimes loosely and pejoratively referred to as cultural elitists, who are primarily concerned with the appreciation rather than the production of art. The cultural elitist view may be said to stem from the work of Matthew Arnold and T.S. Eliot in particular, and one of its most well-known representatives was G.H. Bantock. The view is such that it may be taken to involve hostility to much of what goes on in schools in the name of creativity, because it is feared that the disregard for standards in the work that children produce, that frequently characterizes creativity lessons, renders the work something other than genuinely creative. This partially explains Bantock's dictum that "too much freedom is incompatible with education".[1] Education, for Bantock, must include some reference to the notion of appreciating excellence, and this appreciation, it is claimed, will not be promoted by a situation in which children are free from the controls and limitations provided by the standards of excellence in any sphere. To put it crudely, if a child's writing does not have to meet any standards of coherence or quality, if her freedom is not even limited by such considerations as these, then she is not being introduced to the idea of excellence, and therefore she will be in no position to appreciate it. By definition, then, she will not be being educated. Bantock is not opposed to the aim of promoting artistic creativity, provided that it is genuine creativity, but the stress of his view lies with the notion of appreciation rather than production.

Arnold, Eliot, and Bantock cannot be lumped together without qualification, but all three, I think, would have accepted the broad outline of a thesis such as the following.

There is a body of art that consists of works (whether of music, literature, painting, photography, dance, sculpture) that are manifestly superior to other works. They are superior to other works in the same sphere and they also have an importance that renders them more valuable than works or products of other spheres of human activity. Two points are being made; not only are some books better than other books, as Shakespeare is superior to what Bantock calls "the ephemeral offerings of railway bookstalls",[2] but also good literature in general

DOI: 10.4324/9781003120476-18

is more valuable than such things as bingo. The cultural elitists are hostile both to popular culture (pop music, reality television, thrillers, etc.) and to the utilitarian dictum of Bentham that, provided people derive the same amount of pleasure from either, pushpin (a children's game of chance) is as good as poetry. The body of superior works of art referred to is, in Eliot's terminology, high culture. (I shall refer to it as Culture, with a capital C.) Society should be concerned to maintain the production of Culture and also to promote appreciation of it. But to appreciate Culture requires a developed sensitivity and a disciplined understanding of what is involved in the various works. Understanding, in turn, involves knowledge and intelligence. People do not generally simply pick up a play by Shakespeare and appreciate it. The thesis is prepared to accept the possibility that it is not possible for all individuals to attain the degree of sensitivity, knowledge, and intelligence requisite for true appreciation of these Cultural works; and it is therefore prepared to accept as an unfortunate fact that, in so far as education is to be concerned with initiating people into the high culture, it may have to do so with a minority. It seems to be essentially for this reason that those who hold this view have acquired the negative label of 'elitists'.

In the previous chapter two distinct uses of the term 'culture' were outlined. The danger of not being clear about this distinction can be illustrated by reference to Eliot (although it is only fair to add that there is room for considerable argument over the correct interpretation of Eliot). For despite the title *Notes Towards the Definition of Culture* and a chapter entitled 'The Three Senses of "Culture"', Eliot does not offer a clear and coherent definition of the term and he seems to equivocate between the two senses. (Despite the reference to three cultures, it is hard to locate his third sense.) Eliot argued that in any society there were a number of cultures ranging from high to low. He added that all these cultures were valuable in that their coexistence promoted friction, which in turn kept things alive and productive and prevented a static apathy taking over. Although all cultures have their value, however, it seems that the high culture is in some sense superior. That, at any rate, would seem to be the implication of the term itself and of remarks such as that there are different levels of culture and that, ideally, "the individual shall... take his place at the highest cultural level for which his natural aptitudes qualify him".[3] It is difficult to see how the notion of striving to attain the 'highest cultural level' possible for the individual can avoid being interpreted as involving the claim that 'high' is being used evaluatively. But what is not clear is what makes a culture a high culture, and whether it is not in fact contradictory to talk of a low culture (which, by implication at least, Eliot does), unless Eliot is confusing the two uses of 'culture'. For if we are talking about Culture, and if Culture by definition involves superior works of art, how can there be a low or inferior Culture in this sense? How can one say that Culture consists of a body of superior works of art, but that some Culture may consist of inferior works of art? It looks very much as if Eliot has confused the two uses of the term and that what he means by high culture is Culture, whereas what he means by lower levels of culture are various codes of living or lifestyles, as he clearly does in a celebrated passage in which he remarks that: "[culture] includes all the characteristic activities and interests of a people: Derby Day, Henley Regatta, Cowes, the twelfth of August, a cup final, the dog races, the pin table, the dart board, Wensleydale cheese, boiled cabbage cut into sections, beetroot in vinegar, nineteenth-century Gothic churches and the music of Elgar".[4] In other words, Eliot would seem to be saying that there are various cultures or subcultures in the anthropological sense in any given society, and that the friction between them is valuable, but there are only certain specific works that constitute Culture. The best culture, in the sociological sense, is that which has regard for Culture, in the non-sociological sense.

G.H. Bantock

Whether this is fair to Eliot or not, Bantock is at any rate well aware of the problem and of the danger of confusing two senses of 'culture', and in order to clarify what in his view is really Eliot's position, he explicitly introduces a third sense of 'culture'. This sense of 'culture' lies midway between the sociologist's use of the term and Culture.

> It is applied selectively to important areas of human thought and action. But in itself it is not intended to imply anything about the quality or value of these activities and thoughts. In my meaning of the term, a folk song, a 'pop' song, and a Beethoven symphony are similarly representative of culture.
>
> To speak of '*a* culture', then, in this usage, will be simply to refer to a number of important forms of human thought and behaviour without any distinction of value as between one manifestation and another, and to the pattern of their interrelationship.[5]

This is clear, but the question is whether the introduction of this sense of 'culture' will solve the problem that some find in Bantock's overall thesis.

According to Bantock, in the pre-industrial past there were essentially two Cultures in our society – the bookish Culture or the Culture of the literate minority, and the folk Culture or the Culture of the non-literate majority. Both were Cultures with a capital C and both had their own intrinsic value. Industrialization has killed the folk Culture and we have in its place, for the majority, a commercial and industrial pseudo-Culture. Education should be concerned to preserve the bookish Culture for those to whom it is suited, but it also needs to find and promote a new folk Culture for the majority – a Culture that may be on a different level from 'high culture', but which will nonetheless have value as being a genuine Culture.

But whether this putative third sense of culture is helpful may be doubted. Bantock's basic argument is simply that contemporary mass (or 'industrial') culture, with its detective novels, iPhones, television and rock music is not a Culture, whereas the folklore, folk tales, folk songs, maypole dances, and so on that we associate with the world of George Eliot's *Adam Bede* or the novels of Thomas Hardy are truly Cultural. In order to argue that the industrial culture is in some sense undesirable or inadequate compared to the folk Culture it has replaced, we must in fact drop Bantock's sense of the term 'culture' and revert to the notion of Culture as involving something of value, and argue that the folk songs and dances of the past, though they were not 'high culture' in Eliot's sense, nonetheless had a Cultural quality that their modern equivalents lack. This is precisely what Bantock would claim, but it raises the fundamental question of how one recognizes different levels of Culture as opposed to the products of a culture in the anthropological sense.

At any rate it seems important to distinguish the two separate theses that Bantock is putting forward: (i) that the way of life of pre-industrial society, including such things as its music and other art forms, has been replaced with a way of life, including its art forms, that is unsatisfactory in a number of ways, with the result that one task of education is to promote a new Culture, that has some quality, for the majority; (ii) that Culture in the sense of 'high culture', which happens to have been the interest, historically speaking, of a literate minority, is today in danger of being ignored in society, and in particular in education. Far from an increased emphasis on education and the spread of literacy having spread Culture to the majority "a diffusion of education seems to have had a deleterious effect on the highest cultural standards".[6] Instead of more people having access to Culture, more people seem to be less interested in Culture, and the work that is being produced in the sphere of art is coming up to lower Cultural standards. A vulgar commercialism and a lack of discrimination and taste is in danger of engulfing what Arnold called 'the sweetness and light' that is inherent in great art. The widespread abolition of the grammar schools, which involved selective education according to aptitude and which for a long time maintained the highest Cultural standards, and their replacement with comprehensive or non-selective schools, was just one more step towards the denigration of Culture.

In general terms the argument relating to this second thesis is clear, but not without its problems. First we have to distinguish between what is essentially involved in it and what are merely contingent points. The most obvious contingent point is the whole business of whether this initiation into high culture must in practice be reserved for a few. It is not part of the cultural elitist view that only a select minority are *entitled* to this distinctive kind of education, although critics of it have sometimes written as if it were. Nor, as is absolutely clear from Bantock's preoccupation with the whole question of the folk Culture, is there any suggestion that the majority do not matter. All that the cultural elitists are committed to is the claim that high culture is extremely important and the conditional claim that its importance is such that, if as a matter of fact it has to figure predominantly in the education of only some, it should do so.

Egalitarianism

Some have attempted to dismiss this thesis on the grounds that it is inegalitarian. An egalitarian society is one in which all members of the society receive equal treatment; an egalitarian educational system is one in which all children are treated equally. But equal treatment clearly does not necessarily imply the same treatment; it does not *mean* identical treatment. Or perhaps I should say, more cautiously, that if anyone does mean by equal treatment literally the same treatment for all, regardless of differences between them, it is difficult to see why we should be in favor of equal treatment. For although there may well be good reason for demanding that people should receive identical treatment in a great many more areas than they in fact do receive it in any particular society, it is difficult to accept that treatment should be the same for all in every respect. To advocate such would involve, among other things, a denial of special medical provision for the sick and disabled, a denial of pensions for the elderly, an insistence on identical amounts of food being provided for every individual from the new-born baby to the wrestling champion, and exactly the same education for everybody from the mentally challenged to the child prodigy. If we wish to avoid this absurd conclusion then we cannot say that equal treatment *means* the same treatment. And in reply to the question 'What *does* the claim that everybody ought to be treated equally mean, then?' it is difficult to see how one can do more than follow those philosophers who have argued that the principle of equality is a formal principle that demands that people should be treated the same except where there are differences between them that constitute relevant reasons for treating them differently in particular respects. In other words the principle of equality is one and the same thing as the principle of fairness or impartiality introduced in Chapter 10.

Impartiality involves treating people in the same way in identical circumstances. It does not mean treating people in the same way in all circumstances, which would be being indiscriminate. An impartial person is one who discriminates only with good reason. An indiscriminate magazine editor would be one who accepted anything that was sent in as a contribution for publication; the notion that there might be reasons relevant to the relative suitability of various submissions, such as the quality of the contributions or their relevance to the purpose of the magazine, would mean nothing to him. A partial editor would be one who had his reasons for discriminating between contributions, but whose reasons were bad reasons or reasons that were irrelevant to the purpose of his job. He might, for example, accept a series of bad and unsuitable articles because they were written by his brother. An impartial editor would be one who did the job of distinguishing between submissions for publications, accepting some and rejecting others, on grounds that were relevant to the nature of the task he is supposed to be performing.

The demand that people should be impartial is therefore the demand that people should not treat people differently unless good reasons can be given for so doing. But in calling this principle formal we draw attention to the fact that it only tells us the sort of way in which we should proceed. It does not in itself help us to decide what reasons constitute good reasons for differential treatment in particular cases. But if we accept this identification of the principle of equality with the principle of impartiality, it does follow that there is nothing *necessarily* inegalitarian about proposing different kinds of education for different children.

Elites

At this point some might object that to advocate elites is by definition inegalitarian. However, that is not necessarily the case because there are two distinct senses of 'elite'. The dictionary defines an elite as 'the choice part of society', 'the best part of anything', or a 'select group'. But the words 'select', 'best', and 'choice part' are ambiguous here. What might be meant is either the best part in the sense of the most advantaged, privileged, or best-treated part, or the best part in the sense of the most able or competent part. If the former sense is intended the nature of the advantage might be of several sorts. What seems to be very often implied, particularly by those who regard themselves as anti-elitist, is that elites are groups that are privileged in respect of wealth and/or influence, which in practical and political terms may very often become power. Thus, Russian oligarchs and members of school sports teams might both be said to form an elite in as much as both groups are influential and powerful members of their communities, as well as being granted various privileges. Whether elites in this sense are anti-egalitarian or objectionable obviously boils down to the question of whether one believes that there can be differences between people that constitute relevant reasons for preferential treatment in certain respects. But this is not the sense of elite that seems to be intended by the cultural elitists. What they are anxious to preserve are elites in the sense of groups of particularly able or competent people in various spheres. Thus, Eliot writes that the doctrine of elites "appears to aim at no more than what we must all desire – that all positions in society should be occupied by those who are best fitted to exercise the functions of the positions".[7] It is obviously true that in some societies those who form elites in this sense may also form elites in the other sense of being relatively privileged, and it well may be that some cultural elitists regard this as justifiable (as may a number of other people who have never come across the terms 'cultural elitist'). But that would be a separate question. All that is inherent in the cultural elitist thesis is the claim that individual children have different capabilities and that it is important for education to take account of these differences and to foster and preserve elites, in the sense of highly competent groups, in various spheres of human activity including the Cultural sphere. To regard this elitist theory as necessarily inegalitarian would amount to saying that there cannot be relevant reasons for regarding children as being variously suited to different kinds of education and that it is an offense to the principle of equality to acknowledge that some are more competent scientists, artists, or whatever than others.

The concern to maintain high Cultural standards, even if in practice that means for the few rather than for the majority is not then to be dismissed on the grounds that it is inegalitarian or elitist in the sense of providing unjustified privilege or advantage. On the assumption, then, that the aim of maintaining standards of excellence in various spheres is in itself generally desirable, the question we are concerned with here is the specific question of the desirability of promoting Culture and maintaining Cultural standards. And this question obviously cannot be answered until we have a clearer idea of what constitutes Culture.

The Concept of Culture

What, then, is Culture? Why is it important? What sort of things would we expect of a cultured person? Certain ways of behaving, perhaps, certain interests, certain information? Approaching the matter in this way, Schofield came to the conclusion that a person was cultured in so far as they did 'the done thing'.[8] For example, the done thing in a society might be to open doors for ladies, blow one's nose with a handkerchief rather than one's sleeve and be familiar with Shakespeare rather than Mickey Spillane, Bach rather than Beyonce. But here it seems that we are quietly shifting from one sense of 'culture' to another: to do the done thing is to conform to the culture of one's group and one could therefore be said to be cultured in the anthropological sense. But in general, as was noted at the beginning of the previous chapter, the phrase 'cultured person' does not have the two uses that the word 'culture' does. A cultured person is one who has some smattering of Culture and, although our view of what constitutes Culture will obviously be closely linked to what we value, Culture is not synonymous with what the majority value. The fact that many million more people read and like Agatha Christie than read and like Elizabeth Gaskell does not turn *Murder on the Orient Express* into a work that belongs to our Cultural heritage. (It does of course belong to our culture in the other sense.)

Eliot offered two attempts at a definition of Culture (or high culture, in his terms). "Culture may even be described simply as that which makes life worth living. And it is what justifies other peoples and other generations in saying... that it was worthwhile for that civilisation to have existed."[9] And elsewhere in talking of the need for European men of letters to preserve and transmit their 'common culture' he expands the phrase into "those excellent works which mark a superior civilization".[10]

It is indisputable that, as Eliot says, what we mean by 'Culture' and what we mean by 'those excellent works which mark a superior civilisation' are one and the same thing. Our Cultural heritage consists of those works that are deemed to be admirable. But this kind of definition is not going to help us, given that we live in a society and in an age where there is a great divergence of opinion as to what works, past or present, are the marks of a 'superior civilisation' (whatever that means). What are these excellent works? Who is to decide and how does one decide? Eliot's plea amounts to the injunction that we should be concerned about valuing the works of art that we value. Who could deny that? The problem is that the works that Eliot and Bantock value are not valued, or not to the same extent, by those who object to their view.

Much the same has to be said of Arnold's view that education should be concerned to introduce children to the best that has been thought and spoken in the past. Once again this may serve as an equivalent of what we mean by 'Culture', but it does not help us decide what is the best that has been spoken or thought in the past. (It is also open to the objection that the best from the past *may* be inferior to much of the present. This is not a view that I personally hold, but until we have some criteria for distinguishing good from bad or Culture from chaff there is nothing much that one can say to those who maintain that education should be concerned exclusively with the present, if it is to be concerned with works of art at all.) Arnold did attempt to delineate qualities that go to make the best that has been thought and spoken. He refers to 'high ideals', 'high tone', 'sweetness and light', and the 'Grand Style', for instance. These tantalizing phrases are themselves elaborated on. In his lectures *On Translating Homer* Arnold suggests that the Grand Style is "the result when a noble nature, poetically gifted, treats with simplicity and severity a serious subject". But the problem is that these qualities are themselves value judgments couched in obscurity: What is a noble nature? Why is simplicity valuable? Do we agree that a good play must present high ideals? When Arnold explains what he means by the Grand Style, he has in mind Milton as a master of it. But it would not be absurd to claim that Bob Dylan was an example of a noble nature, poetically gifted, who treats serious subjects with simplicity. It would not be absurd (and indeed since I first wrote these words Dylan has been awarded the Nobel prize for literature) but one feels that Arnold would not accept the example.

The truth is that any attempt to define the qualities that produce a work that belongs to the category of Culture runs up against one of the most perplexing of philosophical problems: how to arrive at criteria for aesthetic excellence. In the chapter on creativity the view that there are no standards, or that self-expression is the only one, was treated rather scornfully. But here is the other side of the coin, and the point that lends some plausibility to that view: if there are standards, what are they and who is entitled to determine them? It is not altogether surprising that Arnold finally observes that one must *feel* the quality of, say, Milton in order to know it. But this capitulation to an intuitive view suffers the defect that intuitive views in other areas do: if it is all a matter of intuition, who are we to tell anybody else what they ought to intuit? In other words, if the cultural elitists were to adopt an intuitionist position, they would automatically defeat their own argument that there are some excellent works, by objective standards, that children ought to be encouraged to come into contact with.

The important question to ask of advocates of Culture is what works they regard as culturally significant and why they do so. Here the cultural elitists do provide some help. Between them they produce a list of examples, which contains such figures as Aeschylus, Shakespeare, Milton, Eliot himself, Yeats, Bach, and Beethoven.[11] It is at once apparent, even from this selective list, that their view of excellent works is more or less equivalent to the list of works that have traditionally been admired by those concerned with education. But whereas Arnold would have found few schoolmasters who would dispute his examples, it is precisely because many teachers today either dispute the value of such works, or at least dispute that they are so valuable as to warrant educational time being spent on them, unless children happen to show an interest in them, that it is incumbent on those who wish to maintain the practice of initiation into the appreciation of such works to explain why this is important. Obviously it will not do to argue simply that they are great works of art. For it is the question as to whether they are, and if they are whether that is important, that is at issue.

Intellectual Quality

Bantock argues as follows: "Some human activities are of greater importance than others because they represent a more deliberate, refined and sophisticated exploitation of human potentiality, as poetry is superior to pushpin".[12] "It is not difficult to show that the study of poetry involves a higher and more deliberate degree of brain organisation, affects more aspects of the personality and produces more valuable consequences – the utilitarian criterion – than the study of pushpin."[13]

He seems to be producing three reasons for encouraging the study of something like a Shakespeare play, rather than leaving the children free to do what they want or to study various other human pursuits: that it requires, and therefore the study gradually promotes, greater intelligence, greater sensibility or sensitivity, and that it has other valuable consequences. But it is difficult to see what these other consequences are supposed to be. One point that Bantock does not mention, which could be another consequence, is that great pleasure might be derived from reading Shakespeare, but then great pleasure might be derived by some from playing video games or reading comics. What are the 'more valuable consequences' that studying poetry may have than playing video games? Surely the only consequences that studying poetry can have (or indeed studying anything else) are the consequences that the study has for the individual in terms of affecting her mental development, her emotional development and her enjoyment. In other words, Bantock is effectively only making two points: that the study of poetry involves greater intellectual ability and greater emotional sensitivity than the study of a good number of other things. To this may be added the claim that it may provide a rich source of enjoyment, which is certainly true but is equally true of a number of other things.

Without going into the problem of what precisely constitutes intellectual ability or what intelligence is, we should surely agree that reading a poem with understanding requires greater intelligence than playing bingo. Bingo is a game of chance and it is frankly difficult to see what P.S. Wilson can possibly mean when he writes: "I am fairly sure that some do, and quite certain that one could... benefit educationally from Bingo", unless he intends to define educational benefit simply in terms of enjoyment. When he adds the more specific claim that bingo "can be done 'seriously' and results, then, in the development of 'conceptual schemes and forms of appraisal which transform everything else'",[14] one is not clear what one can say in reply, except that he is obviously wrong.

Straightaway, then, we may say that the study of literature may be regarded as more worthwhile than *some* other activities on the grounds that it involves things that they do not. It is open to anybody to say that in their opinion intellectual ability and emotional sensitivity are unimportant. But few of us would. We would be much more likely to question the extent to which literature is the best vehicle for the development of these qualities. For instance, it might be argued that although *playing* bingo could not possibly be said to involve or develop intellectual ability (as distinct from serving as a means to some specific and limited task such as learning numbers), some kind of study of the social phenomenon of bingo might involve no less intellectual ability than the study of literature. Going on from there it might be suggested that, given a shortage of curriculum time, it would be more profitable to study such things as detective novels or pop song lyrics than what are conventionally regarded as great works of literature, since such study would hold children's interest more and hence stimulate greater effort and enthusiasm, while still making intellectual demands on the pupils. In reply to this Bantock would seem to be saying that the sort of intelligence required to analyze and understand a Shakespeare play is in some sense superior to the sort of intelligence required to analyze and understand pop lyrics or examine the changing fashions in pop music over a period of years.

I do not see how one could deny that a Shakespeare play (or a Dickens novel or an Eliot poem) is more complex than the average pop lyric or detective novel. But that is not quite the same thing as saying that the study of one requires a higher and more refined degree of intelligence than the study of the other. The assumption seems to be that those who do study, understand, and appreciate great works of literature will therefore be more intelligent in some general sense or have a superior kind of intelligence to those who do not. The problem here is that the notion of a superior kind of intelligence is frankly mystifying. How is this special kind of intelligence to be defined except in terms of the fact that it is related to understanding literature? And to say that that is a superior kind of intelligence would seem to beg the question. If on the other hand we say that people who appreciate literature are more intelligent in other important respects, this raises the simple question of whether it is actually true. Is there any evidence to support the claim that those who have whatever is involved in an intelligent understanding for poetry necessarily have greater intelligence in respect of other aspects of human life and activity? The answer is that there is no evidence at all to support this claim: an individual might display considerable intelligence in Shakespearean criticism and prove relatively incompetent in all other spheres of life. Thus, although one could hardly deny that it requires intelligence to study and understand literature, it is not clear that this amounts to a very strong argument in favor of promoting the study of literature in schools, since there are a great many other activities that also require intelligence.

Emotional Development

The strong card in the cultural elitist hand, therefore, is surely the reference to the development of emotional sensitivity or the schooling of feelings. Despite what has been said in the previous paragraph we surely accept that some intelligence is required for the study of literature, and even perhaps the empirical generalization that people who have such intelligence are unlikely to be devoid of sense in at least some other spheres. The weakness of the argument so far has been that so many other areas of study, which might be selected for quite different kinds of reason, also demand and promote intelligence. But whereas a sociological study of the rise of bingo, or the shifting patterns of pop music, or a purely scientific education, would involve intelligence they would not have much to do with the development of feelings. The real case for concern with Culture in education is surely that the study of Culture involves both the intellect *and* the emotions. Besides the fact that the study of literature makes intellectual demands on us, through it "we can become more aware of the feelings we have and we may also be able to develop new sorts of feeling".[15] There is a tendency for people to lazily identify emotions with feelings. But emotions such as hate, envy, love, jealousy, pride, or fear are not simply feelings akin to a sensation of pain or pleasure. They are to be defined as feelings attached to particular forms of cognitive appraisal; to put the same point in more everyday terms, emotions are feelings associated with particular understandings of what is going on. Envy for example is a negative feeling brought into play by one's reading a situation in a specific kind of way: I am envious if I believe that somebody else has some kind of good fortune that I wish I had (and perhaps think I should have). I am fearful if I have an unwelcome feeling brought about by the assumption that I am in some kind of danger. Worth noting here is the fact that it doesn't make any difference whether my reading of a situation is correct or not. I was afraid even if it turns out that I had no good reason to be. Also, note that though we often think of emotions as feelings, the feeling aspect is the element we know least about. Whether you feel exactly what I feel when you are in love, who can say? What allows people to say that we are both in love is that we are both experiencing some kind of feeling *because we each perceive ourselves similarly to be in a particular kind of situation.*

Understanding *Othello* involves appreciating that Othello is jealous, and that involves understanding that certain kinds of situation generally give rise to negative or hostile feelings towards another. One might say that to understand *Othello* properly, one would have to have experienced jealousy, but conversely one may argue that to introduce children to the character of Othello is a way of introducing them to the concept of jealousy or of sharpening their perception of it and some of its implications.

Of course, just as it was not clear that an individual who had an intellectual grasp of such a play would necessarily display a great deal of intelligence in other spheres of life, so it seems implausible to suggest that it is a necessary truth that those who have emotional sensitivity in the sense that they can put themselves imaginatively in Othello's position and feel what he feels will have or display such sensitivity outside the theatre. We are familiar with the example of certain Nazi leaders who had a deep appreciation of various Cultural works but on whose sensitivity as human beings this had very little effect. One way to dismiss such examples is to argue that the fact that the people in question were so lacking in sensitivity as human beings is proof that their appreciation of Culture was only apparent and not genuine. The trouble with this line of argument is that it makes its conclusion true by definition: appreciation of Culture must involve a high degree of sensibility in individuals in other aspects of their lives because anyone who clearly lacks such sensibility will be said to lack a true appreciation of Culture. Since this is plainly unsatisfactory, it seems to me to be preferable to concede what in any case one would have thought was obviously true: there can be a divorce between people's capacity to feel or experience certain emotions and their tendency to do so in specific situations. One can empathize with the characters of a play, but for some reason fail to empathize with one's neighbors. But to admit this is merely to admit that concern for the study of Culture is not a panacea for all our ills – a point that few, if any, would deny. The basic claim may still stand, and that is that, in so far as literature is predominantly concerned with human emotions and feelings, it is obviously true that to appreciate literature involves understanding and recognizing those emotions and feelings. One might add at this point that generally speaking literature also deals with human relationships and human decision-making, and consequently may also serve to illuminate these dimensions of life. Through literature we may initiate children into experiences that might otherwise lie outside their sphere of awareness. What is finally significant about a Shakespeare play, from the educational viewpoint, is not so much that it is a relatively complex structure and therefore undoubtedly requires some intelligence to grasp its structure, nor the claim that it requires some special type or high degree of intelligence to understand it, but rather the nature of it. For a

Shakespeare play, whichever one you choose, treats of people, their feelings, their relations with one another, their responses to situations, the way in which they act, the reasons why they do so, and the consequences of those actions. It introduces the reader to some of the complexities of people and behavior and thereby may develop the imaginative sensitivity of the audience beyond the limits set by their own experience.

Criteria of Aesthetic Quality

Throughout the above paragraphs it will be noted that I have unquestioningly used Shakespeare as an example of a writer of quality and his plays as examples of works of art or works that belong to high culture. I have done this simply in order to have some example whereby to bring out the sorts of claim that the cultural elitists are making. A Shakespeare play fairly uncontentiously may be said to demand intellectual and emotional maturity for its appreciation as well as being a potential source of enjoyment. It is therefore clear, in broad terms, why the cultural elitists are anxious to promote the study of such works. What however still remains unclear is how one sets about selecting specific works, how one distinguishes between better and worse works of literature, and how one distinguishes between different levels of Culture. What, in other words, are the criteria of excellence within the broad spectrum of works that demand an intellectual and emotional response? Surely popular novels such as those of John le Carré involving themes of loyalty, betrayal, love, friendship, duty, and various moral dilemmas demand an intellectual and emotional response for their appreciation, and yet, one presumes, they are not part of high culture. Why are they not? To this Bantock would reply, as he does in reference to the superiority of Donne's love lyrics over modern pop lyrics, that a Shakespeare play is "more complex, more varied",[16] and "truer" to the complexities of the various emotions portrayed than a Le Carré novel.

  Although there may be dangers in introducing these criteria – (is complexity necessarily a virtue and simplicity never? Arnold, as we have seen, certainly valued simplicity. Is not the criterion of 'truth' going to be very hard to handle in reference to the portrayal of emotions?) – this would seem to me to be an essentially fair comment. The simple and romantic conception of love in many pop songs does not do justice to the reality and complexity of love as it is actually experienced by most of us. To some extent therefore it misleads and distorts rather than develops and expands our sensibility in respect of the business of falling in love and understanding the complexities of our own feelings and those of others. What I confess to feeling very uneasy about is not the distinction between high culture and popular works of literature, poetry, or songs, but the claim that there can be levels of Culture and that the folk culture of the past was of value, whereas the popular culture of today is not. For if complexity, variety, and true representation of the "multi-faceted character of the emotion"[17] in question are criteria for pinpointing work of cultural value, it is very difficult to see why 'Greensleeves' (allegedly partly the work of King Henry VIII) should rank as culturally valuable, whereas modern pop songs do not. To this Bantock would reply by reference to the commercial inspiration and "the emotional falseness of popular culture"[18] today. But the motives or inspirational source of the composer would seem to me to have very little to do with the value of the work produced. (After all, the Homeric poems were composed for the price of a meal by wandering bards, and Mozart was commissioned to write many of his symphonies.) It may well be true that today's pop culture is by and large produced and marketed by hard-headed businessmen, but there is no obvious reason why what they produce should not be as true a representation of some emotion, on the same simple level, as 'Greensleeves'.

There are a number of other interesting questions that one might raise in relation to the cultural elitists: even if we were to grant that adults who appreciate literature are in some general sense likely to be more intelligent and more sensitive than those who do not, does it follow that the *best* way to develop intelligence and sensitivity in children is through study of such works? Might there not be other equally good ways of developing these qualities, which would nonetheless result in individuals being able to appreciate such works as adults? Is the suggestion of the cultural elitists only that the individuals who can take on such an education benefit as individuals or that the community also benefits from the existence of such individuals? Is there supposed to be something inherently good about the existence of great works of art, or are they valuable for the pleasure they give and their educative value? What would it mean to say that the Parthenon was inherently valuable?

But we must call a halt somewhere. It is undeniable that the selection of general criteria for aesthetic excellence is one of the most tantalizing of philosophical problems, and that the cultural elitist position is vulnerable on this point of how one selects great works of literature. Perhaps in practice there is no alternative but to consider specific works and attempt to make specific comments about them, which I take to be what we generally mean by literary criticism. Of course, as we know well, literary critics have to make value judgments as well as draw out what the features of various works are, and they do not by any means always agree in their evaluation. The view that there just are certain great works and we all know what they are is too simple and too naive to be acceptable. On the other hand, we must not confuse the fact that Cultural standards are hard to determine and sometimes difficult to reach agreement on, with the assumption that anything published is as good as anything else published.

In conclusion, it may be useful to note three distinctions: the distinction between a work that is intrinsically superior as a work of art and a work that is superior in terms of the pleasure it gives; the distinction between a work that is intrinsically superior as a work of art and a work that has more educational value; and the distinction between a work that is worth engaging with and one that is worth spending school time on. I happen to be someone who enjoys and values equally both Ibsen and Monty Python, classical and country music, and the films of both Francois Truffaut and the Naked Gun series; but though my evaluation is the same in terms of my enjoyment and I can find much to admire in both of each set of pairs, I regard the first of each pair as superior in terms of art. I also believe that the first of each pair has more educational value. That is to say, I believe that, for example, the plays of Ibsen are both superior to Monty Python as works of art and that engagement with them will contribute more towards one's education than engagement with Monty Python. Having said that, I confess that I have not fully convinced even myself by the preceding argument that, to take another example, the poet W.H. Auden is superior to the singer/songwriter Kris Kristopherson. But perhaps that could be set aside as a problem in philosophy that need not worry us in the context of education. For surely there is one very obvious reason for devoting curriculum time to the former of each pair I have referred to: there is little or no need to devote school time to engaging with pop culture, because the social environment and (by definition) relative approachability and ubiquity of popular culture makes it unnecessary to introduce it to children. By contrast the potential joys and other advantages of appreciating Culture will be denied to most if schools do not introduce them to it.

Notes

1 G.H. Bantock, *Education and Values* (Faber, 1965).
2 G.H. Bantock, *Culture, Industrialisation and Education* (Routledge & Kegan Paul, 1968) p. 15.
3 T.S. Eliot, *Notes Towards the Definition of Culture* (Faber, 1948; rev. ed., 1962) p. 25.
4 Ibid., p. 31.
5 G.H. Bantock, *Culture, Industrialisation and Education*, p. 2.
6 G.H. Bantock, *Education in an Industrial Society* (Faber, 1963) p. 71.
7 T.S. Eliot, op. cit., p. 37.
8 Hugh Schofield, *The Philosophy of Education* (Allen & Unwin, 1972).
9 T.S. Eliot, op. cit., p. 27.
10 Ibid., p. 124.
11 It is incidentally noteworthy that there are still proponents of the 'list' of great works and that the lists continue to refer to the familiar examples. See, e.g., Alan Bloom, *The Western Canon* (Harcourt Brace and Company, 1994), and Charles Murray, *Human Accomplishment* (HarperCollins, 2003).
12 G.H. Bantock, *Education in an Industrial Society*, p. 201.
13 Ibid., p. 94.
14 P.S. Wilson, 'In Defence of Bingo', *British Journal of Educational Studies*, 15 (1). As a matter of fact, bingo is sometimes used in classrooms as a way of teaching, for example, word recognition, new vocabulary, or numbers. But Wilson seems to be making the quite distinct claim that playing bingo can be as useful and effective educationally as studying typical curriculum subjects.
15 G.H. Bantock, *Culture, Industrialisation and Education*, p. 77.
16 Ibid., p. 76.
17 Ibid., p. 76.
18 Ibid., p. 83.

Further Reading

Valuable contributions to this topic include John Gingell & Edwin Brandon, *In Defence of High Culture* (Blackwell, 2000), David Carr, 'On the Contribution of Literature and the Arts to the Educational Cultivation of Moral Virtue, Feeling and Emotion', *Journal of Moral Education*, 34 (2), 137–151 (2005), C. Koopman, 'Art as Fulfillment: On the Justification of Education in the Arts', *Journal of Philosophy of Education*, 39 (1), 85–97 (2005), and Martha Nussbaum, *Not for Profit: Why Democracy Needs the Humanities* (Princeton University Press, 2010).

See R.W. Hepburn, 'The Arts and Education of Feeling and Emotion' in R.F. Dearden et al. (eds.), *Education and the Development of Reason* (Routledge & Kegan Paul, 1972), and Francis Dunlop, *The Education of Feeling and Emotion* (Allen & Unwin, 1984).

Questions

I am not entirely satisfied with my own argument in this chapter. Are you?

If not, how would you set about distinguishing works of Cultural value? Do you agree that, however appealing and benign it may be, popular culture is generally not of great Cultural value?

What reasons would you advance for spending school time on high culture (in Eliot's sense) rather than popular culture?

19 Research into Teaching

Teaching is not perhaps a very philosophically interesting concept, but it is obviously central to the educational enterprise and there are some interesting questions to be raised about the empirical research that is conducted into and around it. When I say 'not philosophically interesting' I mean that it is not an idea that perplexes one, leaves one boggle-eyed or bewildered, or that stands in obvious need of delicate and intricate teasing out. To be sure, one can observe that it is a *polymorphous* term, and that the verb 'to teach' takes two accusatives (so that one teaches somebody something, and the old adage 'I teach children not subjects' is rather robbed of its force). One can question whether it is an *achievement* word such as 'find' (which logically implies success or achievement) or a *task* word such as 'search' (which implies nothing about success or failure) –the issue being whether one can legitimately be said to be teaching provided that one is engaged in certain tasks regardless of the result, or whether one can only be said to be teaching if something is achieved. More generally there are questions to be asked about the logical connections between teaching and learning. But one surely does not lie awake at night despairing of getting an adequately clear idea of teaching, as one might in respect of love, justice, happiness, or indeed education. We know well enough what teaching is.

What is a bit of a mystery is what enables some people to do it well and others not. There is of course a conceptual question here: what counts as doing it well? But that is not what I want to concentrate on. We can reasonably enough say that teaching well means teaching by whatever morally acceptable means will promote and achieve the educational aims that have been discussed throughout this book. That still leaves the question, when we see individuals obviously teaching successfully, of how they achieve what they achieve? By virtue of what are they successful, and what are the best ways for teachers to proceed? On the face of it these are questions to be inquired into empirically. One needs to observe, to look, or assess by means of one or more of the senses, in some organized kind of way, what actually goes on when successful teachers (or indeed unsuccessful ones) are in action. But how is one to accomplish this?

DOI: 10.4324/9781003120476-19

Types of Research

A popular pastime among empirical educational researchers is to contrast, discuss, and argue about the rival merits of what may loosely be termed *quantitative* and *qualitative* research methods. (Many are unhappy with the implications of these and indeed the many other terms sometimes used in the debate, such as 'formal', 'informal', 'systematic', or 'ethnographic'. The main line of demarcation is between those who wish to organize their research more or less exclusively around what can be measured or directly observed, and those who wish to organize it around what can be assessed, the latter allowing of impressionistic judgment and other relatively individual modes of evaluating.) But such debate seems to me largely wasted.

In the first place, as already suggested, in many cases the distinctions are not even clear (there is even something called 'quasi-experimental' research, which a cynic might allege to be a cover-up for what is essentially clearly non-experimental). Until it is absolutely clear what, if anything, the difference is between, say, formal, systematic, and quantitative research and precisely how they are to be contrasted with informal, ethnographic, or qualitative approaches, we cannot have a coherent debate about their relative merits. If, as sometimes seems to be the case, there is some degree of overlap between various purportedly distinct methodologies, the situation becomes even more confused. In the second place this is surely not an argument that makes sense in the abstract, because what is at issue is not some inherent quality in one type of research or another, but the appropriateness of particular modes of research to particular issues. Since educational issues are of many different kinds and logical types, it is to be expected that quite different types of research should be brought into play on different occasions. The question therefore is not whether research into teaching should be conducted by means of quantitative measures (on some such grounds as that they are more 'objective') or qualitative measures (on some such grounds as that they are more 'insightful'), but what kind of research can sensibly be utilized to look into this particular aspect of teaching as opposed to that. That is to say, the form or type of research that should be adopted must be decided by reference to precisely what kind of thing is being inquired into and not to an *a priori* commitment to a particular research model.

Furthermore, much of the argument among researchers themselves is of a technical nature. It is about whether research is being properly conducted on its own terms (e.g., was the sample truly random, the sample size adequate, the reliability rating significant?) rather than about the terms on which it is being conducted. This is rather like the distinction between discussing whether a poem is well written in respect of observing the iambic meter (a technical, measurable matter), and discussing whether the iambic meter is well chosen (an evaluative assessment).

The questionable and misleading nature of this kind of debate (misleading because it wrongly suggests that those involved are being self-critical and analytic at a fundamental level) is intensified by the tendency to misuse or unconsciously take advantage of the ambiguity of some of the terms involved. Here we do run into some genuinely conceptual difficulties. What, for example, is objectivity? We all have a broad and hazy idea of what is meant by the word, but what precisely is meant and how is it related to subjectivity? Are they opposites, incompatible, or what? Some say that systematic observation and other quantitative means of research are to be preferred in that they are more objective. They are certainly less open to individual judgment on the part of observers. But is that necessarily a good thing? Are they more objective in some way that matters? Perhaps calling a method such as systematic observation 'objective' is just another way of saying what the mode of research is (for instance that it concentrates exclusively on the readily observable and pre-specified, at fixed intervals). The question of importance, however, is whether the attempt to understand something such as successful teaching by tabulating the behaviors of the teacher and the students at fixed intervals, in terms of a number of pre-specified observable behaviors such as 'asked a question', 'responded promptly', or 'looked out of the window' is or is not likely to reveal more of the truth more accurately than various other approaches. Calling it 'objective', if that merely draws attention to the mode of observation, does not represent an argument. But if 'objective' is taken to mean something like 'a dispassionate record of the truth', then it is absurd to assume that this method is necessarily more objective than, say, the impressions of an experienced observer. No doubt, in the latter case, one places a lot of trust in the competence and judgment of an individual, and there are many other equally obvious dangers to watch out for, but none of this shows that in principle it is not a better way to investigate such a question, regardless of whether it is more or less objective in some technical sense. And if it is a more appropriate way to investigate a particular issue, the fact that it does not involve the kinds of procedure that allow of high validity and reliability scores is neither here nor there.

In far too many textbooks and courses on research methods the cart is placed before the horse: we are invited to become thoroughly immersed in and to perfect our understanding of one or more approaches to research and to consider their technical strengths and weaknesses *before* we have given consideration to the particular kinds and nature of problems that arise in the context of education and teaching, before indeed we have given thought to what teaching and education are, and, consequently, before we have faced the question of what kind of research would be appropriate to this particular enterprise. (I need hardly add that very often the question of appropriateness is not faced at all, even after the technical aspects have been dealt with.)

In addition, in the realm of methodological discourse, we are commonly faced with ambiguous and confused concepts and a marked absence of any attempt to get to grips directly with conceptual issues.

Conceptual Issues

During the last seventy-five years or so there has been an amazing amount of research conducted into teaching, or particular aspects of it, and it continues unabated. There are a number of books that conveniently summarize some of the research. But, in the light of what has already been said, the philosophical reader is forewarned to expect a lack of real critical consideration. There is criticism, but it is mainly of the technical and rival methodological type just referred to. Whereas, the main problem with the bulk of the research is conceptual, and the nature, limits, and difficulty of conceptualization are evidently not familiar to many people working in the field. Conceptualization, as I hope by now readers will appreciate, cannot be equated with definition, if that means providing a verbal synonym. It is no good saying that 'teaching' is 'instructing' or 'causing to learn' and thinking one has now analyzed the concept. One hasn't. Is it necessarily a matter of instruction? What counts as instruction? Is anything that leads to learning an instance of teaching? Is one not teaching if one's students fail to learn something? What counts as learning? Such questions are real, difficult, and the sort that need answering if we are truly concerned with analyzing the concept of teaching. Nor, if one happens to be dealing with a mysterious, unobservable, concept such as understanding, does one truly explain it by operationally defining it in observable terms. One simply distorts it. Here again, note that behavioral definitions are not inherently objectionable. It depends on the concept. A behavioral definition of something that is essentially to be characterized in terms of behaviors, such as sporting prowess, is appropriate. A behavioral definition of something like love, however, is inappropriate, because being in love cannot satisfactorily be defined in terms such as giving flowers, saying that you are sorry, remembering anniversaries, etc., for they are neither necessary nor sufficient criteria of love.

The conceptual weakness of research into teaching is to be found primarily in three areas; perhaps paradoxically the issue is not about the concept of teaching itself, which, as I said above, is relatively unproblematic. The first and most important thing that one needs to have a sure and clear conceptual grasp of is the educational enterprise itself. The second is the concept or concepts directly at issue (e.g., we may be inquiring into the effects of the teacher's sense of humor in teaching or the student's degree of home support, in which case we need an adequate conceptualization of humor and support respectively). The third is what may be called the particularities of local conditions, by which I mean to refer to such things as what subject is being taught and what group of people we are studying. If we are studying the effects of humor in a Latin lesson, then we need to understand what counts as a good Latin lesson, which may very probably differ in important respects from what counts as a good PE lesson or a good social studies lesson. If we are studying the effects of humor on gifted children, then we need a clear and coherent conceptualization of giftedness, such as is not currently readily apparent in research and writing about gifted children.

Elsewhere I have criticized specific examples of research for failing to conceptualize any of the above three areas adequately, and I maintain the strong thesis that the bulk of such research is valueless in view of its logical and conceptual shortcomings.[1] However, here I want only to make the point generally – as befits a philosophical textbook concerned with principles rather than particulars. Whether particular pieces of empirical work, and if so how many and to what extent, are guilty of the errors and confusion that I claim are widespread, readers can judge for themselves at another time. The question here and now is whether it is correct to argue that conceptualization, in the sense that we are concerned with, is vitally important in the three areas mentioned.

Conceptualizing the Educational Enterprise

The case for insisting on the need for an adequate conceptualization of the educational enterprise seems to me as good an instance of logical necessity as one is likely to come across. It just does not make sense to conduct empirical research into teaching, in any manner or mode, without a clearly articulated conception of the educational enterprise. For research into effective teaching requires criteria of success. (That is to say, we need to know what criteria have to be met for something to count as an instance of successful teaching.) But the success that we are supposed to be interested in is educational success. A good teacher is, by definition, one who contributes to the successful education of her students. Therefore, in order to judge whether someone is a good teacher, you have to have a very clear idea of what counts as being successfully educated.

This is so obvious a point that one may briefly inquire why it needs to be stated so bluntly, and why it is not acknowledged or lived up to in practice, as I maintain it is not. There seem to be three rather similar and closely related explanations of why people do not proceed in ways that show an appreciation of the need for a clear conceptualization of the educational enterprise. The first is that they do in fact have such a conceptualization, but have not chosen to articulate it. But, in so far as this is the case, it is unsatisfactory. It is not sufficient that the researcher should have an adequate conception. We, the public, need to know what a particular researcher understands the educational enterprise to involve and in what he considers educational success to consist, in order to be able to judge for ourselves the plausibility of his research. If he says that his research leads him to the conclusion that x is a good teaching technique, even if we trust his research so far as methodology goes, we need to know to what sort of educational ends this technique is a good means. If we do not know his ends, we are in no position to decide whether we too approve of the means or teaching technique at issue.

Secondly, and I believe that this is the most usual explanation, the researcher may see the need for sound conceptualization of the educational enterprise, and try to meet it, but fall short because she is not really sure what is involved in the clear analysis and articulation of a concept. Here we run, once again, into the difference between analyzing a concept and providing various other types of definition. I hope that it is clear from the course of this book that analysis is to be distinguished carefully from a whole host of superficially similar, but nonetheless quite distinct, activities, such as providing examples, metaphors, verbal synonyms, and similes. The fact is that analytic ability has to be cultivated, and, if research programs are going to be improved at the level of conceptualization, researchers are either going to have to become philosophers or philosophers become researchers.

Thirdly, sometimes there is a view of the educational enterprise implicit in research that is clear enough, but is highly questionable. (There is, of course, always some idea implicit, since, if nothing else, the researcher's idea of educational success can be identified with success in respect of the instruments and measures used. But the idea implicit is by no means always clear or coherent; nor is it always recognized, even by the researchers themselves.) What I am getting at here is the extent to which, if certain educational research is to be taken seriously, we would have to assume that being well educated consists of things such as being able to draw facile pictures, to solve artificial and sometimes trivial puzzles, to recognize various sounds, to recall information, and to look attentive. For many research programs into teaching estimate student achievement largely or solely by reference to performance at such tasks and to other equally banal standardized tests of achievement.[2]

Conceptualizing the Object of the Research

It is equally evident that the particular object of one's research interest must be conceptualized properly, and the same rules of proper analysis apply: giving examples must not be confused with providing criteria, nor must any other substitute for proper analysis be accepted. For instance, if I want to inquire into the effects of the teacher's sensitivity, I need to make it quite clear what criteria have to be met for something to count as an instance of being sensitive. Establishing the criteria or formulating the conditions (necessary and sufficient if possible) for determining instances of sensitivity is *not* to be confused with giving examples of sensitivity, paraphrasing what it is to be sensitive by recourse to a thesaurus, defining it in the manner of a dictionary as 'keenly perceptive; reacting to stimuli', likening it to something else, or describing it metaphorically.

Then, having established exactly what it is, I need to note precisely what kind of thing it is, because it is also necessary to establish that what one is interested in can be meaningfully, and in some appropriate manner, monitored. It is not necessary that it should be directly observable, but it is necessary that the question of whether we choose to rely on direct sightings, indirect indices, or judgment, should be decided by the nature of the concept rather than the methodological orientation of the researcher. Is it, for example, the kind of thing that can be directly observed or at least its presence equated with directly observable behavior? Or is there a good argument to show that while it is not to be identified with any set of directly observable phenomena, its presence may be inferred from directly observable evidence? Is it, rather, the sort of thing that can only reasonably be detected by the judgment of the well-practiced observer? (If so, how does one recognize or develop the 'well-practiced observer'?) Is it the kind of quality that individuals can reliably recognize in themselves, so that a questionnaire might be appropriately used? Only when such issues have been sorted out am I in a position to determine what kind of research method would be appropriate in this particular case. Prior to coming up with an adequate analysis I am in no position to adopt an appropriate research methodology.

Conceptualizing Local Conditions

The requirement that local conditions be adequately conceptualized is partly related to the technical matter of variables. If we do not specifically take account of the fact that we are, for example, studying a history lesson for gifted children, then we may fail to see that our conclusions are based on data that are significantly attributable to the fact that it was history and not physics, or that the students were gifted. In order to take account of such variables, we need a clear definition of them. But it also arises partly from the claim, argued for in Chapter 13, that there are few if any generic teaching skills that are both significant and in danger of going unrecognized. It is highly unlikely, for instance, that using the blackboard, irony, drills, debate, essay-writing, punishment, praise, discovery methods, student interests, are either desirable or undesirable *in general*. It is likely to depend on what subject is being studied, what you want to achieve (which may differ depending on the level of study as well as the nature of the subject), and on the differences between students in terms of such things as age, preparedness, and aptitude.

Conclusion

If we bear the above points in mind, we can reasonably proceed to undertake empirical inquiry into some aspects of teaching. But it may be worth suggesting, if only as a counter-balance to the current fashion for trusting empirical inquiry into everything: (i) that a lot of questions about teaching, though undoubtedly empirical in some degree, just don't lend themselves to empirical research, and certainly not to research of the formal, systematic variety; the question of when and where humor has what effects in teaching, for instance, is both interesting and empirical, but I doubt very much whether one could successfully research the question in such a way as to yield practical guidance to teachers; (ii) that folk wisdom to the effect that good teachers are, if not born, at any rate educated rather than trained or made, is true, and that there is no appreciable set of techniques or skills that will make a poor teacher good or prove necessary to a good teacher. It may, more plausibly, be suggested that there are some rules of thumb that will prevent a poor teacher from being a disaster. Indeed, it may be that this is the truth that explains the long life of otherwise unimpressive research in this area: we have such a distorted conception of education and so many poor teachers that perhaps it pays to discover, laboriously, ways of controlling largely disaffected classes; and (iii) that one can come to recognize a lot about good teaching by a process of reasoning. If you know what you are trying to achieve, in what context, with what subject matter, and you know something about yourself and your students, then you ought to be able to work out some sensible and desirable ways to conduct yourself.

In my most pessimistic moments I imagine a school founded on the claims of empirical research into teaching in terms such as the following. (The reader should note that what follows is an extreme characterization, drawn in order to highlight some dangers.) It would consist of teachers adopting a number of specific techniques and tactics, behavior and orga- nizational ploys, routines, and rules based on the claims of empirical research. Teachers would proceed to a considerable extent formulaically rather than by intelligent response to situations. Paradoxically, given the emphasis on the scientific objectivity of such research, what particular techniques teachers selected would be largely a matter of chance. This is because, if we take the research of the last fifty years seriously at all, there is a great deal of contradictory evidence on a number of specific issues. So in the end, when deciding to adopt this or that approach to the teaching of reading, for example, "you pays your money and you takes your choice".

Some of the rules of thumb adopted, such as that one should use students' first names, will on the face of it be trivial. (The research on this topic for what it is worth asserts that it is not trivial. I would respond that in the first place we don't need expensive research to tell us that using first names is the norm and to depart from the norm would obviously be likely to upset or offend, at any rate in the elementary school. In the second place, the offensiveness or other- wise of using surnames, at any rate for older children, is clearly the con- sequence of social or cultural factors. Those who go to secondary boarding schools, where surnames are the norm, have no problem with being addressed by their surname. Indeed, many, rather irritatingly perhaps, persist with the practice through life.) Some of the rules will be very difficult to interpret: for example, be 'with it', show warmth, and be considerate may be good advice, but it is far from clear what counts as being 'with it', warm, and considerate (the conceptual issue again). Some principles appear to be logically necessary truths dressed up as empirical findings, as for example, when teachers are told that they should be interesting or clear. Part of what we mean by good teaching is surely teaching that is interesting. (Although even here one must be careful and not assume that what is in fact merely a sensible generalization is some kind of law. That a teacher should strive for clarity seems at first glance an obvious truth, but there may be circumstances in which it would be educationally beneficial for the teacher to be deliberately obscure. Faced with able and motivated senior students, for example, a teacher might abandon clarity with the intention of driving students to pursue research on their own.) The bulk of the rules of conduct, because of the nature of the research that lies behind them, will enjoin discrete, fairly mechanical behaviors of the type, 'look people in the eye', 'do not lecture or instruct', 'ask five different kinds of question', 'recapitulate the work of the previous class at the beginning of the following one', and 'require students to follow five or six specific steps when they are going to write an essay'.

Not only do the majority of such principles seem to me to miss altogether the essence of what teaching is about and requires, and to be in themselves somewhat 'poor things', but there is also the added fear that, since, by and large, the research is conducted in such a way as to assume that these skills are generic and these rules of universal application, teachers in this imaginary high school will adopt them routinely in every class, without any thought for what is being taught to whom and why. Furthermore, because this school with its endless repetition of lessons that start with recapitulation, then move through five types of questioning, with a great deal of eye contact, minimal instruction, and so forth, has, by definition, bought into the empirical research paradigm, it follows that questions such as "What is education?" will not be on its mind. The 'education' it provides will be the skill-training, information-processing kind of enterprise, that suits the industrial, military, and management models from which much of the research is derived, rather better than it suits the kind of education that we have argued for in this book. Nor are teachers of this type likely to be the sort of people who, throwing caution to the wind, capitalize on particular situations, doing what they see an opportunity to do rather than what they have been prepared to do by rote. Putting it very plainly, there is not, so far as I know, a shred of evidence that doing any of the things enjoined by empirical research (that are truly empirical claims and that involve specific behaviors) *as a matter of routine* will be in any way advantageous, if our ideal is to produce educated people of the type formally characterized in Chapter 6.

I should stress again that I have depicted an extreme possibility. I do not deny that there are various useful rules of thumb, principles, and precepts to be offered nor that it is possible for individuals to make intelligent and flexible use of rules and routines. My point is that the dominance of the idea of a science of teaching militates against such intelligent and flexible use.

Of the two broad divisions of research referred to above, and notwithstanding what was said there about the folly of judging in the abstract, I wish that there were rather more of the informal variety, because I think it more appropriate a mode of research for a greater number of more important and worthwhile educational questions. Whether, for example, a teacher is being humorous, is being taken to be humorous by her students, and is consequently being paid attention to, seems to me more plausibly answered on the strength of the judgment of one who, in the light of experience and understanding, has watched and come away with a judgment, than by any measure of humor and its effects that I am familiar with.

However, neither that example nor any other single instance is of particular interest to me in this context. My concern is with the spirit of the age (particularly as it affects education), which I take to be anti-philosophical at a time when what it most clearly needs is more competent philosophizing. Whether empirical research into teaching can in principle yield much information of importance may be open to doubt, in the light of the points made above. But it is certain that we cannot reasonably rely on such research so long as it falls as short conceptually as it has done heretofore.

Finally, the question may be raised of whether a good teacher needs herself to be well educated. I don't think that one can respond to this by stating unequivocally that she must be. There are, surely, examples of teachers who successfully contribute to the education of individual students by imparting understanding of and enthusiasm for their subject without themselves knowing much more than their specialist subject. And of course, students may develop of their own accord some of the characteristics of the educated person such as being transformed, or acquire breadth as a result of the curriculum provided rather than any individual teacher. But even the aim of meeting the breadth, the transformation, and the cognitive perspective criteria of the educated person will be more likely to succeed if individual teachers are themselves educated and hence able to make direct interventions designed to develop a broad integrated understanding that changes the individual's outlook on life. And the commitment or caring criterion is, I think, something that the good teacher must necessarily possess, since one logically cannot be a good science or history teacher if one is not imparting commitment to the procedures and norms of either subject in addition to information. Thus, we may conclude that, though it may not be logically necessary, ideally teachers ought themselves to be well educated.

Notes

1 See, in particular, Robin Barrow, *Giving Teaching Back to Teachers* (Wheatsheaf, 1984).
2 Think, for example, of the creativity tests referred to in Chapter 16, IQ tests, and simple tests of memory, variants of all of which have been used in research into teaching.

Further Reading

Pride of place here must go to Paul Croll, *Systematic Classroom Observation* (Falmer Press, 1986), which presents a strong critique of my argument (see especially Chapter 7). Paul Croll is a friend of mine and a person for whose scholarship generally I have the greatest respect. However, we have strongly divergent views on research into teaching, a field in which he is admittedly a renowned specialist. There are however two specific claims he makes about previous iterations of the argument I have provided here that I wish to respond to.

First, he writes: "Barrow [in The Philosophy of Schooling] makes the astonishing claim that it is impossible *a priori* to describe teaching styles in terms of... clusters of teachers [e.g., traditional, progressive]... and suggests that it is equivalent to dividing teachers on the basis of eye colour... This extreme claim cannot be taken seriously" (p. 169). He is quite right to take me to task for saying that researching into differences between progressive and traditional teachers is "as if you were to divide teachers into those with blue eyes and those with brown eyes". The analogy is absurd and I am duly chastised. However, my mistake was in the analogy and not, I think, in the point I was actually making. That point was that categories such as 'progressive' and 'traditional', the generality of which means that they involve a number of criteria (A, B, C, D, E, F, etc.) and the lack of precision of which allows that not all criteria are always met (so that one teacher may be classified as progressive because they exhibit criteria B, C, D, and E, another because they exhibit A, B, D, and F), create two serious problems. (i) It is sometimes difficult to know how to classify an individual: how many criteria, and which ones, necessarily have to be met to establish that a given individual is progressive? This problem could of course be solved by a tighter conceptualization of progressive, but my point is that that is not in fact being provided. (ii) So long as the definition remains broad, which it will inevitably be so long as we divide teachers into a mere two or three clusters or categories, we have no way of knowing which of the criteria A, B, C, D, E, F etc. was actually the cause of whatever outcome we observe.

Secondly, Paul writes that "To say that [the outcomes we observe] might all be due to some variable that no one has thought of is like rejecting a philosophical argument on the grounds that it might have a logical flaw that no one has yet spotted" (p. 173). But it isn't; this time it is he who has produced an incorrect analogy. My argument is that there are hundreds of variables that are not taken into account, any of which might (and some of which almost certainly will) be significant. This is not at all the same thing as saying that there might be a flaw that would invalidate an argument. The former is of the form: there is an x that might be relevant. The latter is of the form: there might be an x that is relevant. We can do nothing about that latter until somebody spots the flaw, but we can and should do something about the former, namely conceive of and control for more variables. To take but one example, I would suggest that one factor that may have some effect on how the student reacts to a given teacher has nothing to do with their teaching methods or style, but is rather the opinion that the student's parents have of the teacher. I liked the teachers that my parents (meeting with them on parents' evenings, etc.) admired, liked rather less those they were unimpressed by, and to some extent prospered more with the former. Yet, as far as I know no research program has ever even considered whether this factor may play a part in the outcomes they observe.

On the concept of teaching see William Hare, *What Makes a Good Teacher?* (op. cit.), David Carr, *Making Sense of Education: An Introduction to the Philosophy and Theory of Education and Teaching* (Routledge, 2002) and *Professionalism and Ethics in Teaching* (Routledge, 1999).

For a broad overview of the field, see Tony Townsend & Richard Bates, *A Handbook of Teacher Education* (Springer, 2007). A useful summary of research, up to 1974, is provided by M.J. Dunkin & B.J. Biddle, *The Study of Teaching* (Holt Rinehart & Winston, 1974). C. Wittrock (ed.), *Handbook of Research on Teaching*, 3rd edition (Macmillan, 1986) is comprehensive. See also P. Smeyers & R. Smith, *Understanding Education and Educational Research* (Cambridge University Press, 2014). On qualitative research see N.K. Denzin & Y.S. Lincoln (eds.), *Handbook of Qualitative Research* (Sage, 1994).

To engage further with the debate see, R. Barrow & L. Foreman-Peck, *What Use is Educational Research? A Debate, IMPACT*, No. 12, Philosophy of Education Society of Great Britain (2006), Jack Martin, 'In Defence of Robin Barrow's Concern about Empirical Research in Education', *Philosophical Inquiry in Education* 26 (2), 137–145 (2019), D. Rowbottom & S. Aiston, 'The Myth of "Scientific Method" in Contemporary Educational Research', *Journal of Philosophy of Education* 40 (2), 137–156 (2006), and C. Chambers, *The Seven Deadly Sins of Psychology: A Manifesto for Reforming the Practice of Scientific Practice* (Princeton University Press, 2017).

See also Ellen Condliffe Lagemann, *An Elusive Science: The Troubling History of Education Research* (University of Chicago Press, 2000).

Questions

Summarize and evaluate the argument of this chapter.

Read Chapter 7 of Paul Croll's book (cited in Further Reading) and consider its argument in relation to the argument of this chapter.

What do you think is necessary to meaningful research into effective teaching methods?

20 Conclusion: Theory and Practice

Remarks such as "That's all very well in theory but it won't work in practice" suggest that theory and practice are two distinct realms with little or no bearing on each other. And it is not uncommon to hear people dismiss philosophy as being 'just theory' with the implication that it is of no practical value. But this distinction must be rejected.

Let us begin by clarifying what is meant by 'theory'. It is clear that there are different kinds of theory. Thus, there are (i) mathematical theories. In pure mathematics one encounters the theory of equations, the theory of probability, the theory of numbers, and so on. Such theories exhibit a number of theorems (or results) derived from certain basic premises or postulates and the kind of derivation is usually described as deduction. Thus 'a is greater than b' and 'b is greater than c' yield the deduction 'therefore a is greater than c'. Generally speaking, pure mathematicians are not concerned that their highly organized, tightly welded abstract theories find practical application; indeed, very often they betray lordly indifference to the possibility. But this fact does not cause the 'practical' man or woman, nor in particular the 'practical' teacher, much worry. Mathematical theory is not what they have in mind when they inveigh against theory, and they would not regard the pure mathematician's disregard for practical application as an example of the thesis that theory and practice are poles apart and utterly unrelated. Besides, they are probably aware that mathematical theories *do* find application in the 'real world' via (ii) the theories of the well-developed natural sciences of which physics is, perhaps, the paradigm.

With respect to theories of type (ii) it is once more manifest that the slogan "Theory gets you nowhere" is not directed against these. For it is clear that the theories of natural science *have* got us somewhere if not where all of us want to be. Controlled experiment forms an integral part of natural scientists' procedures and the possibility of their research finding technological application is therefore always present. The breathtaking technological advances of recent decades serve as dramatic reminder of the successful marriage of theory and practice as far as natural science is concerned.

Not surprisingly, the success story of natural science inspires others working in different fields. If there can be a science of nature, why should there not be a science of humankind? And if it is possible to adapt the methods of

DOI: 10.4324/9781003120476-20

natural science to the human or social sciences, will not the success achieved by natural scientists attend the efforts of the social scientists? So we get (iii) social scientific theories deserving of separate classification because of their inbuilt methodological deficiencies – for example, the fact that they treat of human beings and not of inert matter, and the fact that moral considerations act as a restraint on experimentation. And, lastly, we have (iv) the kind of theorizing undertaken in this book, differentiated from (iii) in that whereas psychologists and sociologists may undertake empirical investigation in the form of surveys and experiments we, as philosophers, do not. Theorizing for us consists in no more than a sustained attempt to 'think things through' with particular regard for analysis of the concepts behind the words which are the principal medium of thought. Our kind of theorizing harks back to one of the senses of the Greek word from which 'theory' is derived, namely contemplation.

There are of course bad theories of every type. But the bulk of mathematical, scientific, and historical theory provides a true account of certain facts about the world in which we live and as such is of immense practical value. Some areas of inquiry, in producing less robust theory than others, as I would argue literary and much social science theory do, may leave something to be desired. Nonetheless, it misses the point to say that theories about human conduct and literature are of no practical value simply because they are theories. The basic sociological theory that large parts of human behavior are brought about as a result of social environmental factors is both obviously correct and of extreme importance. Even a theory such as the psychological theory that many if not all adult states of mind are governed by repressed sexual attitudes, which I personally find totally unconvincing, has some practical value in that it gives us a potential understanding of certain particular cases.

Theories of types (iii) and (iv) tend to attract the 'practical' teacher's scorn of course because sociologists, psychologists, and philosophers, unlike mathematicians and natural scientists, treat specifically of educational matters. Though I have been critical of some aspects of the research behind type (iii) theories (Chapter 19), I certainly do not accept that psychological and sociological questions and answers are of no practical value. But I shall not attempt to defend type (iii) theorizing against the practical person's strictures – sociologists and psychologists are well able to look after themselves. I shall concentrate on defense of the 'thinking things through' kind of theorizing as exemplified in the preceding chapters of this book.

Is philosophical theory of any practical value? To put it more colloquially, what can philosophy do for you or me? Does philosophy provide any answers? Yes, of course it does – to its own questions. Is critical thinking a normative notion? Yes. Does it make sense to say "She is six foot tall so she must be well educated"? No. Is the nature of scientific inquiry logically distinct from the nature of philosophical inquiry? Yes. Is imagination a skill that can be developed simply by practice in any context? No. However, it is the case that many philosophical questions yield not simply provisional answers (as strictly speaking all disciplines do), but also open rather than definitive answers. An important mantra for philosophers should therefore be 'many, but not any', since often analysis, though unable to prove that one particular conception is the 'correct' one, will be able to rule out many suggested interpretations of a concept. For instance, in Chapter 6 an answer to the central question 'What is to be educated?' was set out. Was the answer proven to be correct or the only possible one? No. But I hope it was established that it was a particularly reasonable answer, and that many alternative answers such as that education is essentially a matter of physical fitness, of possessing a mass of information, or of moral virtue are not convincing. Even when philosophy offers no clear-cut answers there is surely practical value in its contribution. In discussing religion, we did not 'prove' the truth or falsity of any particular religion, but the conclusion that one cannot reasonably claim to know the truth of one's religion was surely clearly established, and that should have a very significant practical effect on one's attitude to and behavior in respect of other religions. If I have no more and no less grounds for assuming the truth of my religion than you have for assuming the truth of yours, then going to war over the issue seems singularly pointless.

First, then, let us consider the objection that thinking things through in philosophic fashion is unrelated to what people *do*. Taken at its face value this is surely an untenable position. Suppose, for example, a teacher said, "I don't get my children to learn their tables by heart because I don't want to indoctrinate them", and suppose that the teacher then gave thought to the notion of indoctrination and came to the conclusion that getting children to learn their tables by heart did not constitute indoctrinating them, would we not now expect a change in that teacher's *action* in the classroom? Again, suppose a teacher held the belief that the purpose of education is to get children through examinations but that thinking about the concept of education brought about a change in her belief about its purpose, would we not now expect to find changes in what she actually did in the classroom? Or suppose that this teacher abandoned, as a broad guide to action, the precept 'Get them through their examinations' and substituted the precept 'See that they develop'. Would we not feel justified in asking what is involved in seeing that children *develop*, and if it were the case that the teacher could not tell us, would we not now counsel further thought on her part about the concept of development? Far from theory being unrelated to practice we have here an instance of theory – thinking about what it is to develop – being a necessary prerequisite to action. Until the practical consequences of acting in accord with the precept 'See that they develop' are spelled out there *cannot be* any action in accord with it. How can there be *selection* of activities to be carried on in schools without prior thought being given to the question of what ought to be done and what ought not to be done, and why?

Often those who denigrate theorizing of type (iv) show themselves to be inconsistent. This is the case, for example, when the objection to theory is expressed in some such way as, "You get on with your philosophizing and leave me to get on with educating". For, presumably, anyone who makes a remark such as this either must have some conception of what it is to educate, in which case they must have done some thinking, or else they have done no thinking at all, in which case it is difficult to see what they want to get on with. I suppose that an anti-theory advocate might finally claim that there is no need to think about the meaning of education in order to 'get on with educating', because he simply does what other people tell him to do. It's true that a claim like this would be coherent, but at what cost? For the picture with which we are now faced is of a person content to serve as a mere agent, a mere tool of others, content to carry out instructions emanating from superiors in the institutional educational hierarchy. And even then, hated theory will not have been disposed of; it is just that theorizing will now be carried on by the superiors, and, of course, it may be of a most unpalatable kind.

There are two main clusters of educational problems that await 'thinking through' and the basis of the division is made in accordance with the relative remoteness and relative nearness of the problems to classroom concerns. Thus, problems to do with equality of educational opportunity, the future of private schools, the rights of parents as far as the education of their children are concerned, the place and relative importance of vocational education, and so on are examples that would figure in the first cluster. It is unlikely that a teacher of chemistry or of history would find that thinking about problems like these affects in any significant way their teaching of chemistry or history, their principal classroom concern. But in spite of the relative remoteness of such problems, a strong case could surely be made for saying that all teachers nonetheless *ought* to be aware of them, to have thought about them, and to be prepared to take an informed view on them. It is at least arguable that this is a duty incumbent upon any person who would count themselves a member of a profession, apart from the fact that if educators are not prepared to think about such problems other people will and, further, will *act* on the basis of their conclusions.

The second cluster of problems has, in general, to do with the classroom. As far as this cluster of problems is concerned, it has already been suggested that it's a very odd teacher indeed who can get by without any kind of thinking designed to illuminate day-to-day teaching – the teacher as mere agent. But now let us examine this more specific objection to theory in greater detail. Consider some examples of everyday classroom actions involving what is done and how it is done. Teachers of young children often read stories to them and often these stories have a moral point or punchline; some teachers favor the asking of questions by pupils, others tend to regard questions as no more than pointless interruptions to the free flow of exposition; different teachers operate different kinds of sanctions – punishment for essentially the same type of misdemeanor takes diverse forms; some teachers set great store by 'creative' activities (free expression in painting, writing, etc.), others set greater store by the mechanics of an activity (spelling and punctuation, say, in the case of writing). Examples like these could be multiplied almost indefinitely. Now, how can it be that thinking about these activities and techniques is of no assistance? Thus, suppose I ask a teacher who does not favor questions, "Why don't you allow questions to be asked?" eliciting the reply, "Because they learn more if I don't allow questions". I then say, "Do they understand what they learn?" and a dialogue then ensues about what it is to understand – and what it is to learn – the upshot of which is that the teacher may be prepared to take a somewhat different approach and finds, perhaps, that there is a more precise definition of what he or she is doing, or ought to be doing. Again, with respect to the telling of stories, perhaps a teacher chose stories with a moral punchline in accord with a desire to do something in the way of moral education. Would not thinking about the whole notion of moral education help to suggest other techniques that might be tried, serve to render more clear what it *is* to educate morally? It is very difficult to believe that reflection on curriculum and teaching techniques does not provide, and never will provide, assistance to a serious-minded teacher intent on doing a good job.

So it should be unnecessary to say "Teachers ought to think about the why and wherefores of their everyday classroom practices" for the simple reason that such thinking is part of what is meant by 'teacher', not in the sense of 'child minder' or in the institutional sense of 'one whose job consists in going daily to a school', but in the normative sense of 'good teacher'.

At this level, theory and practice are intimately interconnected and the rigid dichotomy between them finding expression in 'Theory is one thing, practice another' is a false dichotomy. Obviously, theory will modify practice and practice will modify theory. The notion of theorizing about classroom activities if one is not going to *try out* the theory and refine and modify it in the light of practice makes no kind of sense, or, at the very least, it is difficult to see what the point of the theorizing is meant to be. As a matter of fact, teachers' objections to theory of the kind under discussion are usually objections to failure on the part of theorists to have sufficient regard to the practical side of the equation. The familiar complaint runs along the lines of arguing that lecturers in education have never known what classrooms and children are like, or have forgotten what they are like. Objections of this kind are not in reality objections to theory *per se* but the danger is that they will be mistakenly seen as such and result in decrying, not the present arrangements relating to, say, teaching practice, but the very act of thinking about teaching.

There is an even more specific interpretation of the 'theory is unrelated to practice' thesis. Someone might accept all that has been said so far but go on to observe that I have missed the point, which is that what is wanted from theory is a set of directions enabling all teachers to control their children, to keep discipline, a set of directions telling teachers what to do with youngsters who don't want to learn anything, are rebellious, and so on. Clearly, philosophical theorizing alone cannot provide direct, detailed specifications of this kind. I simply cannot see theory providing someone equipped with all the personality defects

ever unearthed by psychologists with foolproof means of controlling and sti-
mulating the interest of recalcitrant pupils. Nevertheless, careful thinking might
ameliorate the conditions under which some teachers operate. Consider, for
example, some of our practical arrangements governing the young probationer
teacher. As far as one can judge it seems to be the case that a number of schools
still operate in accordance with the principle that new entrants to the profession
have to prove their worth by showing that they can handle the roughest,
toughest classes there happen to be. Either they crack under the strain or, if they
survive, they are eventually rewarded by being assigned to some of the 'A' forms
when another unfortunate arrives. Is such practice justified? Is it not the case
that questions of control and discipline ought not to be left to inexperienced
young teachers to work out alone but that the staff as a whole should deal with
them in concert, taking care that new members are shielded to some extent from
direct confrontation with very difficult children and certainly supported if they
run into difficulties? And is it not the case that teachers as a body ought to bring
before society as a whole awareness of the disciplinary problems that exist in
some schools as a reminder that the onus is not upon teachers alone to resolve
these problems? Or, to take another example from the business of initiation into
teaching, is it really acceptable that newly qualified teachers should be placed
'on call' and expected to teach subjects for which they have no qualifications at
all, as commonly occurs in some jurisdictions? Surely these are questions that
need to be *thought* about.

Finally, let us return to the general objection to theory of type (iv) and, for
that matter, to theory of type (iii), that such theories do not provide *certainty*.
They are grievously deficient in this respect compared with mathematical and
scientific theories. Thus, it might be said that we have not provided *proof* that
education is this rather than that, or ought to be concerned with this rather than
that. Similarly, psychologists have not *demonstrated* that streaming is a more
efficient way of organizing for teaching and learning than non-streaming, or
that learning by discovery is more effective than learning by instruction. This is
quite true. We have not provided proofs of the mathematical variety – the
paradigm of proof – but could we, in logic, do so? It has to be recognized and
faced up to that the matters of which we have treated, involving fundamental
questions of value at every turn, are not matters which can be treated mathe-
matically or in accord with the procedures of natural science. Proof in the sense
of mathematical demonstration, the QED of Euclid, is not to be had here and
in its place, as was argued in the chapter on rationality, we can only offer *reasons*
for thinking this rather than that. As Aristotle observed: "the man of education
will seek exactness so far in each subject as the nature of the thing admits, it
being plainly much the same absurdity to put up with a mathematician who
tries to persuade instead of proving, and to demand strict demonstrative reasoning of a public speaker".[1]

Because of this methodological fact – that mathematical proof is not to be
had in all spheres – it must be the case that there will be differences of opinion
on educational issues. In this book we have sought to show that people who are

prepared to exercise their reason and powers of critical thought, and who are prepared to work to sharpen them, may come to firmly based opinions of their own – may, indeed, come to agree about some of those issues. And if they find agreement on some other issues hard to achieve they may come to accept the inevitability of disagreement and learn to live with it. As Sir Alan Bullock, speaking to the Commonwealth Universities Congress, once wisely observed, "there have always been differences of opinion and cultural splits. The problems discussed in our universities are open-ended. There are no definite answers. If you do not like this pluralism you should not have been born; because it is what life is about".[2]

Notes

1 Aristotle, *The Nicomachean Ethics*, I (iii), 4.
2 Alan Bullock, reported in *The Times*, August 15, 1973.

Further Reading

See R.F. Dearden, *Theory and Practice in Education* (Routledge & Kegan Paul, 1984), Chapter 6, by Harold Entwistle, in J.W. Tibble (ed.), *An Introduction to the Study of Education* (Routledge & Kegan Paul, 1971), Chapter 7 of *Introduction to Philosophy of Education* by James Gribble (Allyn & Bacon, 1969), and P.H. Hirst's paper 'Educational Theory' in J.W. Tibble (ed.), *The Study of Education* (Routledge & Kegan Paul, 1966).

For a full list of the many useful articles published in the *Journal of Philosophy of Education* (previously *Proceedings of the Annual Conference of the Philosophy of Education Society of Great Britain*) see vol. 15, no. 2, 1981, and indices published in subsequent volumes.

Question

Only one question here:

Do you or do you not agree that philosophy has relevance to educational practice? (Give your reasons!)

Appendix

This Appendix consists of the Prefaces to the second, third, and fourth editions, which are retained largely for historical reasons. Apart from registering when various specific changes and additions were made, they provide a record of the continual debate among philosophers as to the precise nature of analysis, and remind us of the constant need for those who are committed to the view of rationality that underpins this book to defend it against those who, however incoherently, seem to question it, whether in the name of relativism, nihilism, Marxism, sociology of knowledge, or postmodernism.

Preface to Second Edition

The invitation from our publishers to update and revise our *Introduction to Philosophy of Education* gives rise to the question of the nature of philosophy, for it is not the kind of subject that dates in the way that physics or even history may do. There are revolutionary thinkers in philosophy who open up entirely new paths of inquiry, but they are exceedingly rare, and even they do not often falsify the past so much as move away from it. Philosophy is less about generating knowledge of new matters than about providing greater understanding of what we are already familiar with. Seldom are there new discoveries or new interpretations that make previous work in the field unacceptable. What, for example, Plato had to say about love or justice over two thousand years ago has not been invalidated, replaced, or rendered obsolete by the work, of, say Wittgenstein in the last century. Plato's writings really do have as much pertinence today to the questions with which they are concerned as any contemporary work, in a way that the writings of early Greek doctors or scientists, for all their intrinsic interest, do not. There can of course be specific criticism in philosophy that shows arguments thought to have been sound to be untenable, but that kind of shift of view scarcely applies at the level of an introductory text.

Out initial aim was to provide an introduction to the business of philosophizing in the context of educational problems; in line with that aim we concentrated on pursuing an examination of the main concepts in the domain of education (or, as I should now prefer to say, schooling, since I take education to be merely one of many possible concerns of school, although most of the topics treated here are to do with the more specific concept of education). The intention was to conduct a rigorous investigation of the ideas of education, knowledge, culture, etc., so that a fuller picture of them and a greater awareness of the implications of each concept would emerge, or sometimes, so that the inadequacy of an idea or slogan might be exposed. In so far as what we originally wrote was to the point and coherent, the passing of time – at any rate, so brief a period of time – does not much affect it. If there was the logical possibility of distinguishing between influence generally and indoctrination specifically five years ago, there will be still. If our conception of education involved knowledge and understanding then, it does now in all probability. If the creativity of a Beethoven was distinct from the self-expression of a young child last year, there will be good reason to maintain that distinction this year. So, in design and broad outline this edition retains the format and flavour of the first, not because we are complacent, but because material changes in the world do not often affect conceptual truths and points of logic.

Nonetheless some changes have been made. First, there are a number of small but not insignificant stylistic alterations; and a number of grammatical infelicities have been corrected. Allusions and references have in many places been brought up to date: nothing dates quite as obviously as the name of a defunct pop group or a forgotten political event. Examples, too, have sometimes been brought up to date, although here again it must be remembered that the function of examples in philosophy is very often such that neither their being up to date nor their practical likelihood matters very much. For instance, when a philosopher considers whether a historian who knows nothing other than history should be considered as educated, he is not interested in the likelihood of there actually being such a person, but in whether, *if* there was, he would count as educated. He is interested in what might intelligibly be conceived, more than in what happens to be the case in the physical world. It is important to realize at the outset that examples are used for the purpose of testing logical possibilities rather than actual probabilities in order to avoid the mistake of assuming that philosophers are out of touch with the everyday world. When we ask whether a person could be in two places at the same time, we are not questioning the possibility of a physical body such as yours or mine being entirely in Oxford while also being entirely in Cambridge; rather we are raising the question of the senses in which a person might conceivably be said to be in two places at the same time. (Suppose your body minus your heart is in Oxford, but your heart is keeping another body alive in Cambridge.) In other words we are really raising the question of what constitutes being a person, and not asking about material factors in the everyday world at all. When we ask whether an individual could be considered creative if he were to spill paint accidentally onto canvas in such a way as to produce a beautiful pattern, we are not concerned with whether anyone has done or might do such a thing, but with throwing light on what is involved in the notion of being creative. (Again, *if* someone did that, would we classify it as a creative act?) Likewise, nobody that I know of would behave in some of the ways used as examples in the chapter on rationality in this book, but to consider examples, however bizarre, allows us to fill in the details of, or to question, our conceptions. (Incidentally, one reference that I have not bothered to update is that made to the launching of the first sputniks. It is true that some readers may not have heard of sputniks, but in terms of technological breakthrough, which is the point of the reference, some of the early steps in the space race represent more significant achievements than later, more dramatic steps. For that reason the example does not need bringing up to date, and for that reason younger readers ought to be presented with it.)

Once or twice changes in our own thinking brought about by thought and discussion and with the passing of time have necessitated alterations to the substance of an argument. Or issues to which we were not previously alert, such as the widespread immoral treatment of animals, have impinged on our consciences and required a mention. However, such changes in substantive content are not extensive, if only because, while the original text was the work of two of us, this revision has been solely my responsibility.

The main weakness of the original edition, in my view, was that we did not draw a very clear distinction between words and concepts or between verbal and conceptual analysis. More simply, we did not, perhaps, make it entirely clear what we took philosophical analysis to involve. In particular, we made a number of references to 'linguistic usage' and to 'objectivity' and 'correctness', without making it clear to what extent linguistic usage *determines* conceptual meaning (as opposed to reflects it, coincides with it, influences it, etc.), and without explaining in what senses of the words an analysis can be said to be 'objective' and/or 'correct'. On this broad but vitally important matter of methodology Woods and I have, we think, slightly different views although we have never satisfactorily resolved wherein the difference lies. This may partially explain the slight vagueness, not to say odd sign of tension, about our procedure in the previous edition.

I have argued extensively elsewhere that although there are a number of very important questions to be asked about verbal matters (the features and functions of words and our use of them), it is important to distinguish them from conceptual questions.[1] Questions about linguistic usage may lead to illuminating answers of direct relevance to conceptual issues, and should therefore be asked by philosophers. But none the less they are distinct from questions about concepts as such, and should therefore not be the philosopher's only interest. As words and concepts are not identical, so linguistic analysis cannot be coextensive with conceptual analysis. We may ask how people tend to use the word 'educated' and that will certainly throw light upon what is generally involved in being educated, at any rate as conceived by our culture. We may find that all people use the term in exactly the same away, or we may find that, despite variations, there is a common core to all uses of the word. Consequently we might, if we chose, talk of a correct or objective sense of the word 'educated' (i.e. the sense of the word sanctioned by usage in our culture). But such linguistic exercises, though they may in some cases incidentally reveal all that there is to be said about the concept behind the word (the idea behind the label), do not necessarily do so, and in fact are less likely to do so in proportion to the complexity and sophistication of the idea in question. Two problems, at least, may very likely remain – problems that need tackling and which very obviously belong to the domain of philosophy: people may use a word in widely different ways, sometimes to the point at which there does not appear to be even a common core, and people's use of a term may fail to reveal a clear and coherent conception on its own terms. Thus 'educated' might conceivably mean something quite different for two people (in which case we are dealing with distinct concepts labelled with the same word), and anybody's notion of being educated, including one's own, might just be insufficiently clarified and worked out. I should be strongly inclined to conclude that talk of a correct or objective concept is therefore meaningless, unless one merely means a widely shared concept. One may reasonably ask whether my use of the word 'educated' is correct according to standard practice in my culture, but the question to ask about my concept of being educated is how well formulated or articulated it is.

The task of the philosopher, having taken what hints and clues he can from linguistic patterns, is to arrive at a set of clear, coherent, and specific concepts. We need to clarify our concepts in order to assess them; until we painstakingly spell out what we understand by being educated we can say nothing about it, and obviously our unpacking must lead to a clear exposition, so we know that we are saying something and what it is. Coherence is necessary, both within and between concepts, so that our ideas make sense and can stand up: we do not want a conception of being educated that when clearly articulated turns out to be self-contradictory or to carry with it implications that we cannot for one reason or another accept. Specificity is necessary in order to facilitate talk with teeth in it. That is to say, in order to be able to make telling comments on the world, in order to gain a fuller understanding, one needs to develop an armoury of specific as opposed to general concepts. The ability to discriminate between the various species of a genus, in any field, rather than to see the world only in terms of genera, represents power when it comes to knowledge.[2]

In line with the distinction referred to between words and concepts, the device of using quotation marks round single words or phrases, rather overworked in the first edition and not adopted consistently, has here been systematized. When the word is being referred to, quotation marks are used; when the concept is being referred to, they are not used. Thus we discuss the logical features of knowledge, but the emotive force of the word 'knowledge'. Occasionally quotation marks are also used as 'sneer quotes' to suggest an ironic or otherwise not quite literal use of a word or phrase.

Another change I considered was that of replacing the generic use of the word 'he' (to mean 'a person') by 'she' or by some newly coined neutral term. But I rejected this in the end on the grounds that correct English provides us with the word 'he' meaning 'a person of either sex', and it would be more appropriate for the few who do not appreciate this to learn it, than for the rest of us to devise new terminology. To replace 'he' by 'she', as some authors now do, seems the worst of all worlds and a good example of the incoherence of what is sometimes termed 'reverse discrimination'. If 'he' were an immoral or otherwise unacceptable usage, then so must the use of 'she' be immoral, as well as incorrect.[3]

One or two additional comments, sometimes substantive, have been made, but economic factors have necessitated that most of them be added as notes at the end of the chapter in question.

But what, the novice may ask, about the effect of recent currents of thought and shifts of ideology and perspective? Marxism, for instance, has made great inroads in the philosophy of education in Australia since this book was first written. In Britain in the same period interest in phenomenology and existentialism has increased. In the study of education a number of sociological critiques have tried to suggest that the type of philosophy here practised is just one more class-based act of special pleading. Should not these and other similar tides of thought be reflected in some way in a new edition? The simple answer is, no. The various movements, ideologies, and methodological critiques that come and go are attempts to interpret the world in one particular way. They are therefore to be contrasted with, rather than opposed to, a book such as this which does not seek to explain the whole field of education, let alone the world or human experience, but to contribute to a greater understanding of some ideas and arguments related to education.[4]

Of course some work in other fields does suggest criticism of our methodology. Some, for instance, have argued, though quite unconvincingly, that knowledge is a *purely* social construct, and that our attempt to be detached and objective is necessarily but one more socially determined pose. Others, more reasonably, have made points to the effect that our procedure is in various ways less value neutral than we might wish. These latter kinds of criticism, involving argument directly related to certain practices or assumptions, are fair comment and, in so far as they are convincingly argued, to be taken note of. But a general sociological thesis, presented without reference to the arguments of particular philosophers, to the effect that the would-be autonomous and independent-minded philosopher is actually inevitably the product of his social environment, no more requires a philosophical rejoinder or the abandonment of philosophical practice, than a Freudian account of why an individual seeks love in the ways he does obliges the lover to start loving in a new way. It is, incidentally, most unfortunate that, given this quite common tendency to fail to see the difference between sociological attempts to explain, psychological types of explanation, philosophical inquiry, and historical accounts of events, and the consequent tendency to believe any one of them to be more significant than it is, we have for the most part failed to institutionalize the study of at least these four subjects as crucial to the study of education. Had we done so with more success there might be fewer people around who believe that to explain why somebody believes something in sociological terms is to dispense with the question of whether the belief is reasonable. (At the University of Leicester, while preaching the importance of the disciplines, we have in fact moved from requiring students to study all four ten years ago, through a period of requiring that they study only one, to a state in which they study two. This is to be welcomed, I suppose, on the grounds that half a loaf is better than none. But the adage is misleading. When the point of the exercise is to develop in people a capacity to recognize logically different aspects of a matter, giving people awareness of only half the possibilities is more like giving them half a sixpence than half a loaf.)

It was, then, never the purpose of philosophy (our conception of it, that is) or a book such as this to offer to interpret the world. Its aim was, and remains, 'to attempt to show philosophy in action' with 'the stress on how to do philosophy'. For this reason it is of secondary importance what particular concepts and arguments are focused upon. We might have elected to add chapters on topical themes, but to have done so would only have been to reduplicate work done elsewhere. As to the original issues we chose to discuss, it is difficult to see how a philosopher of education could not but throw out at least passing reference to education, understanding, and knowledge, and we still believe that rationality, culture, creativity, indoctrination, and the notions of readiness, discovery, needs, and wants (collected together in Chapter 10), deserve to be carefully considered by any prospective teacher.

Robin Barrow
University of Leicester
1982

Notes

1 See in particular my *The Philosophy of Schooling* and Robin Barrow (ed.) 'Five Commandments for the Eighties' in *Educational Analysis*, vol. 4, no. 1, 1982.
2 See Robin Barrow, *Injustice, Inequality and Ethics* (Brighton, Wheatsheaf, 1982) ch. 1.
3 [For the third edition I have left this paragraph and left the generic 'he' in the body of the text. I recognize, however, that, rightly or wrongly, I am likely to lose this argument in practice, in the long run.]
4 [But note, since these words were first written, a recent review of the author's *Critical Dictionary of Educational Concepts*, which refers to an 'individualistic lack of interest in the social dimension'. *Times Higher Education Supplement*, 29 May 1987.]

Preface to Third Edition

In the Preface to the second edition of this book I wrote 'At the University of Leicester, while preaching the importance of the [foundation] disciplines, we have in fact moved from requiring students to study all four [philosophy, psychology, history, and sociology]..., through a period of requiring that they study only one, to a state in which they study two.' Time passes, and now Leicester, in common with many other departments of education, requires nothing in the way of disciplined academic study. Indeed, both Ron Woods and myself, in common with other theoretically inclined educationalists, have now left the University of Leicester, nor is it likely that we will be replaced.

That, as some readers may appreciate, is about par for the course. It is particularly gratifying, therefore, to be invited to produce a third edition of this *Introduction to Philosophy of Education*, at a time when philosophy departments in universities are being closed down and education departments are all too often turning their backs on anything except 'hands on' courses dictated by government (to what good purpose we have yet to be told). The fact is not only that having some adequate grasp of philosophy is essential for making sense of daily educational activity, and sorting out the coherent from the absurd, but also that, *mirabile dictu*, there is a market for it!

Mention of the previous Preface brings me on to the point that Woods, who is now happily cultivating his garden both literally and metaphorically, and who for that reason left the preparation of this edition to me, has none the less voiced an opinion on that Preface. He thinks that it should be omitted from this edition. 'I cannot think', he writes, 'that a rarefied dispute about philosophic techniques is of interest to anyone except people like you and me – and we are rare!' He is referring to the comments made there about the distinction between words and concepts, and he may well have a point, at least so far as the manner of drawing attention to that issue goes. None the less, I have retained the Preface, including the passage in question, though with a few modifications and omissions. This is because, in my judgement, the question of what philosophical analysis is – what one is trying to analyse, why and how – is supremely important. It is obviously important theoretically since an understanding of what one is about must have some effect on the doing of it. But it is also important in practical terms, since lack of competent philosophizing in educational contexts is due partly to ignorance of what is involved.

In particular, many, if not most, people still seem to equate analysing a concept with defining a word in the sense of attempting to provide some verbally synonymous phrase for the word in question. The Preface to the second edition draws attention to the view that (i) philosophical analysis is ultimately concerned with the clear and coherent articulation of ideas rather than with definitions of words (although the latter may have a part to play in contributing to the former), and (ii) consequently, so-called ordinary language philosophy and linguistic analysis can be at best only part of the business of philosophy. To illustrate this as succinctly as possible: while our style of philosophy here is indeed closely associated with the clear use of everyday language, the book is not concerned simply with attempting to tabulate how people generally use such words as 'education', 'creativity', and 'culture'. Rather it is concerned with trying to explicate and unfold ideas or concepts such as those of education, creativity, and culture. The object is to explore and iron out obscurities, contradictions, confusions, absurdities, and so forth that may be involved in particular people's hazy grasp of the ideas in question, rather than to say how various words either should be or are used.

What Ron Woods will feel about this tenacity on my part, I do not know. But I do wish to take this opportunity to record my affection and admiration for him. He is, *au fond*, a very private man, but he was a fine colleague and I miss him a great deal professionally.

In this edition I have made minor revisions throughout and updated the Bibliography (which incidentally was previously inaccurately and absurdly called 'a comprehensive bibliography of worthwhile writing in the field' – it was not comprehensive, nor is it now; furthermore, some indubitably worthwhile writing was not mentioned, and some of what was mentioned was not obviously worthwhile). But the major change is to be found in the addition of two completely new chapters (Chapters 3 [8] and 11 [19] on 'Curriculum Theory' and 'Research into Teaching', respectively).

These chapters are not in quite the same mould as the rest of the book. The original chapters are all concerned with the analysis or elucidation of a concept (or concepts), with the aim, as was stated in the introduction, 'to attempt to show philosophy in action' with 'the stress on how to do philosophy'. While the new chapters do add a little to the general discussion of conceptual analysis (including some quite important points referred to but not illustrated in the Preface to the second edition), they are more concerned with claims about the confusion and logical incoherence of much of the current practice in the domains of curriculum and empirical educational research.

Curriculum is a branch of educational study that has come into its own more or less as institutional interest in philosophy has declined. This seems to me very sad. (And I suspect the change in their official fortunes is connected. Work in curriculum very often looks like a combination of bad philosophy and bad science, but it's very much easier to pass oneself off as a curriculum expert than a competent philosopher.) If curriculum is a relatively flourishing area, empirical research is rapidly becoming a *sine qua non* of respectability. Lecturers and professors are increasingly evaluated by reference to the amount of grant money they bring into a department (even if it is quite literally wasted) rather than by reference to an estimate of the wisdom they purvey. Yet, as I shall argue, a great deal of empirical research in education is misconceived, inappropriate, and quite simply irrelevant to advancing our understanding of the educational enterprise and thereby contributing to good practice.

I hope that the new chapters do not upset the pattern and the flow of the book as a whole too much. But it seems to me that philosophers should be applying themselves more than they sometimes have in the past to the practices and assumptions of those around them, that it is important in an introductory text to draw attention to the huge practical value of philosophy (as pinpointing, and hence allowing one to avoid, gross folly of one sort or another), and that their addition should therefore improve the utility of the book in respect of courses in education departments.

I toyed with the idea of cutting out some of the original chapters, as I did when preparing the second edition, but again felt disinclined to do so. Some of the words that form the chapter headings may be less in vogue than they once were, but the concepts and the issues surrounding them are quite certainly still around. For example, people do not actually say 'I believe in child-centered education' in the dewy-eyed way they did in the innocent 1960s and early 1970s. Nonetheless, and whatever words they use, plenty of people do still emphasize the importance of children's needs, interests, and readiness and other features that once were referred to as the tenets of child-centered education; and furthermore they act in the light of their beliefs about such things. Consequently, it is as important as ever to get individuals to think more closely and carefully about these concepts and others that are discussed in Chapter 8 [4 & 5], but it is no longer entitled 'Child-Centred Education'. Similarly, 'creativity' may not be on educators' lips to the extent that it was when the book first appeared, but creativity tests are still an integral part of such things as empirical research into teaching quality, and a very large number of teachers, particularly at the primary or elementary school level, still proceed to put an inordinate amount of time and effort into what are hazily thought to be creative activities.

Of course, the fact that educationalists in general are still concerned with certain concepts does not necessarily mean that philosophers are. A case in point is provided by indoctrination. With the exception of my good friend Tasos Kazepides, philosophers have more or less stopped writing on the concept, because so much was written (a lot of it very good stuff) in the 1960s. But the issue of indoctrination is obviously still very much with us – one thinks of the upsurge of fundamentalism and creationist legislation in America, the recent trial of a teacher in Canada who maintains that the holocaust did not exist, and some of the 'educational' aspirations of the Department of Education and Science in Britain[1] – and in a textbook such as this it is therefore right and proper to study the concept.

There are certainly some omissions that might ideally be rectified. For example, there is no chapter on intelligence, which, quite apart from the fact that IQ tests are still with us and that the vogue word 'giftedness' at times seems a mere synonym for it, is surely one of the basic or key concepts of the educational enterprise. I decided against adding something on this particular topic, because I think that ideally it requires a fuller, book-length, treatment. (Within the limits of a chapter, a useful analysis is provided by John Kleinig in his *Philosophical Issues in Education*.) But more generally, having flipped through my own recent *Critical Dictionary of Educational Concepts*[2] for possible ideas, I decided against any attempts to cover the ground more thoroughly than we did initially. Philosophy is not about jumping on each passing wagon. The educational philosopher's task is to select the seemingly central or key concepts, those that help to constitute and organize his field, and stick with them.

In short, I am back with the contention that whatever one's particular views may be, anybody who professes to be able to talk reasonably about education and to proceed in practical terms in ways that can be shown to be reasonable, will need to be able to show that he has a pretty good grasp of such concepts as education, understanding, indoctrination, rationality, culture, needs, interest, and wants, which in one way or another are central to the enterprise in question. Such concepts remain the core of this book.

Robin Barrow

Vancouver

1988

Notes

1 I have in mind the charge that some would make, to the effect that recent initiatives combine to transmit the values of free enterprise and industry as if they were uncontentious. One might add the concern of some that such subjects as peace studies and sex education may become exercises in indoctrination.
2 Robin Barrow & Geoffrey Milburn, *A Critical Dictionary of Educational Concepts* (Wheatsheaf, 1986).

Preface to Fourth Edition

Philosophers sometimes refer to a ship that needs repairs over the course of a long voyage, in order to illustrate certain problems or questions about identity. The wooden ship leaves harbour and, while at sea, certain planks have to be replaced. A short time later some others have to be replaced; a few days after that, some more; and so on, until by the journey's end all the planks that went to make up the original ship have been replaced. Is this the ship that was originally put to sea or an entirely different one? Whatever the answer to that question, this book is beginning to resemble that ship.

Since the launching of the first edition in 1975 five completely new chapters have been added, one has been thrown overboard, and the remaining text has been subjected to repeated overhaul. Nonetheless, I hope it can be said that the book remains recognizably the same one that Ron Woods and I set out to write thirty years ago. That is to say, I hope that it still provides a helpful introduction to the business of philosophizing in the sense of engaging in conceptual analysis and coherent reasoning about education, while providing a plausible answer to some specific educational questions and establishing at any rate the groundwork of an argument for a particular view of what education is all about and what it therefore demands of us.

In this revision, three new chapters entitled, respectively, 'Thinking about Education', 'What is it to be Human?' and 'The Postmodern Challenge' have been added. 'Thinking about Education' attempts to set the stage by briefly

examining the context in which philosophical thought about education oper-
ates, stressing in particular the rational tradition in Western thought to which
philosophical analysis belongs, and the wider concerns of schooling of which
education is merely a part, albeit, it will be argued, the major part. It seems
important also to address the question 'What is it to be Human?' in view of
much recent research, particularly in genetics, and in order to locate education
as a peculiarly human activity. It seemed necessary to add the brief chapter on
'The Postmodern Challenge' not in order to address any theses associated with
any particular individuals, but to combat the stultifying effect of certain propositions, such as that there is no truth or that nothing can be known, which,
rightly or wrongly, are often classified as postmodern in tenor and which, if
accepted, would undermine the key foundations not only of the positive educational argument of this book but also of the philosophical activity that it is
concerned with. The chapter on 'Understanding' of previous editions has been
dropped, not because we do not continue to believe that education is primarily
and essentially about understanding, but because a great deal of the overall text
is concerned directly and indirectly with issues to do with understanding and
knowledge, and, given a need to cut something at the publisher's behest, it was
felt that a direct examination of what 'understanding' means could be fore-
gone. Beyond these major changes, the bibliography has been brought up to
date and the remaining text has been subjected to various fairly minor revisions
and one or two paragraph length additions.

I should like to conclude with a comment on the updating of references
and examples. I have, by and large, attempted to bring specific examples
of, for example, films up to date, so that the 'Straw Dogs' of 1975, which
became 'The Texas Chainsaw Massacre' of 1988, now becomes 'Crash'.
This is simply to help the majority of readers recognize the reference! And
though, for example, a few references to the game of Bingo are retained,
because as a matter of fact for a period educational philosophers used it as
an iconic example and argued about its specifically educational potential,
most of them have been replaced by reference to, for example, video-
games, since clearly it is the latter that represent a potential challenge to
education today rather than Bingo. But, and this is important, by and
large the philosophical references – the author cited, the arguments
explored – have not been changed.

A very minor reason for this is that after discussion with the publisher it
was agreed to produce a new edition of this work rather than a new
introduction to philosophy of education altogether, since, strange as it may
be, this book has proven itself capable of weathering changes of fashion
and focus over time. If all the topics and the arguments relating to them
had been brought up to date, drawing on new material written exclusively
in the last ten years, then clearly it would not have been a new edition; it
would have been a new book – a different ship.

A major reason is related to the original aim of the book: to introduce the
business of philosophizing about education. To that end, provided the

examples are not so foreign as to be incomprehensible to the reader, it really doesn't matter what issues, what authors, or what arguments one uses, since the primary purpose is to illustrate philosophy in action and to have material on which to practice (i.e. get thinking). That reason would be sufficient to justify continuing to examine, for example, Peters' work on the concept of education or Hirst's work on forms of knowledge. Indeed, in the latter case, Hirst himself, if he hasn't actually repudiated his original thesis, has certainly moved way beyond it. But that does not stop it still being an intriguing and persuasive thesis, and one which may serve as an excellent way of introducing the question of the nature of knowledge and the significance of the question for curriculum. But sufficient though that reason alone would be, I must in honesty add one more. While philosophy of education continues to thrive, not very much has been done in recent years that really adds to the primary analytic work done thirty to forty years ago, at least at a basic level. If I look at a recent issue of the *Journal of Philosophy of Education*, for example, I see a number of excellent articles, but none of them speak to the issues in this book. This is not to set the stage for a confrontation between different types and styles of philosophy. It is simply to say that this book is predicated on the belief that it is desirable that all teachers and educators should recognize the importance of, and become reasonably adept at, analysing the key concepts in education; that, and secondarily suggesting a particular view of what such analysis leads us to recognize as genuinely educational, is what this book is about, and most of the work focused on that was indeed done some years ago. Does this make the book old fashioned? No. This – analysing the key educational concepts – is something that each generation has to do for itself anew.

Robin Barrow
Vancouver
2005

Index

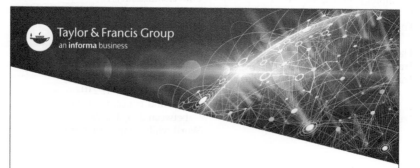